RENT UNMASKED

*How to Save the Global Economy
and Build a Sustainable Future*

A basic principle of economics holds that it is highly efficient to tax rents because such taxes don't cause any distortions. A tax on land rents doesn't make the land go away. Indeed, the great nineteenth-century progressive Henry George argued that government should rely solely on such a tax. Today, of course, we realize that rents can take many forms – they can be collected not just on land, but on the value of natural resources like oil, gas, minerals, and coal. There are other sources of rents, such as those derived from the exercise of monopoly power. A stiff tax on all such rents would not only reduce inequality but also reduce incentives to engage in the kind of rent-seeking activities that distort our economy and our democracy.

Joseph E. Stiglitz
The Price of Inequality
(2012: 212-213)

Works by Mason Gaffney

The Mason Gaffney Reader (2013)
After the Crash: Designing a Depression-Free Economy (2009)
The Corruption of Economics (1994 with Fred Harrison)
Land and Taxation (1994, Nicolaus Tideman ed.)

RENT UNMASKED

*How to Save the Global Economy
and Build a Sustainable Future*

Essays in Honour of
Mason Gaffney

Fred Harrison (Editor)

SHEPHEARD-WALWYN (PUBLISHERS) LTD

Robert Schalkenbach Foundation
211 East 43rd Street, Suite 400
New York, NY 10017
www.schalkenbach.org
www.earthsharing.org

First published in 2016 by
Shepheard-Walwyn (Publishers) Ltd
107 Parkway House, Sheen Lane,
London SW14 8LS
www.shepheard-walwyn.co.uk
www.ethicaleconomics.org.uk

British Library Cataloguing in Publication Data
A catalogue record of this book
is available from the British Library

ISBN: 978-0-85683-511-7

Typeset by Alacrity, Chesterfield, Sandford, Somerset
Printed and bound in the United Kingdom
by Short Run Press, Exeter

Contents

A TRIBUTE TO MASON GAFFNEY

Conflict Resolution and Ethical Economics

WORLD WAR 3 is not possible – is it? When the proposition was advanced in 2012 (Harrison 2012: 206), the world was locked in a deep depression, but statesmen were reassuring their constituents. Since then the President of the European Union (Donald Tusk, a historian by profession) observed that Europe was experiencing 'some very dangerous moments in our history. It is like the day before the World War One' (Holehouse 2016). And Russia's Prime Minister, Dmitry Medvedev, informed a German newspaper that the conflict in Syria was in danger of erupting into 'another world war' (*Handelsblatt* 2016).

The global economy is locked into a void which evokes the Depression of the 1930s. We shall call this void the 'suppressed depression', a term that came into use in 1937 but long since forgotten. How we got here is the story of the failures of governance. The blueprint for what we can do about it is the subject of this volume. The ethical economics which could resolve the conflicts that constitute a world at war with itself have been most meticulously analysed by Mason Gaffney.

The financial implosion of 2008, and the failure of policy-makers to adopt appropriate remedies, turned the global economy into a hostage to malevolent forces. Those forces, centred on global real estate, had been allowed to gather strength and momentum over the past century. They culminated in the sub-prime mortgages which threatened to crush the banks and financial institutions which purchased those toxic mortgages

1

as 'collateralised debt'. Now, *working within the existing economic paradigm,* law-makers are helpless. They resorted to monetary policy to prevent the West's banks from collapsing. They pumped up the money supply to levels so high that it became difficult to keep track of the zeros at the end of the numbers. Their fears are justified: governments and central banks no longer have at their command the tools which could cushion the downward spiral.

It need not have happened.

Remedial action could have been taken at any stage in the build-up to the crisis. One policy alone could have charted a course to sustainable prosperity. That policy would have rebalanced the global economy on the twin axes of ethics and efficiency. It could have been promulgated in response to any of the crises that were building towards the seizure of the western financial sector in 2008.

➤ The Black Monday stock market crash (1987)
➤ Japan's real estate boom/bust (1989)
➤ Recession at end of the 18-year business cycle (1992)
➤ The Asian financial crisis (1997)
➤ The toxic mortgage boom/bust (2007)
➤ Implosion of the post-Marxist economies (2010s)

Any of these episodes could have been forestalled; or, failing which, could have been used to reconstruct economies on sound foundations. Repeatedly, policy-makers ignored the advice of high-profile authorities like Nobel Prize economist Joseph Stiglitz, and the guidance offered by contributors to the present volume. They explained how to eliminate inequality of incomes while raising growth, in harmony with the reconstruction of communities and natural habitats. That advice was ignored. The richly-rewarded advisers to governments are missing something. What?

In a speech in Paris on April 8, 2015, Joseph Stiglitz sketched the issues.

[M]inor tweaks in the economic system are not going to solve the problem... The underlying problem is the whole *structure* of our economy, which has been oriented more at increasing *rents* than increasing productivity and real economic growth that would be widely shared in our society ... one has always to think about issues of *shifting* so that, for instance, just a tax on capital might be shifted, and a lot of the models have shown this would happen, but a tax on land, rents, would actually address some of the underlying problems. This is the idea that Henry George had more than a hundred years ago, but this analysis that I have done ... goes one step beyond Henry George. Henry George argued that a land tax was non-distortionary, but this analysis says that *a land tax actually improves the productivity of the economy because you encourage people to invest in productive capital rather than into rent generating.* Well, the result of the shift in the composition of the savings towards more productive investment leads to a more productive economy and in the end leads to a more equal society.

(Stiglitz 2015, emphasis added)

The italicised concepts in the Stiglitz speech are forensically examined in this volume.

To understand the grave implications of the new reality, we need to unmask rent. The emphasised sentence on the 'land tax' identifies the nub of the solution to the debt crisis. No-one has contributed more to the task of forensically examining the nature of rent, and the associated solution to society's problems, than the professor whom we rate as the foremost authority on the economics of real estate: Mason Gaffney. And so, *Rent Unmasked* must serve two purposes.

The first is to honour Mason Gaffney, academic and activist who dedicated his life to shedding light on the issues that his peers, for the most part, have preferred to shroud in darkness. The debt crisis provides a fitting backdrop against which to evaluate his works of a lifetime. The second purpose is in keeping with Professor Gaffney's wish that the contributors to this volume should analyse the state of our world both theoretically and empirically.

In relation to the debt crisis, we will explain how the transformation of the tax regime could elevate consumption and investment in the global economy by something of the order $14 trillion. That would be the *additional* value that would flow from the increased productivity to which Stiglitz referred in his Paris speech. That is the magnitude of the added value that people would generate as the barriers created by the Treadmill Taxes were dismantled. It is the sole strategy capable of pulling the indebted world back from the precipice. Part I of this volume explores the theoretical issues, and we lay out the empirical evidence in Part II. In Part III, we discuss the need for the prophetic voices that would mobilise people behind the democratic mandate that is needed to drive policy-makers in the direction of remedial action.

Box 1

The Ride to Nowhere

Mason Gaffney was exposed to the authorised version of economics at Harvard. His unwillingness to accept the conventional doctrines on taxation stemmed from an accident. As a 14-year old he was riding his bicycle when he was struck down by a car. His left leg was seriously damaged. The books brought to his bedside included Albert J. Nock's *Henry George: an Essay*. That was in 1937. Two years later he received a flyer from the Chicago branch of the Henry George School. A free class on economics was offered at his local 'Community House'. The teacher, John Lawrence Monroe, was persuasive. So Mason decided to study economics at Harvard. There, he was put under pressure to ignore Henry George. He recorded his professor's advice:

> You see, my boy, this Henry George lived at a time when the country was growing rapidly, when land values were skyrocketing and great fortunes were being made from speculation. Not being a 'trained economist,' George attached disproportionate importance to this … er … er … land question. Land is, of course, of minor importance in 'economics,' and speculation, well … of trifling significance.
>
> (Gaffney 1942)

But Mason had traversed the Road to Nowhere, the highway along the North Shore west of Chicago. For mile after mile, 'developers' had sunk capital into streets and sidewalks … with not a house in sight. Farmers had sold their acres in the expectation of reaping windfall capital gains. The profits did not materialise. Instead, the fields remained barren, bereft of farms and families.

By applying common sense and the principles he had learnt at his Community House, young Gaffney was able to decode the source of behaviour that was economically anti-social, ecologically damaging and fiscally perverse. Governments, by the way they administer the public purse, encourage land speculation. Urban sprawl, it appeared to Mason, reduced the productivity of the economy and forestalled the creation of employment opportunities.

Burnished into his mind was the sign erected at a junction with Arlington Heights Road. This proclaimed: 'The Idle Rich of Today Bought Acres Yesterday'.

But he was sympathetic towards his Harvard professor. He wrote: 'His salary, after all, is paid in part from the proceeds of the foresight of certain friends of the institution who bought up much of the land on which the slums and business districts of Cambridge now stand.'

Mason was due to major in Economics. He tired of what he called 'the drivel' and switched to History.

The Perversion of Classical Economics

The thesis developed in this volume is based on a shocking proposition. The dismal failures of governance ultimately stem from one source: the intentional manipulation of classical economics. That distortion turned Mason Gaffney into a rebel with an honourable cause (Box 1). For what had originated as a method for diagnosing economic behaviour and prescribing effective government policies was perversely compromised for the private benefit of a self-serving minority. The outcome is the convergence, in the 21st century, of what the US intelligence community calls mega-trends. These are global problems (both social and ecological) that have reached such scale and intensity that they collide with, and fuse into, each other (National Intelligence Council 2012). This creates the kind of chaos that becomes an existential threat to humanity.

The western financial system began to implode when property prices peaked in 2007. It was rescued by politicians who shifted the costs of their negligence onto their citizens. People lost jobs by the millions. Homes were repossessed, and savings and pensions disappeared. The culture which created the disaster was put on a life support system, nursed so that it may return to wreak havoc on another day.

The Depression of the 2010s followed.

The most comprehensive interrogation of the intellectual crimes and policy failures which nourished this tragedy is to be found in the life-time's work by Mason Gaffney. He was unrelenting in his investigations, for even in the darkest hours of his career as a non-conformist professor he remained resolute in his belief that economics as a scholarly discipline could – and *must* – be rehabilitated (Box 2).

Ethics and Economics   Classical economics originated with the French Physiocrats and thinkers of the Scottish Enlightenment, among whose ranks was the moral philosopher Adam Smith. They saw the Big Picture, and they became the architects of a system which holistically integrated people's private interests with the financial formula that would deliver honest governance. They understood that individual rights were inextricably bound up with social obligations. Not for them the linguistic contortions of medieval schoolmen. They cut to the chase. People should be free to get on with their lives (*laissez faire*); but they should also honour their responsibilities to society.

The organising mechanism for achieving this prospectus was based on

Box 2 • The Professor they Could Not Gag

Mason Gaffney's studies at Harvard were cut short when he was called for wartime service. He joined the US Army Air Corps and reported for duty at Fort Grant, in northern Illinois. He was shipped out to the Pacific, but on his return to the States he decided that Harvard was not the place to complete his studies. He earned his BA at Reed College, in Portland, Oregon, before moving to Berkeley for a PhD.

Mason's early years combined teaching and social activism. In the 1960s, he marched to support the Civil Rights of African Americans. In 1969 he joined Resources for the Future, Inc., a Washington, DC-based think tank that was commissioned to address the problem of resource scarcity. His relationship with colleagues was warm until he began to question their methodology. He was told to shut up or go away. In 1973 he was invited to head a new think-tank sponsored by the provincial government of British Columbia. The BC Institute for Economic Policy Analysis encouraged research into pollution control in the market economy. Again, Mason came under pressure from those who favoured the privatisation of natural resources as the best route to conservation.

In 1976 he moved to the University of California, where he engaged with environmentalists who were seeking policies which could protect natural habitats. As professor of economics at the university's Riverside campus, and Chair of Economics in 1978, his working relationship with authority was never going to be easy. The university favoured agribusiness over family farms. He found himself defending his department against the ideologues who were the mouthpieces for businesses built on the landed interest. The guardians of the IMF/Washington Consensus had a long reach, and they were gunning for the professor who objected, on scientific and ethical grounds, to what is now called rent-seeking. He refused to compromise, lecturing on, and publishing articles about the West coast rent-seekers who purloined public value through their legal rights to water, timber, oil or fisheries.

Public subsidies for 'bridges to nowhere' infrastructure were a *bête noire*. They enriched the owners of land in the catchment areas of the investments, causing the professor to comment adversely on the waste of public funds for proposals like the Peripheral Canal project in the arid lands east of Riverside. Why, he asked, reward corporate land owners for raping the earth?

When state-wide property taxes were further compromised by Proposition 13, to enrich residential land owners, Mason was dismayed to witness a deterioration in the educational attainment of students graduating from California's cash-starved schools (Gaffney 2011). In the year Professor Gaffney prepared to retire (2014), *Time* magazine used new White House metrics to rank his university as No.1 in the USA.*

* http://time.com/71782/make-your-own-college-ranking/

the rents which everyone helped to create. These *ought* to fund the services that were provided by public agencies. The classical economists understood that, when rents are privatised, the result is parasitism. Adam Smith was too polite to call his noble patrons *parasites*, but he left his readers in no doubt about the realities. He described landowners in these terms:

> They are the only one of the three orders whose revenue costs them neither labour nor care, but comes to them, as it were, of its own accord, and independent of any plan or project of their own. That indolence, which is the natural effect of the ease and security of their situation, renders them too often, not only ignorant, but incapable of that application of mind which is necessary in order to foresee and understand the consequences of any public regulation.
>
> (Smith 1776: Bk 1, Ch XI: 277)

Private claims on socially-created rent were not only unjust. They also damaged society when those who claimed to own the nation's rents controlled the reins of power. In what were then Europe's two leading nations – the monarchies of France and Britain – the landlords were counsellors to kings and administrators of the state. There was one peaceful way only to deconstruct that powerful edifice: synthesising the scientific approach to the production of wealth with an ethics-based public administration.

The starting point for this project was the rigorous definition of the agents of production: land, labour and capital. National income was divided into rent, wages and interest. To achieve optimal outcomes, the new economy had to synthesise

> ➤ *a free-market* that served the common good as well as the private benefit; with
> ➤ *governance* that was grounded in the norms of both efficiency and justice.

When correctly aligned, classical economics and the art of public administration would deliver material prosperity and social solidarity. In this vision of the world, there need be no poverty: people willing to work could not be prevented from doing so. There need be no unhealthy communities: society would grow organically, adjusting naturally to the opportunities that presented themselves during the Agricultural and Industrial Revolutions.

Classical economics was a revolutionary prospectus. It was a direct challenge to the vital interests of the landed aristocracy. This meant that, sooner or later, the classical model – and its promise of the Good Life for everyone – would have to be subverted. To achieve that outcome, the heavy lifting was performed by individuals who became known as 'neoclassical economists' (Gaffney 1994). The proximate cause that animated them was the emergence on the world scene of an American journalist.

Henry George published *Progress and Poverty* in 1879. He set the type himself in his printing works in San Francisco. The book became the first best-selling text on economics. Its message was lethal. There was nothing *natural* about poverty and mass unemployment, social division and the urban sprawl that blighted natural habitats. These were symptoms of a malevolent financial regime. The antidote was a financial formula.

✔ Abolish taxes on people's earned incomes.
✔ Enable and require people to pay for the services they receive from nature and from society.

Henry George's analysis laid the foundations for what became the first global reform movement in history. The time had come to embed justice in the public's finances. The income at stake was the rent that flowed (in the main) through the land market. This was a direct threat to the material foundations of the class that monopolised power, and to its supporters (such as mortgage-granting financiers).

The social movement that mobilised behind *Progress and Poverty* could not be neutralised through physical coercion. The beneficiaries of the Land Grab of old had to take control of the narrative. The way to achieve that was by burying two concepts: land and rent. Professors of economics on both sides of the Atlantic stepped forward to oblige. The outcome was the sterilisation of economics as a problem-solving discipline. Students were inculcated with a doctrine which, conceptually speaking, cut the ground from beneath their feet. The political impact was devastating. Legislatures of the West devoted the 20th century to palliatives rather than structural reform. That is why the social and economic problems that Henry George catalogued in the 19th century remain with us in the 21st century.

The Inconvenient Truth   A pathologically traumatised society needs to heal itself with appropriate therapies. Recovering healthy minds begins by excavating the closest approximation to truth. Archaeologists collaborate in one such exercise, by digging up the carcasses of ancient urban settlements with the aid of trowel and brush. They sweep away the sands of time to try and understand how humans collaborated to create the earliest civilisations. Mason Gaffney became one of his generation's foremost excavators in the realm of public policy. He de-constructed the linguistic contortions of the academicians who had mangled the tools of their trade, exposing the way in which they rationalised turbulence in the out-of-control economy. One of their excuses is 'market failure'. Because the experts cannot blame governance, they need a scapegoat. The failures were blithely attributed to the market. Gaffney would have none of it. And so, when economics as a science fell into general disrepute in 2008, he explained that blaming the market distracted attention from the inconvenient truth.

But people cannot be blamed for imbibing the *clichés* of their tutors or economic commentators. That is why Prof Gaffney patiently explained to his students that technical terms had to be rigorously analysed. In relation to rent, it was crucial to understand that net income was a composite value. It represented the services provided by

> *nature*: this stream of income emerged with the first agricultural revolution some 10,000 years ago. Nature's rent remained the largest portion of net income all the way through to the Industrial Revolution. Rent, which assumed different forms through the ages (from labour power to payments in kind, and then cash in the commercial society) made possible the innovations which crystallised as urban civilisation.

And then there was a shift to rents generated by

> *society*: from the 18th century, rents increased in absolute terms, and as a proportion of total income, through investment in the infrastructure associated with industrialisation. New water and sewerage systems improved the health of the population, education funded by governments, and other public investments, resulted in the exponential increase in the flow of rents generated by the collective efforts of people working through their public agencies.

But those streams of rents had been shorn of their social status by the feudal patricians. People were socialised into accepting the legitimacy of rent as private income.

Beyond the Kafkaesque Conversation There is a worldwide awareness that our globalised civilisation is defective in some profound way. What is now fast being reduced to a mono-culture appears helpless in the face of mounting crises. The world's financial arteries have been corroded. Gains are eclipsed by painful losses to the wealth and welfare of every society on earth. Conversations that purport to diagnose the problems are distorted at all levels.

- ✤ Policy-makers wrestle with shortfalls in revenue from taxes on wages and consumption; when (as Gaffney continues to insist) that revenue ultimately comes out of rent (ATCOR).[1]
- ✤ Economists agonise over their forecasts, using tools like 'inflation'; when the comprehensive indicator of the state of health of the economy is the net income that people produce.
- ✤ Media commentators celebrate the rise in 'house' prices; when the increases are in the price of land (bricks-and-mortar depreciate), a fact which they continue to ignore for diagnostic purposes.

The first step in releasing ourselves from this Kafkaesque nightmare is the unmasking of the role played by rent in our lives. Rehabilitation of that one concept would empower people to rethink the state of our biological, social and cultural condition. For *there is no shortage of resources to invest in everyone's welfare.*

People are willing to work to pay for decent personal lifestyles and congenial communities; to fund state institutions and neighbourhood law enforcement; to enjoy recreation and the fulfilment of education. But, collectively, they realise that their labour alone is not sufficient. They need the partnership of public agencies. The inability to fully

---

[1] In addressing the claim that rent did not generate sufficient revenue to become the Single Tax advocated by Henry George, Mason Gaffney revisited the writings of the earliest commentators. People like John Locke had explained how a tax on the wages of peasants reduced the net income that they could pay to their landlords as rent. In other words: there was no escaping economic reality, no matter how the noble lawmakers tortured fiscal policy to diminish the amount collected *directly* from rent through the Land Tax. In addressing this issue (1970: 157-212), Gaffney coined the acronym ATCOR – All Taxes Come Out of Rent. He reviewed the international evidence to assure governments that restructuring the tax system would deliver revenue that was 'enough and to spare' (2009: 328-411).

Box 3 • The Resilliance of Truth

When Mason Gaffney retired from teaching in 2014, at the age of 89, he was in the company of a small but impressively qualified network of people who refused to be deterred by the guardians of the rent-seeking society. This group included

- **in academia: Joseph Stiglitz** The Nobel Prize economist who had served as Senior Vice President of the World Bank coined the term 'Henry George Theorem' in 1977. His advocacy of rent as public revenue continued in speeches, articles and in his books (most recently in *The Price of Inequality* [2012]). His academic peers, for the most part, remained aloof.

As professor of economics at Columbia University, Joseph Stiglitz was enlisted as adviser to two political parties in Europe that challenged the austerity policies imposed by the IMF: Syriza, which formed the Greek government in 2015, and Podemos, which made a bid for power in Spain in 2016. But their leaders failed to adopt the Henry George Theorem.

- **in the mass media: Martin Wolf** As the chief economics commentator of the *Financial Times*, he explained to the House of Lords economic affairs committee that there were three reasons why the housing crisis would benefit from 'the Henry George type argument'. He noted, for the benefit of their lordships: 'I have been arguing this for 15 years completely unsuccessfully' (Wolf 2015).

For his 'services to financial journalism' Martin Wolf was made a Commander of the British Empire in 2000. He was enlisted as a member of the UK government's Independent Commission on Banking in 2010. But the commission's report failed to explain the link between fiscal policy and the funding of land-led property boom/busts by banks.

Authoritative confirmations of the wisdom of rent-as-public-revenue continue to surface. These include the report by the commission headed by Nobel Prize economist Robert Mirrlees (2011). The inability of policy-makers to respond to such advice reveals the existential nature of the threat facing society. When the lines of communication are polluted by misinformation, we should not be surprised when terrible accidents explode in our midst.

Politicians continue with their charade – of claiming to serve the common good – by deploying false doctrines. One example is the 'efficient market hypothesis'. The world was assured that rational individuals and spontaneous market-clearing activity would deliver macro-economic stability. The era of disruptive booms and busts was consigned to the past. By such techniques of self-deception, specialist advisers to governments have lost the capacity to understand and communicate the significance of what they see and hear around them. Everyone else pays the price.

consummate this partnership stems from the damage inflicted on the information membrane which knits us all together. That membrane is fragile, and its future is wholly dependent on the goodwill of people who refuse to be disheartened (Box 3).

Mason Gaffney, by his persistence in sharpening the discipline of economics, has empowered future generations with the means to rip off the mask that conceals reality. By learning to deploy the key tools associated with the concept of rent, we can all participate in the ultimate adventure: the elevation of humanity onto a higher evolutionary pathway.

References

Gaffney, Mason (1942), 'Taking the Professor for a Ride', *The Freeman*, November.

— (1970), 'Adequacy of Land as a Tax Base', in Daniel Holland (ed.), *The Assessment of Land Value*, Madison: University of Wisconsin Press.

— (1994), 'Neo-classical Economics as a Stratagem against Henry George', in Mason Gaffney and Fred Harrison, *The Corruption of Economics*, London: Shepheard-Walwyn.

— (2009), 'The hidden taxable capacity of land: enough and to spare', *International Journal of Social Economics*, Vol. 36(4).

— (2011), 'Sleeping with the Enemy: Economists who Side with Polluters', *Mother Pelican*, Vol 7(9). http://www.pelicanweb.org/solisustv07n09page5.html

Handelsblatt (2016), 'Medvedev warns of new world war', February 17. https://global.handelsblatt.com/breaking/exclusive-russias-medvedev-warns-of-new-world-war

Harrison, Fred (2012), *The Traumatised Society*, London: Shepheard-Walwyn. For Harrison's 2013 analysis of 'When did World War 3 begin', view his YouTube video: https://www.youtube.com/watch?v=Nbw_INDttic

Holehouse, Matthew (2016), 'Migrant crisis could trigger Brexit, fears EU's Tusk', *Daily Telegraph*, February 10. http://www.telegraph.co.uk/news/worldnews/europe/eu/12151092/Migrant-crisis-could-trigger-Brexit-fears-EUs-Tusk.html

Mirrlees, James, *et al* (2011), *Tax by Design*, Oxford: Oxford University Press.

National Intelligence Council (2012), *Global Trends 2030: Alternative Worlds*, Washington, DC.

Smith, Adam (1776), *The Wealth of Nations*; Edwin Cannan (Ed.), Chicago: University of Chicago Press, 1976.

Stiglitz, Joseph (2010), *Freefall: Free Markets and the Sinking of the Global Economy*, London: Allen Lane.

— (2012), *The Price of Inequality*, London: Allen Lane.

— (2015), Speech, New Economic Thinking conference, Paris, April 8. https://www.youtube.com/watch?v=OPTBr9LExRs

Wolf, Martin (2015), Testimony, House of Lords Economic Affairs Committee, December 1. http://parliamentlive.tv/Event/Index/a2ece60a-e20e-4718-84f1-30a9ff6541bd

PART I

Last Man Standing

A rapacious financial process was conceived by Europe's aristocracies in the late Middle Ages. It mutated to the point where its practitioners could capture the nation-state, giving the lords of the land the power to create a self-serving model of property rights and taxation. That model could be sustained for as long as it was possible to appropriate other people's territories. Colonisation assuaged their rent-seeking appetite and at the same time provided a refuge for people who were violently displaced from their homelands in Europe.

The global depression of the 1870s signalled that the ignoble social experiment had exhausted itself. The limits of territorial aggrandisement were reached with the closing of the western frontier and the annexation of vast territories in the southern hemisphere. The tenure-and-tax nexus generated a systemic disorder that was no longer controllable. One man, Henry George, valiantly fought to mobilise a global reform movement behind a social paradigm that would restore justice and social stability. But despite his achievements, his model of ethical economics was rejected by Europe's leading nations. The outcome was two world wars, a Cold War and the experiments in Marxism.

The world has changed since Henry George traversed the seven seas. Nevertheless, the core financial principles on which classical economics had been established remain at the heart of a paradigm fit to guide humanity through the next phase of social evolution. In Part I, the authors rehabilitate a model of property rights and public finance which, in important respects, was revised and enriched by Mason Gaffney. That model's twin planks of personal freedom and honest governance evoke a new way of living in the 21st century.

The emerging alternatives are horrendous to contemplate.

1

Beyond Socialism:
Science and the Culture of Society

FRED HARRISON

T
HE WESTERN frontier was closed in 1890. According to the US Census, all the land had apparently been settled by migrants coming from Europe, to the east, and from China, to the west. And yet, just a buggy ride out of San Francisco, vast tracts of land lay unused. That puzzled Henry George. How could poverty afflict people who were willing to work? The frontier journalist investigated and analysed the facts in *Our Land and Land Policy* (Peddle and Peirce 2016). In what would become known as the Gilded Age, the crisis of inequality was exposing the ligaments of a flawed social system. Henry George decided to do something about it by advocating what would become known as the geoclassical model of property rights and taxation (O'Donnell 2015).

The problems that were embedded in society in the 19th century remained fossilised throughout the 20th century, and they threaten existential consequences in the 21st century. And yet, the means exist to solve the problems baffling policy-makers. All they need is an honest re-appraisal of the metrics of rent, the net income produced by societies that evolved above the level of subsistence.

What prevented people in the past from re-ordering their communities to the benefit of everyone, releasing the creative potential that would drive cultural evolution to ever more satisfying heights of accomplishment?

Was it malice aforethought or ignorance? Or were the outcomes – visible in the violent ruptures in the social fabric of our world today – accidental? Governments, and people of goodwill, need a realistic appreciation of what it would take to scope out the blueprint for a new future. One starting point is to examine the errors made by those who, in the past, sought a fresh start. What lessons may be learnt so that the mistakes are not repeated?

The opportunity to observe and influence epochal change at close quarters is exceptional. Ordinarily, we have to rely on understanding such events through the prisms and prejudices of historians. But in our lifetime we have twice been privileged with that opportunity. Both transformational episodes resulted from the capitulation of the communist model of society. There occurred in Russia and in China the unique opportunity to test the doctrines that might replace the communism which had failed as the antidote to capitalism. This would be an engagement in as close to laboratory-like circumstances as it is possible to get when dealing with human beings.

The two communist societies were inspired by Karl Marx's theory of history. His methodology was based on what he called materialism, which was supposed to set his vision apart from the utopian versions of socialism. His model was given a fair chance to prove itself. Joseph Stalin in Russia and Chairman Mao in China were determined to give Marxism a clear, unimpeded run at transforming the course of history, even at the cost of depriving tens of millions of people of their lives. Those two architects of communism could not claim that their endeavours were subverted by hostile external forces: they operated in isolated spaces, behind Iron and Bamboo Curtains. Flaws in the theory negated their experiments.

With the collapse of communism, there was a clear choice between two competing models of society. One was the reversion to capitalism, the defects in which had originally provoked Marx into developing his economic doctrines. Alternatively, Henry George's model could be adopted. His was an ethics-based resolution of the physical with the moral worlds, an integration of the private and public sectors on the back of a financial mechanism that respected the core human values of individualism and socialism, each sector fulfilling their functions to secure the stable growth of culture in the direction favoured (on democratic principles) by the people themselves. The testing ground for each of these models was to be found in the realm of property rights and the consequential distribution of income.

❖ The property rights championed by what was then called The Washington Consensus were based on the claim that the market economy worked best when land and man-made capital were privately owned, with government revenue raised by taxing wages and entrepreneurial profits. Privatisation, therefore, became the mantra for the relaunch of Russia as far as the governments in Washington, DC, London and Brussels were concerned.

❖ The geoclassical theory stressed that capital was best treated as private property, but that land should remain in public ownership. This was a nuanced approach to privatisation led by fiscal policy: it entails exclusive occupation of public land combined with the payment of rent into the public purse – the model that had prevailed in the British colony of Hong Kong for more than a century – would combine with the de-taxation of wages and profits (Purves 2015).

The 1990s was the ideological battleground for the contest that would seal the fate of the peoples who had venerated Karl Marx. In the event, Moscow was captured by the Washington Consensus. China was not subjected to similar external influence. The failure of the Politburo in Beijing turned on the inability to grasp the difference between the ownership of an asset (land, which was retained in the public domain), and how the revenue streams from that asset could be sliced-and-diced by non-owners with political connections.

Disappointment with the transformation in Russia and in China is based on outcomes ranging from the eruption of the billionaire oligarch class to the extensive poverty in both countries, and the undemocratic power exercised by authoritarian governments. All the socially significant symptoms may be traced back to the misappropriation of socially-created rents. That record provides the guidelines for the policy reforms that would empower Western democracies to fulfil the goals that are formalised in their social contracts.

Russia: The Clean Sheet

In 1985, after he was elected as General Secretary of the Central Committee of the Communist Party, Mikhail Gorbachev began to signal that something was wrong with the Soviet experiment that had been launched by Lenin in 1917. Reform was needed. His catchword was *glasnost* (openness). This afforded western economists and political philosophers with a golden opportunity. They could commend optimal policies for elevating wealth and welfare within the territories of the Soviet Union. Here was the chance for a fresh start without bloody upheavals. Not since the Clean Sheet proclamations of the civilisations of antiquity had any society experienced the opportunity to effect social renewal in a non-violent way. Restoring social equilibrium could be by taking into account the 'facts on the ground', with policies that could stimulate the economy without having to alter the legal status of land. The best of brains in the West knew how a market economy could be grafted onto the back of land held in the public domain – *they had to look no further than Hong Kong!* The people of Russia were ready to listen and learn.

The first initiative on behalf of the geoclassical model took place in August 1990 at the University Club of New York, on the corner of 5th Avenue and West 54th Street. The conference was sponsored by the New York-based Robert Schalkenbach Foundation. A delegation from the Soviet Union listened to presentations from speakers that included Professor William Vickrey of Columbia University. He had studied New York's mass transit system and had concluded that the network could be fully funded out of the rents generated by the residents of the city. That empirical evidence convinced him of the wisdom of paying for social services with the rents generated by public agencies (Vickrey 1999).

In his presentation to the Soviet delegates, Mason Gaffney explained that the Soviet Union could have both common land and private markets. He coupled this economic insight with a warning: trouble came with anything less.

> Privatizing property and freeing markets in Soviet nations should not be imitative but integrative, synthesizing a new economy from the best of capitalism and socialism. The centerpiece of policy proposed here is social collection of land rent to finance government. Selling land quickly without reserving tax power is rejected as being financially disastrous and politically abject and submissive to alien buyers. The policy of taxing land in perpetuity is shown to make land markets work better.
>
> (Gaffney 1990: 22-23)

This doctrine resonated with the people of Russia. They were wedded to one primordial sentiment: their land was something special, which belonged to them all. This was the key to understanding how they could remain true to that almost spiritual ethos, while liberating themselves within a new market economy that would protect the social fabric which they had sacrificed so much to create.

And so, beginning in 1991, teams of geoclassical activists criss-crossed Russia to explain how the transition to a new kind of market economy could remain faithful to the people's social aspirations. Personal energies could be liberated within a vibrant market-based system for producing wealth and distributing income. Here was a golden chance to transform the economy in an orderly way. The formula: combine the freedom of labour to work without the burden of taxation; allocate tax-free capital to rehabilitate the shattered state of industry; and use land and natural resources to generate rents to fund infrastructure and the costs of running what would metamorphose into a liberal democratic form of governance. Russia's federal politicians and municipal administrators were provided with the conceptual tools for

✔ *preserving their hard-won social solidarity* while creating the cultural space for the emergence of individualism; and
✔ *embedding the market in an ethics-based commercial economy* that was fit to compete with all-comers in global markets.

That this model was credible was attested by the prestigious signatories to an Open Letter addressed to Mikhail Gorbachev, who had become President of the USSR. Among them were three Nobel Prize economists: Franco Modigliani, Robert Solow and James Tobin (Tideman *et al.* 1991: 225-230). William Vickrey also signed the Open Letter: he was awarded the 1996 Nobel Memorial Prize in Economic Sciences with James Mirrlees, the emeritus professor of economics at Cambridge University who was subsequently to endorse the virtues of a public charge on land values (Mirrlees 2011).

Throughout the 1990s, the channels of political influence were kept informed both within the federal Duma and directly to the population through such organisations as the Union of Russian Cities.

It was a race against time. Evidence of what was happening to the population's net income rippled through the streets. 'Mafia' organisations emerged to demand 'protection money' from kiosk traders who began to trade in goods imported from the West (making jeans available for the first time!). They set up their stalls outside the metro stations of Moscow and St Petersburg. The most valuable locations were at the entrances to the busiest stations where the footfalls were highest. But the municipal

Federal Duma Hearings on Land Policy, January 1999: L to R: Fred Harrison, Victor Chernomyrdin (Prime Minister of Russia 1992-1998), Professor Nicolaus Tideman, Mason Gaffney, Ted Gwartney, Vyashislav Zvolinsky

governments undercharged for the kiosk licences. That meant the rents were 'up for grabs'. Ruthless characters moved in to charge 'protection money'. The scale of the exactions varied according to the location of each kiosk. By default, public policy was privatising the socially-created rents and consequently sponsoring the corruption of culture.

Within Russia, the lead role in explaining the geoclassical model to government was taken by Dr Dmitry Lvov, the Secretary of the Economics Department of the Russian Academy of Sciences. He had direct access to all the leading politicians, including President Boris Yeltsin's prime ministers like Viktor Chernomyrdin. Lvov was supported by activists from around the world: they came, on a *pro bono* basis, from Australia, South Africa, Denmark, the UK and the USA to explain the theory and undertake empirical studies.

At hearings in the federal Duma in Moscow in 1999, organised by Vyacheslav Zvolinsky, Chair of the Committee on Natural Resources, Mason Gaffney drew on evidence from western experience to warn of the risks of creating fiefdoms ruled by oligarchs.

> [S]ome poor regions, like the American State of New Mexico, or Canada's Prince Edward Island, are ruled by small oligarchies of wealthy people who create their own region's poverty by the extreme inequality of resource ownership. It is folly to 'tax poor people in rich regions to subsidize a few rich people in poor regions,' as often occurs (Gaffney 1999).

To help municipal officials to visualise what could be achieved, a team of geoclassical economists assessed the taxable capacity of land in Novgorod, the old Russian capital. Between them, they combined the professional skills of property assessors and high finance. Ted Gwartney, who was working for Bank of America as a commercial appraiser, flew in from California. Foreign exchange dealer Ronald Banks arrived from London, and property valuer Peter Meakin travelled north from South Africa. They were attracted by a unique challenge. The Soviet Union had banished the market in land. So, in the early post-Soviet years before market evidence could accumulate to assist for valuation purposes, assessment would have to be based on the relative merits of each plot of land. Western real estate techniques were combined with knowledge gleaned locally from people who identified their preferences about where to live and work.

The Mayor of Novgorod was delighted with the outcome. The land would be retained in public ownership, but it would be privately possessed on secure tenure rights. Sufficient revenue could be raised to fund public services, and there was no need to impose additional taxes. Left alone, the citizens of Novgorod could work and save to nurture the new arts of commercial entrepreneurship while renewing the stock of buildings in the town. Before implementation, however, a delegation from the West arrived in town. The US Government offered to fit out the Mayor's offices with free computers. The gift was conditional: he would have to adopt the conventional property tax, one that also taxed buildings. And, he was informed, there would not be sufficient revenue from the property tax on real estate, so taxes would have to be levied on wages and profits. The Mayor accepted the gift.

The International Monetary Fund entrenched its ideological battalions outside the Kremlin. It symbolically occupied Red Square with the financial firepower of the Washington Consensus. Its mission was to ensure that the privatisation of land would be embedded in Russia's new constitution (Harrison 2008). The outcome was the oligarchy, a class of political insiders who acquired proprietary rights over the rents from Russia's fabulous natural resources. The peoples of the steppes were left to reap the wild wind.

Dystopia: Mao's Legacy

Russia and her satellites (notably Poland) had been urged by western economists like Jeffrey Sachs, the Special Advisor to the UN Secretary General, to swallow a dose of 'shock therapy'. This was the medicine prescribed by the advocates of the Washington Consensus to facilitate the transition out of the command economy. In its early stages, China was not subjected to similar external influences.

The need for reform became apparent to Du Runsheng (1913-2015), an agricultural economist who had been purged by Chairman Mao because of his opposition to the Soviet-style collectivisation of land. Catastrophic decline in the output of food caused terrible suffering in some rural areas. Du Runsheng, a civil war veteran, drafted a policy document in 1980 that would allow peasants to farm their own plots (he became known as the 'father of land reform'). At the same time, Deng Xiaoping announced that foreign investment would be allowed in four Special Economic Zones. Architects of the post-Mao system claimed that they could meld planning with market forces, both of which were 'ways of controlling economic activity' (Gittings 2005). It was a delusion. By the second decade of the 21st century, the people of China were locked deep in the same rent-seeking dystopia as the post-communist settlement that prevailed in Russia.

Guardians of Marxist orthodoxy believed that, by retaining the title deeds to the nation's land and natural resources in the public domain, they could remain faithful to their communist ideals. The scale of the delusion became visible in the form of ghost towns. Labour and capital were systematically wasted on an epic scale to build urban settlements where no-one wanted to live or work.

> Between 1996 and 2003, the urban population increased by just over 27%. The built urban area was increased by 370%. That vast over-investment continued up to the global crisis of 2008. Result: a vast country pock-marked with vacant skyscrapers.
> China plans further construction that could accommodate a population of 3.4 billion, nearly three times the population of 1.3 billion (Tang 2015: 72). The population was predicted to reach its peak in 2017, and then begin to decline.

Given the pursuit of riches through rent-seeking, it is not surprising that the legacy is one of the world's highest levels of income inequality. According to research at Peking University, the richest 1% of households own a third of the country's wealth, while the poorest 25% own 1% of the wealth. Among the world's 25 largest countries by population (according to the World Bank's Gini coefficient, which measures inequality), only South Africa and Brazil have a worse record (Wildau and Mitchell 2015). An estimated 99m people live in poverty, surviving on an annual income of less than $360.

Apologists for the capitalist paradigm would dismiss China's horrendous waste of resources as evidence of bureaucratic interference with the market economy. But the people who corrupted government officials and constructed the cities were developers whose behaviour was identical to entrepreneurs in countries like Ireland and Spain in the years leading to the 2008 crisis.

Local governments forcefully acquired land from peasant farmers, which they then leased to raise money to fund infrastructure. The developers were not interested in providing useable accommodation for the people of China. They used construction as the means to extract rents in the form of capital gains. The emerging middle class learnt that the best way to accumulate a fortune was to create portfolios of apartments that they were willing to leave untenanted on the assumption that prices would continue to rise.

Some of the contributors to the present volume worked to explain the more efficient transition mechanism to personal prosperity and social wellbeing (Löhr *et al*, 2014; Gwartney 2014). Too late: the damage was done. The rate of increase in the price of residential land in Beijing tells the tragic story (Graph 1). Mason Gaffney provided the autopsy (Gaffney 2015).

Graph 1

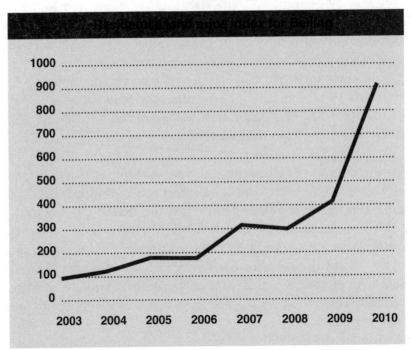

China failed to deploy, during the formative post-Maoist years, a property tax that would ensure fairness with efficiency. Instead, it employed the fiscal system that rewarded land speculation.

China's land-based financing mechanism is one of the main causes of other urban issues that we face today. Skyrocketing housing prices, growing local debts, excessive land-taking, growing tension between the farmers and municipal governments over land-taking, and widening gaps of income and wealth distribution between urban and rural populations are among the major issues.

                                                                    (Zhi 2015: 31)

Poverty was incubated alongside the atmospheric pollution that assaulted people's health and their natural habitats. People's savings, locked up in apartments and houses that were surplus to requirement, were not available for consumption. The unbalanced economy is the mirror image of the capitalism against which Marx had directed his venom. The corrupted financial culture solidified in the something-for-nothing social psychology which, in the capitalist West, resists justice-based reforms.

Parameters of a Scientific Theory

Marx played up the scientific status of his theory (Engels 1880). The claim was spurious. For all the documentation that went into *Das Capital*, Marx's work was based on observations about past events. He converted these into a narrative about the inevitability of unfolding history to produce the conclusion he favoured (Popper 1962).

Analysis of historical trends *can* generate patterns which may, indeed, provide the clues for predicting future events. But to qualify as a scientific theory, hypotheses must be testable under conditions in which the claims can be disproved. On this score, the rent thesis has attained the scientific status that Marxism lacks (Box 1:1).

Marx's political philosophy was based on a struggle to the death. A negotiated transformation of capitalism was not possible. Henry George's philosophy, on the other hand, was based on evolutionary transformation facilitated by the democratic process. Incremental reform of the public's finances would synthesise the public and private sectors into a harmonious whole. George knew that capital was also a victim of the rent-seekers.

By his own test – the verdict of history – Marx's philosophy has been relegated to the archives as a curiosity of the 19th century in whose name millions of people were deprived of their lives in the 20th century. That leaves one theory with which to guide future action. The name of Henry George has become the metaphor for the reforms that are capable of rescuing the global economy. Joseph Stiglitz, in a major report on how to reconstruct the US economy, wrote that

> [T]here is a range of pro-growth and pro-equality tax reforms that can both raise revenue and rebalance misaligned incentives. One general principle of taxation – known as the Henry George principle – is that we should tax things that have an inelastic supply, like land, oil, or other natural resources. The 19th century progressive Henry George argued that because land does not disappear when taxed, it can be taxed at high levels without

Box 1:1

Science and the Culture of Society

In the 1930s, Homer Hoyt demonstrated that land values in Chicago rose and fell in an 18-year cyclical pattern (Hoyt 1933). This pattern surfaced in the US economy throughout the 19th century. Further investigation revealed a similar periodicity in countries as geographically and culturally dispersed as the UK, Japan and Australia (Harrison 1983). But the pattern, while illuminating, was based on ex post analysis: looking back in time, and assuming that history would repeat itself. Cynics could claim that 'this time is different' – one of the mantras in the run-up to the Crash of 2008. And you cannot disprove a theory grounded in retrospective evidence.

So, when (in 1997) the present author made strenuous efforts to alert the Blair Government that house prices would peak 10 years later, in 2007, followed by a depression (Harrison (1997: 27; 2010), economists in the UK Treasury could delude themselves with the doctrine promoted by US Federal Reserve chairman Alan Greenspan: that this time it was different. History would not repeat itself. History, apparently, had come to an end! And Gordon Brown, the Chancellor of the Exchequer, had (after all) banished the 'boom/bust cycle': we had his word for it, repeated many times at the Despatch Box in the House of Commons.

The 18-year business cycle needed a scientifically robust explanation for the periodicity: an explanation which could be tested in real time. This was provided in 2005, in the form of the hypothesis that the 5% long-run interest rate shaped the 14-year property cycle within, and determined the outcome of, the 18-year cycle (Harrison 2005: 199-201). If correct, the 1997 forecast that the cycle which began in 1992 would terminate in 2010 was scientifically based. As yet, no economist has attempted to falsify the hypothesis. Why they have chosen not to apply scientific methods to test this scientific explanation for cyclical recessions is a matter for conjecture. What is beyond doubt is that academic economists, who presume to guide law-makers, inform the public and educate future generations, are derelict in their duty to act as scientists.

negatively distorting the economy; there is effectively no supply response. Even better, we can tax factors or behavior that do harm the economy.

(Stiglitz 2015: 71-72)

Henry George did not seek to negotiate change with the power-brokers. He spoke to the people, and his message was direct: it was up to them to reclaim their birthright. That was why professors of economics had to erase the significance of rent as an economic category. With the reworking of their technical language (see the chapters by Feder and Cleveland in this volume), the 20th century suffered from Flat-Earth economics. Statistics in official records (such as those of the US Government) could not honestly represent what was happening 'on the ground'. The data on capital gains from land was not just incomplete; it was false (Hudson and Feder 1997). This made it impossible to visualise how to heal the fractures in the economy and in society, for the law-makers no longer lived in a three-dimensional world.

This tragedy was poignantly expressed by a bewildered Mikhail Gorbachev. In recording the dismay of statesmen who had ended the Cold War, he wrote: 'We are often asked the following question: what went wrong? Our generation ... carried out its mission. But then why is today's world unquiet, unjust and militarised?' (Gorbachev 2016). The answer is evoked by an episode that terminated the Soviet Union. Gorbachev had insisted that, in dismantling the command economy, land should remain in public ownership; with secure private possession matched by payment of rent into the public purse (Noyes 1991:4). It was not to be: the putsch against him heralded the era of Yeltsin and the oligarchs who captured the rents of Russia.

If society is to be rescued from the state of turpitude into which it has been driven by the culture of rent-seeking (Harrison 2015), people who shape the public discourse have to come to terms with the Last Man Standing: Henry George.

References

Engels, Friedrich (1880), *Socialism: Utopian and Scientific.* www.marxists.org

Gaffney, Mason (1990), 'Concepts and Procedures for the Social Collection of Rent in the Soviet Union', revised as 'Privatizing Land Without Giveaway', Conference on Social Collection of Rent in the Soviet Union, New York City. http://www.earthrights.net/docs/privatize.html

— (1999), 'The Taxable Surplus of Land: Measuring, Guarding and Gathering It', Moscow, Duma Parliamentary Hearings on Land Revenues, January 19, 1999. Published in Russian in Zvolinsky, Vyacheslav (ed.), 'Nalogooblagayemi izlizhek, sozlavayemii zemlyei: izmyeryeniye, primnozhyeniye, sochranyeniye i sbor,' *Prirodniye resurci – natsionalnoyeh bogatstvo Rossii (Natural resources – the national wealth of Russia)*. Moscow: The Duma.

— (2015), 'A Real-Assets Model of Economic Crises: Will China Crash in 2015?' *American Journal of Economics and Sociology*, Vol 74 (2).

Gittings, John (2005), *The Changing Face of China*, Oxford: Oxford University Press.

Gorbachev, Mikhail (2016), 'Where did it all go wrong?' *Russia Beyond the Headlines*, April 28.

Gwartney, Ted (2014), 'Land Rents As a Sustainable Revenue Base for China', *Journal of Translation from Foreign Literature of Economics*, January.

Harrison, Fred (1983), *The Power in the Land*, London: Shepheard-Walwyn.

— (1997), *The Chaos Makers*, London: Othila Press.

— (2005), *Boom Bust: House Prices, Banking and the Depression of 2010*, London: Shepheard-Walwyn.

— (2008), *The Silver Bullet*, London: theIU.

— (2010), *2010: The Inquest*, London: DA Horizons. Available at:
   http://www.sharetherents.org/wp-content/uploads/2013/09/2010-The-Inquest-FINAL.pdf

— (2015), *As Evil Does*, London: Geophilos.

— (2016), *The Economic Consequences of Kate Barker*, London: Geophilos.

Hoyt, Homer (1933), *One Hundred Years of Land Values in Chicago*, Chicago: Chicago University Press.

Hudson, Michael, and Kris Feder (1997), *What's Missing from the Capital Gains Debate? Real Estate and Capital Gains Taxation*. Levy Institute Monograph #32.
   http://michael-hudson.com/wp-content/uploads/2010/03/97Missing zCapitalGainsDebate_ppb32.pdf

Löhr, D., Fu, S., Zhou, L. (2014), 'The Qingdao Land Regime – Lessons Learned', *Journal of Translation from Foreign Literature of Economics*, Special Issue on Land Value Taxation, English version online: http://se.xmu.edu.cn/jzyc/UploadFiles/201437183177055475115776.pdf

Mirrlees, James, *et. al.* (2011), *Tax by Design*, Oxford: Oxford University Press.

Noyes, Richard (1991), *Now the Synthesis: Capitalism, Socialism and the New Social Contract*, London: Shepheard-Walwyn.

O'Donnell, Edward T. (2015), *Henry George and the Crisis of Inequality*, New York: Columbia University Press.

Peddle, Francis K., and William S. Peirce (2016), *The Annotated Works of Henry George: Vol 1*, Madison: Fairleigh Dickinson University Press.

Popper, Karl (1962), *The Open Society and its Enemies*, 5th edn., Vol.2, Princeton: Princeton University Press.

Purves, Andrew (2015), *No Debt, High Growth, Low Tax: Hon Kong's Economic miracle Explained*, London: Shepheard-Walwyn.

Stiglitz, Joseph (2015), *Rewriting the Rules of the American Economy*, New York: Roosevelt Institute.
   http://rooseveltinstitute.org/rewrite-rules/

Tang Liming (2015), 'Local governments' hunger for land threatens sustainable development', *Chinareport*, November.
   http://www.newschinamag.com/magazine/local-governments-hunger-for-land-threatens-sustainable-development

Tideman, Nicolaus, *et al* (1991), 'Open Letter to Mikhail Gorbachev', reprinted in Richard Noyes (Ed.), *Now the Synthesis: Capitalism, Socialism & the New Social Contract*, London: Shepheard-Walwyn

Vickrey, William (1999), four chapters in *Land Value Taxation* (Editor: Kenneth C. Wenzer), NY: M.E. Sharpe/London: Shepheard-Walwyn.

Wildau, Gabriel, and Tom Mitchell (2015), 'China income gap among world's widest', *Financial Times*, January 15.

Zhi Liu (2015), 'Strengthening Municipal Fiscal Health in China', *Land Lines*, October.

2

Economics from the Ground Up: Public Revenue and the Structure of Production

KRIS FEDER

M ASON GAFFNEY argues that taxes and the excess burdens they cause are at the expense of economic surplus, which is captured in rent.

➤ Taxes reduce site rents by the sum of tax revenue and excess burden.

➤ A direct tax on rent is efficient; it imposes no excess burden, and it reduces rent in private markets by the amount of the tax.

➤ Taxes on other bases are shifted to rent by market adjustments that erode surplus. In particular, the ratios between land, labor, and capital employed in production are highly sensitive to relative prices and taxes.

➤ Long-lived capital, which turns over slowly, is associated with lower output, lower payrolls, higher interest costs, and higher land requirements per job compared to capital of short life. Existing tax regimes favor slow turnover and favor both capital and land over labor.

➤ Excess burden manifests as adoption of inappropriate technologies, underemployment of labor, and overuse of Earth's limited resources.

A. Design Flaw

AROUND THE WORLD today, national economies suffer a deep structural imbalance. To varying degrees in different political and economic systems, labor is underemployed while the services of nature are perilously overexploited. Capital seems most abundant where it is least needed. The evidence of dysfunction includes economic and social polarization, stagnant wages despite rising labor productivity, escalating public and private debts, a dearth of working capital, recurring booms and busts, and a headlong rush toward global resource depletion and ecological catastrophe. The political therapies usually applied may alleviate symptoms, but the malady is chronic; symptoms return, complicated by the side effects of the medicine itself.

Conventional political discourse is framed as a contest between Left and Right, liberal and conservative, communism and capitalism. This is a false dichotomy. Both conservative and progressive ideologies are superficial and incomplete. Communism may have proved a failure, but capitalism is ailing – and has yet to correct the injustices that give socialism its allure. In American politics, each of the dominant parties survives because it grasps enough of the truth to sound plausible and because, despite repeated failures, it gets re-elected after each failure of its rival. Possessing no theories that can withstand serious scrutiny, opponents take cover behind easy slogans or divert attention to side issues. Legislators talk past one another in partisan standoff. Reinforcing gridlock, the rent-seeking elite uses the political process to secure and enhance its privileges.

Conservatives know that the price system has no parallel in allocating scarce resources, a point that progressives often neglect, but they seem blind to the limitations of markets and apparently cannot distinguish parasitic incomes from productive ones. They see that government can do great harm, but their insight amounts to the conviction that regulations are always too taxing and taxes are always too high. Conservatives proclaim the sanctity of private property as though property were an end in itself, not an institution designed to promote work and saving. They forget the words of John Stuart Mill, ambassador of classical liberal philosophy:

> Private property, in every defence made of it, is supposed to mean the guarantee to individuals of the fruits of their own labour and abstinence. The guarantee to them of the fruits of the labour and abstinence of others, transmitted to them without any merit or exertion of their own, is not of

the essence of the institution, but a mere incidental consequence, which, when it reaches a certain height, does not promote, but conflicts with, the ends which render private property legitimate.

(Mill 1848: II.1.17)

Progressives, for their part, decry rising inequality and declining social mobility. They call for redistribution, by which they mean progressive income taxes, government benefits targeted to low-income families, and direct market interventions such as minimum wages or rent controls. They underestimate the deterrent effect of taxes on economic activity and ignore the possibility that progressive tax rates are offset, in the long run, by market adjustments to the wage scale. They appear not to notice that price controls work by reducing economic output, or that stimulating demand while stifling supply may produce little but inflation. Both sides make much of the need to promote small businesses, the 'job creators,' but neither knows how.

On the question of macroeconomic stability, Republicans prescribe austerity to ride out recessions and tax cuts to unleash aggregate supply. Democrats favor a Keynesian approach, prescribing government deficits to shore up demand during downturns, presumably offset by budget surpluses during expansions. Each treatment protocol addresses symptoms, not causes. Neither can be expected to produce economic stability and security.

All this is really not necessary. Competition and resource scarcity will always be with us, but the design flaws at the root of the economy's structural imbalance can be repaired. Rather than asking how much efficiency and freedom to sacrifice for the sake of justice, the geoclassical approach asks what share of economic output properly belongs to individuals and what part to the community and nation. It diagnoses the economy's dysfunction with reference to the institutions by which humans share the Earth – among themselves, with future generations, and with other species. It focuses particularly on the surpluses jointly produced by communities of people and their governments, linked together in networks of production and exchange. Geoclassical analysis reconciles the elements of truth in opposing ideologies (Gaffney 1994b:40-44), offering policies to raise wages and employment, shrink the nation's ecological footprint, improve the allocation of capital, and reduce public debts without starving the public sector (Box 2:1). The geoclassical approach aligns private incentives with public purposes, making markets perform better and initiating systemic transformation from the ground up.

Box 2:1

Mason Gaffney and
Geoclassical Economics

I adopt the term 'geoclassical,' once suggested by Fred Foldvary, to denote the modern school of thought that finds its inspiration in the work of Henry George. Geoclassical economics traces its roots to classical political economy. Classical economists concerned themselves with grand questions of growth, distribution, and sustainability. They recognized three productive factors – land, labor, and capital – and thought that economic growth is ultimately constrained by land scarcity. David Ricardo gave us the law of rent; others extolled the virtues of taxing land. Adam Smith wrote:

> Both ground-rents and the ordinary rent of land are a species of revenue which the owner, in many cases, enjoys without any care or attention of his own. Though a part of this revenue should be taken from him in order to defray the expences of the state, no discouragement will thereby be given to any sort of industry. The annual produce of the land and labour of the society, the real wealth and revenue of the great body of the people, might be the same after such a tax as before.... Nothing can be more reasonable than that a fund which owes its existence to the good government of the state should be taxed peculiarly ... towards the support of that government.
>
> (Smith 1776:V.2.75-76)

Geoclassical economics (GCE) offers a framework for studying the interplay between individual and collective action. It recovers the classical focus on the role of land (geo), long abandoned by neoclassical economics (NCE). Mason Gaffney, the leading expositor, revives certain classical themes that George overlooked, notably the relationship between capital turnover and employment. Drawing also on ideas from Knut Wicksell and Austrian economics, Gaffney has developed a robust geoclassical theory of capital which runs through his theory of the real estate cycle and forms the basis for the analysis presented in this chapter.

Henry George thought that Earth's limits to growth were remote. Land scarcity was a consequence of public policy, and what was needed was to transfer idle lands from speculators to the landless. Much has changed since 1880. Global population is over five times larger; the US population over six times. An industrial structure dependent on cheap fossil fuels has given us ecological destruction and climate change. Resources once abundant are growing scarce, yielding spectacular rents to the holders of what is left. The geoclassical

The argument of the present chapter is that all taxes are ultimately paid out of the economy's surplus. The public sector can tap surplus directly in ways that improve efficiency and generate full employment. When surplus is tapped indirectly by ill-designed taxes, however, much of the surplus is dissipated as taxpayers adapt to warped price incentives. Such taxes press the economy to produce less and employ less labor with any given resource base. They slow capital turnover, freezing capital in unproductive forms and creating artificial scarcity. They impose a dead-weight loss, or excess burden, eroding the tax base as they distort the allocation of resources.

The surplus of a territorial community is rent. Taxes come out of rent. Excess burden also comes out of rent, and Gaffney demonstrates that excess burden is much larger than conventionally thought. *Inappropriate tax structures diminish the economy's rent surplus by the sum of tax revenue and excess burden.* A tax applied directly to the narrow base of rent, because it creates no distortion, can generate more revenue than a tax applied to any other base. It directs the economy to employ more labor where labor is offered in abundant supply and to economize on nature's gifts as they grow scarce.

B. Income and Taxes

An error typical of many public revenue systems is to base taxes, in whole or in part, on sales or cost or components of cost, rather than on the excess of income over costs. Mason Gaffney shows how sales, VAT, and US income taxes produce enormous inefficiencies (Gaffney 2013, 2011, 2009, 1976). His approach is to examine how taxes affect the intensity of land use on a particular site. Political jurisdictions are defined as fixed areas of land, so the effects of tax changes can be replicated across all sites in the tax jurisdiction to study the aggregate response.

It is important to follow the reasoning behind this critique of conventional tax policies, if electorates are to be informed to the point where lawmakers can come to terms with the need to abandon obsolete doctrines in favor of radical fiscal reform. A simple tabular model is offered to illustrate the contrasting outcomes between benign ways of raising the public's revenue compared to the damage inflicted by the taxes that are currently employed by governments.

Suppose that a parcel of land can be used in one of three ways, A, B, and D (reserving 'C' for cost). Define the variables:

G = Gross income per period

C = Cost per period

N = Net income per period (G – C)

T_N, T_G, T_C = Tax revenue raised from a proportional tax on the base of N, G, or C

NAT_N, NAT_G, NAT_C = Net income after tax with a proportional tax on N, G, or C

Columns (1) and (2) of Table 2:1 shows hypothetical values for gross income and cost for each land use. Columns (3) through (9) compute net income, taxes, and net income after tax for each tax base.

Table 2:1

Taxes on Net Income, Gross Income, and Costs

	(1)	(2)	(3)	(4)	(5)	(6)	(7)	(8)	(9)
	Gross income	Cost	Net income = G – C	Tax on N at 20%	Net after tax = N – T_N	Tax on G at 20%	Net after tax = N – T_G	Tax on C at 25%	Net after = N – T_C
	G	C	N	T_N	NAT_N	T_G	NAT_G	T_C	NAT_C
Land use A	100	80	20	4	16	20	0	20	0
Land use B	25	15	10	2	8	5	5	3.75	0.25
Land use D	10	2	8	1.6	6.4	2	6	0.50	7.500

(Based on Gaffney 2011, 1999)

Use A is the best use of this site. Though it has a relatively high ratio of costs to sales, it yields the most net income (N = 20). It is also the most intensive use; it has the largest sales and creates the most jobs. The lowest use is D, which yields a net income of N = 8. It generates little income, but its cost is near zero. For efficient resource allocation, the land should be devoted to use A, and *this will be the market outcome in the absence of taxes.*

Suppose we impose a 20% tax on net income. Columns (4) and (5) show the tax and net after-tax income for each land use. This tax does not affect the ranking of land uses, so efficiency is not compromised. Sales are $100 and tax revenue is $4.

Suppose we impose the 20% tax on *gross* income. Columns (6) and (7) show the results. The tax on gross income reverses the ranking of land uses. NAT is now lowest ($0) for use A and highest ($6) for use D. The land is devoted to use D, so efficiency is lost. Sales are just $10 and tax revenue a mere $2.

Sales, VAT, and excise taxes are based on gross income. They create a powerful bias against enterprises that generate high sales, employment, and net income. They favor low-intensity land uses that generate few jobs and little income. Columns (8) and (9) show that a 25% tax on cost, like a 20% tax on G, wipes out the net income from land use A, but gives an even greater advantage to D. A payroll tax is a tax on a component of cost and has the additional effect of encouraging the substitution of land and capital for labor in the input mix that composes cost.

Although gross income is a broader base than net income (five times larger for use A), a tax on N can raise more revenue than a tax on G would. A tax on gross income can go no higher than 13.33% without shifting the land into a lower use,[1] so it can yield at most $13.33. A tax on net income, however, can run to 100% and rise to $20, the maximum net income for this site. A tax on any other base distorts factor proportions, reduces output, and diminishes the available tax revenue.

C. The Great Revolving Fund

Of Gaffney's major contributions, the most underappreciated may be his rediscovery of the enormous variation among enterprises in the degree to which capital, natural materials, and land sites substitute for or complement labor, and his analysis of the staggering implications for tax policy. The thesis explored here is that a given stock of capital generates more gross income and larger payrolls as it turns over faster. The speed of turnover is constrained by a tax on gross income. The ratio of interest income to wage income is raised, output is reduced, and the negative impact is felt in the labor market as fewer people are employed.

Capital is wealth that yields a future return of cash or in-kind income. Capital allows us to adopt technologies that raise the value of what labor and land can produce, at the cost of a time delay between the start of

---

1 A tax of 2/15 or 13.33% of gross income takes 13.33 with land use A and $3.33 with B. Net income after tax is $6.67 for either use.

production and final consumption. Robinson Crusoe can catch more fish if he first spends three weeks building a canoe, but he cannot begin until he has stockpiled food to last through the days when he does not fish: food-capital is depleted, day by day, as canoe-capital takes shape. Capital also allows us to exploit the values created by biological growth, which takes time. Through saving, lending, and leasing, capital permits individuals to adjust the timing of production and consumption in cooperation with others who have complementary preferences. In an efficient market, investment is carried to the margin at which the rate of return to capital equals the rate at which people are willing to trade off present for future consumption. When an enterprise borrows to finance investment, market interest motivates owners of wealth to postpone some consumption so that others may invest or consume income they have not yet produced. When an enterprise sinks its own funds, the 'opportunity cost' of capital is the foregone interest that it might otherwise have earned by lending its capital to other investors.

Physical capital is produced by applying labor to materials. Gaffney analyzes two general types.

'Flowing' capital, such as a machine or the stock of flour in a bakery, depreciates or is used up over time and must eventually be replaced. Flowing capital is not worth the trouble of producing it unless its lifetime gross income covers not only the invested principal (its cost of production) and operating costs, but also the time cost of capital, that is, interest. A depreciating capital good is fully amortized when accumulated revenues net of current costs, if saved at interest through its economic life, are sufficient to replace the invested sum. Unlike physical capital, these set-asides for depreciation (capital consumption allowances) are liquid and fungible, so they can be reinvested elsewhere as opportunities arise. The frequency with which flowing capital is used up or fully depreciated and replaced is the rate of capital 'turnover'.

'Growing' capital, such as crops or livestock, appreciates over time. Appreciation is a flow of income that is not realized until harvest or sale (unless by borrowing against the rising value of the asset). Growing capital is not worthwhile unless sales revenue covers the accumulated interest cost of the capital sunk at planting time, as well as replacement (replanting) cost. The frequency with which growing capital is harvested and replanted is the rate of capital 'turnover'.

Gaffney shows that – with instructive exceptions – capital that has a high turnover rate has a high 'valence' for labor (Gaffney 2003), that is, its employment entails a high ratio of wage cost to interest cost. There are two reasons for this pattern. First, fast-turning capital must be replaced frequently, and labor is employed in producing replacement capital. Only enterprises expected to yield *gross* income sufficient to hire this labor will be undertaken. Second, fast-turning capital is generally 'working capital,' largely complementary with labor as it is used. Gaffney attributes this insight to the classical economists and especially to Swedish economist Knut Wicksell.

> Wicksell saw capital soaking up any surplus labor. 'If ... more labor is available than can be employed ... a *shorter* period of production ... is adopted, and the capital which was before insufficient is now able to give employment to all workers.' He saw social capital as a wage fund, but a fund which can sustain any rate of flow because it revolves. This Great Revolving Fund does not limit wages. By recycling faster it employs more workers up to any needed number, and it speeds up when stimulated by lower wage rates and higher interest. In the idiom of modern macro-economics, this increases replacement demand. Aggregate demand can fall short of full employment if capital turns slowly, but quicker replacement corrects things and fills the gap. Thus 'the existing capital must just suffice to employ the existing number of workers.' The greater replacement demand is financed by greater capital recovery, and matched by a greater flow of finished goods, so it is not diluted by inflation.
>
> (Gaffney 1976:139-140; citing Wicksell 1954: 127, 160)

In short, employment is *not* linked tightly to the volume of capital or net investment as standard models assume. Capital can combine with more or less labor, over a wide range, depending on relative prices. 'We do not need to find a new theory, but to resurrect one' (Gaffney 1976:106).

Flowing Capital   Consider first the case of flowing capital, which yields a stream of income as it depreciates. We are interested in the long run effect of a tax levied by a political jurisdiction, so let us see how taxes affect capital turnover on a representative parcel of land. Suppose that the land manager can borrow at an interest rate of 2% to finance con-struction, and that he has three development options:

Option A   Build and rent out 20 modest straw houses for a construction cost of $100 ($5 each). Give each house a small yard. Replace each house every year. Gross income is large compared to other options, but so is cost.

Option B Build a grand brick house for a construction cost of $100. Surround the house with a spacious yard. Rent it to a well-to-do family. Every 50 years, the owner or his heir replaces the depreciated old house with an identical new house.

Option D Build a parking lot. Gross income is low, but cost is lower. G (gross income) is a large multiple of C (cost).

Capital invested in straw houses turns over faster than capital invested in brick houses or parking lots. To be worth building, a house must yield an annual service flow (gross income) that covers the rent of land, interest on the invested capital, and a capital consumption allowance. Depreciation is a small component of annual cost for a brick house or a parking lot, but the service flow of a straw house must be sufficient to replace the entire $5 principal in a year.

The alternative outcomes are illustrated in Table 2:2. Annual depreciation is capital value (K) multiplied by the rate of turnover (d). The rate of turnover is the reciprocal of capital life: 1.00 for a straw house, 0.02 for a brick house, and 0.04 for a parking lot. Annual cost (C) is the sum of depreciation and interest cost, excluding rent for now. Annual net income (N) is gross income (G) minus cost. Note that interest is less than 2% of total cost for straw houses but half of the cost for brick houses. Option A is the most intensive use; it houses 20 times as many families and employs 50 times as much labor in construction as the brick house option. It employs 500 times as much labor as the parking lot.

Table 2:2 • Flowing Capital, Turnover, and Taxes

(1)	(2)	(3)	(4)	(5)	(6)	(7)	(8)	(9)	(10)	(11)	(12)
Land use	Life (years)	K	dK = K/LIFE	iK = 0.02K	C = dK + iK	G	N = G − C	TAX G (t = 20%)	NAT (= N − TAX$_G$)	TAX G (t = 40%)	NAT (= N − TAX$_G$)
A Straw houses	1	100	100	2	102	120	$18	24	− 6	48	− 30
B Brick house	50	100	2	2	4	10	6	2	$4	4	2
D Parking lot	25	5	0.20	0.10	0.30	5	4.70	1	3.70	2	$2.70

Option A is also the most efficient option, yielding net income of $18. Option B yields $6 and option D is the worst option, yielding just $4.70. *If there are no taxes, the land manager builds straw houses.*

Now suppose that a tax of 20% is levied on gross income. Because straw houses are replaced every year, gross income must be high. The tax reduces net income from option A by $24, leaving negative net after-tax income (NAT). Because brick houses are durable, option B is viable with little gross income. A brick house is still preferred to a parking lot. The land manager builds a brick house; tax revenue is $2. The net income yielded by the site falls from $18 to $6 and gross income, which includes payroll, shrinks to just one twelfth of the untaxed amount. If the tax rate is doubled to 40%, the order of preference is reversed. A parking lot – the least efficient use of this site – becomes the most attractive option. Gross income shrinks to just one twenty-fourth of the untaxed amount. Thus a tax on gross income favors a less efficient and less intensive land use. By contrast, a tax on N can yield up to $18, the maximum achievable net income. Because it does not distort land use, a tax on net income has greater revenue capacity than a tax on the larger base of gross income.

Growing Capital   Growing capital ties up capital until harvest or sale before any is recovered. Appreciation must be sufficient to pay interest and rent and to recover the invested principal (next cycle's planting cost). Suppose the owner of a patch of fertile land is considering whether to plant trees or carrots. Timber is ready to cut in 50 years; carrots are harvested each year. Table 3 shows hypothetical gross income, planting cost, interest cost, and net income for each land use option. Total cost in column (5) uses an interest rate of 2% continuously compounded (C = 100ert) and rounded to the nearest dollar. The bottom row shows income and cost over 50 carrot crop cycles, for direct comparison with the timber enterprise.

The carrot farm is the more efficient option. Over 50 years it yields a net income of $400, compared to $78 for the tree farm. The carrot farm is also the more intensive land use; it employs 50 times more labor and yields a gross income over four times larger than timber. *The same capital, turning over faster, generates more income.* Wages are a larger share of cost and interest is a smaller share: interest is (172/272) = 63% of cost for the tree farm but just (2/102) = 2% of cost for the carrot farm. Capital's share rises and labor's share falls as the interest rate rises – slightly for the carrot farm; dramatically for the tree farm (see Appendix 1).

Table 2:3

Growing Capital, Turnover, and Taxes
(Interest Rate 2%)

(1)	(2)	(3)	(4)	(5)	(6)	(7)	(8)
Land Use	Gross Income G	Planting Cost	Interest Cost	Total Cost	Net Income N	TAX$_G$ 20%	NAT 20%
A Timber (50 year rotation)	350	100	172	272	78	70	8
B Carrots (1 year rotation)	110	100	2	102	8	22	– 14
B Carrots (50 rotations)	5,500	5,000	100	5,100	400	1,100	– 700

Columns (7) and (8) show the effect of a 20% tax on gross income. Now the tree farm becomes the land manager's choice; the carrot farm is sub-marginal. The revenue raised is $70, payable when the timber is cut in 50 years.

The tax on gross income, as in the case of flowing capital, aborts the more intensive land use. Employment on this land parcel is much reduced. The differential effect of a tax on realized gross income (or payroll or any other part of cost) is even starker for growing capital than for flowing capital. In both cases, a tax proportioned to gross income (G), due at harvest or sale, bears more heavily on enterprises with faster capital turnover. *When the effect is generalized across all parcels in the tax jurisdiction, we expect lower aggregate employment, less output, and more capital per worker.* A tax on net income, by contrast, does not distort land use; productivity is not impaired and the economy's aggregate rent is higher. In Table 2:3, a tax of up to 100% on net income can yield up to $400 in revenue over 50 years.

This is not to suggest that people must all live in straw huts to achieve full employment, or that the market will give us carrots but no lumber. Nor do the tables account for differences in factor ratios employed to produce bricks and fertilizer or to process trees and carrots into finished goods. It is the function of markets to adjust the relative prices of things, fitting quantities demanded to quantities supplied. If there were too many straw houses and not enough brick to satisfy people's tastes, then price and gross income would fall for straw houses and rise for brick. In Table 2:2, if the gross income of straw houses fell from \$120 to \$100, then the net income would be wiped out, straw houses would become submarginal, and the land manager would build a brick house instead. In Table 3, less than a 10% decline in gross income makes the carrot enterprise sub-optimal. The lesson is that, given relative demands and costs, a tax levied on gross income can press land into suboptimal, low-intensity uses. Gaffney writes:

> I would not recommend that all our investing go into working capital like carrots, and none into fixed capital like roadbeds, harbors, telephone poles, plant and equipment. There is an equilibrating market mechanism that finds, or at least seeks, an optimal balance. If capital is scarce and labor surplus, this should lead to higher interest rates and lower wage rates. The combination leads investors into working capital, and away from fixed capital, until the 'valence' of capital for labor shall have risen, soaking up the surplus labor. There is no need to go any further and reverse the bias in favor of labor. The operation of a free market with flexible prices to serve as equilibrators should do the job. The idea is to make jobs not by waste but in the process of mixing inputs more efficiently. Based on that analysis we can then see how to invest so as to put capital where the jobs are, to invest so that the 'job-creating efficiency', if you will, of capital and land is higher – not a maximum, but an optimum where idleness is only voluntary and the amount of capital suffices that people save voluntarily. It is the price system that weighs these compensating factors in the same balance and lets us achieve an optimal total deployment and mixture of labor, capital, and resources.
>
> (Gaffney 2003)

D.. All Taxes Come Out of Rent

Net Income of Households and Enterprises   A tax on net income is efficient because it does change the land manager's preferred enter-prise. The production plan that maximizes net income (N) also maximizes after-tax net income, $(1 - t)N$. Economically marginal activities, which cover costs (pay wages) but yield zero net income, owe no tax, so no worth-while enterprises are driven away. Because supply is not withdrawn, prices are not pulled upward. It is natural to infer that the net incomes of households and firms, as well as landholders, can be taxed with no loss of efficiency. Nevertheless, taxes based on the net incomes of house-holds or business enterprises fall far short of ideal.

For households supplying labor, the calculation of net income should deduct the expenses of earning income, which may be broadly or narrowly interpreted. Gaffney makes the case that a considerable proportion of median household income is expended on the necessary costs of raising children and maintaining the household (Gaffney 2005a). Net income accounts also for the imputed income from owner-occupied homes and other in-kind flows. In deducting costs, fine determinations would have to be made, such as whether spending time with the kids is consumption or cost. Thus household net income is ambiguously defined, partly unobservable, and probably small. If income devoted to the expenses of maintaining a household and reproducing a family is treated as taxable income, excess burden will appear as an erosion of skills and capabilities appropriate to adults' roles as workers, entrepreneurs, citizens, and parents.

Business net income has similar shortcomings as a tax base. Again, imputed income is hard to measure. How much of the salary that an entrepreneur pays herself is foregone earnings – the opportunity cost of withholding her time and talent from the market? Is monopoly profit net income, or must we first deduct the rent-seeking expenditures by which the monopolist elbowed its way to dominance?[2] Moreover, tax neutrality requires that if net incomes are taxed then losses must be compensated by a subsidy at the same rate. Insofar as markets are competitive, however, little revenue would be raised this way. Resource mobility ensures that over the long run revenues just cover opportunity costs and economic profit tends to zero. One might suppose that average profit is slightly positive to induce entrepreneurs to accept investment risk; but then the risk premium appears as a necessary cost of production, and so not surplus. If losses are not deducted, then the expected marginal after-tax reward of risk-taking enterprise diminishes and some socially warranted risk-taking is presumably discouraged. Thus a tax intended to fall on business net income may produce an excess burden because investment and innovation are risky.

ATCOR and EBCOR in Models with Flowing and Growing Capital

In our models of flowing and growing capital, we compared alternative uses for given parcels of land, but we did not account for rent. We rectify that now, recognizing that 'net income' (N) as defined in the tables is the maximum annual amount that an enterprise can afford to

---

2 If there is competition for the chance to achieve monopoly status, as by lobbying a congressman or buying a taxi license, then part of the monopoly "profit" recoups these costs.

pay for the use of the site. If market rent were any higher, net income after payment of rent would be negative. Thus N represents the *bid-rent* of an enterprise. In spatial equilibrium, each land parcel is allocated to the enterprise that outbids all others. Rent is the opportunity cost of turning a site to one use rather than its best alternative use; it is the bid-rent of the runner-up enterprise in the contest for access to land, which is the amount that the winner must offer to meet the competition. (The gap between the highest and second-highest bids is probably negligible in active land markets.)

Mason Gaffney's ATCOR thesis is: *All taxes come out of rent.* EBCOR says: *Excess burden comes out of rent.* Together, ATCOR and EBCOR mean that any tax reduces rent below the untaxed level by the sum of the tax revenue and the excess burden. To see this, observe that:

1. The rent of a parcel of land is the net after-tax income of the successful bidder[3] for the land:

$$\text{RENT} = \text{NAT of winning bidder}$$

2. Excess burden (EB) is the decrease in net income that occurs if the tax causes the land to be turned over to a lower use:

$$\text{EB} = \Delta N \text{ from tax-induced change in land use}$$

Table 2:4 summarizes the results from Tables 2:2 and 2:3. A tax on gross income favors capital that turns over slowly. For flowing capital, a 20% tax changes land use from brick houses to straw; a 40% tax favors the parking lot. For growing capital, a 20% tax changes the preferred crop from carrots to timber. Columns (5), (6), and (7) illustrate ATCOR/EBCOR:

$$\text{TAX}_G + \text{EB} = \Delta \text{RENT}$$

If the tax base is net rather than gross income, the thesis holds trivially. Excess burden is zero and rent declines by the exact amount of the tax. All taxes come out of rent, but whereas direct taxes on rent are efficient, taxes on other bases are shifted to rent in an economic process that destroys a considerable part of the rent surplus.

---

3 Ignoring the gap between the highest bid and the second-highest.

Table 2:4

ATCOR and EBCOR with Taxes on Gross Income

ATCOR/EBCOR and Flowing Capital (from Table 2)

(1)	(2)	(3)	(4)	(5)	(6)	(7)
Tax rate t	Winning bidder	N	NAT = RENT	TAX_G	EB = ΔN	ΔRENT
0	**A. Straw houses**	18	18	0	0	0
0.20	**B. Brick house**	6	4	2	12	14
0.40	**D. Parking lot**	4.70	3.70	1	13.30	14.30

ATCOR/EBCOR and Growing Capital (from Table 3)

(1)	(2)	(3)	(4)	(5)	(6)	(7)
Tax rate t	Winning bidder	N	NAT = RENT	TAX_G	EB = ΔN	ΔRENT
0	**B. Carrots** (50 rotations)	400	400	0	0	0
0.20	**A. Timber** (50 year rotation)	78	8	70	322	392

ATCOR and EBCOR in Market Models

In market models, the ATCOR/EBCOR thesis is strictly correct when labor and capital are perfectly elastically supplied in the long run. The supply of a factor is perfectly elastic if a rise in demand for it raises the quantity employed without pulling up price and a fall in demand reduces employment with no downward pressure on price. A factor that is perfectly elastically supplied will withdraw rather than absorb any share of a tax. Enterprises in a competitive economy earn approximately zero economic profit over the long run, so they cannot absorb tax costs either. To stay in business, enterprises compensate for payroll taxes either by raising product prices or by paying less for other inputs.

Enterprises faced with a wage tax in a single jurisdiction cannot raise the prices of products that compete in national or global markets.

For goods and services sold locally, the standard analysis says that the wage tax may be shifted forward to consumers in higher prices. 'Consumer surplus' falls. Consumers, however, faced with higher prices in the tax jurisdiction, are able to offer less for land there, shifting the tax backward to land. After all, consumers are the same people supplying the labor to produce consumer goods. If they will not bear the tax by submitting to lower wages – either because they cannot live on less or because they are mobile and free to take their business elsewhere – then they are unlikely to submit to a reduction in real wages by another path. The standard partial-equilibrium market analysis does not account for this.

A wage tax cannot be shifted to capital if capital, like labor, is perfectly elastically supplied. It must be shifted to land: ATCOR. Land as site, the sense used here, is perfectly immobile. However heavy its tax burden, land does not starve or fall into disrepair, and it cannot flee the jurisdiction; its supply is perfectly inelastic. A wage tax causes rents to fall by more than enough to absorb the tax because as people and enterprises withdraw, resources are diverted to less productive uses or dis-employed altogether: EBCOR. A parallel argument applies to a tax on capital. Appendix 2 uses an aggregate Cobb-Douglas production function to show that a tax on labor raises the equilibrium gross-of-tax wage by the amount of the tax and depresses rent by the sum of tax revenue and excess burden.

How elastic are factor supplies? It is true that much capital is locked up in durable forms with limited adaptability for new uses. Capital affixed to land, like houses and shops and streets, may appear to be perfectly immobile. Unlike land, however, capital turns over – it wears out or is used up, and must be replaced with capital of comparable value if productive capacity is to be maintained. In the normal state of business, capital yields enough income (net of operating costs) to finance eventual replacement. If an office building is located in a city that imposes a wage tax, then when the time comes to tear down the building, the owners may relocate the offices to a tax-free city and recycle the present site for a less labor-intensive enterprise. Meanwhile, capital consumption allowances set aside from gross income can be reinvested anywhere, in whatever enterprise promises the best after-tax return. Today, with electronic communications, financial capital is highly mobile in the short run, even across most national borders. Investors will be repelled from a jurisdiction where after-tax returns to capital are lower than elsewhere.

Rents will fall in the high-tax jurisdiction until capital flight ceases as after-tax returns are equalized across borders.[4]

As for labor, workers are mobile among local jurisdictions. Some can be expected to emigrate if one city or state taxes wages at higher rates than its neighbors (other things being equal). The demand for land falls in the high-tax location and rises elsewhere; rents adjust accordingly. Workers acquire specialized skills that are not always easily transferable among occupations, and social considerations limit geographic mobility across a national or global economy; but even in a national economy with no migration, labor supply may be highly elastic. The supply of low-skilled labor may be perfectly elastic along a wage floor determined by a minimum legal wage, or by the value of the public assistance available to the unemployed. The Physiocrats of 18th-century France, who first developed the thesis that All Taxes Come out of Rent, observed that the wages of ordinary labor tended to hover around 'subsistence'. It seemed evident to classical and pre-classical economists that the natural rate of wages was just sufficient to maintain the labor force.

In today's distressed economies, the main reason to suspect that labor supply is highly elastic is that unemployment and underemployment are persistently high. If the demand for labor grows in an economy with a fixed population, then as employment approaches the maximum that the population can supply, higher wages must be offered to draw more people into the labor force.[5] If, however, the demand for labor is low and unemployment high, wages may remain quite flat as demand rises over some range. With a large reserve army of the unemployed, employers need offer no more than the going wage to attract job applicants.

The widely-reported official unemployment rate understates the slackness in the labor market. The U-6 measure tracked by the United States Bureau of Labor Statistics counts 'total unemployed, plus all persons marginally attached to the labor force, plus total employed part time for economic reasons, as a percent of the civilian labor force plus all persons marginally attached to the labor force'. U-6 runs nearly twice the official

---

4 According to the US Census, 12% of employed civilians moved in 2014-2015. Of these, 35% moved out of county and 3.7% moved abroad. *Geographical Mobility*: 2014 to 2015, http://www.census. gov/hhes/migration/data/cps/cps2015.html. About 5 to 7% of Americans switch from one job to another each year. Job-to-Job Flows (J2J) Data (Beta), http://lehd.ces.census.gov/data/j2j/ R2015Q2/j2jr/us/graphs_adj_national_totals.pdf.

5 Rising wages suggests rising costs of bringing qualified labor to market, in which case the thesis still stands: labor will not bear a tax. In general equilibrium models of a closed economy, however, the distinction between cost and net income is murkier.

unemployment rate (U-3, 'total unemployed, as a percent of the civilian labor force'). U-6 peaked at over 17 percent in late 2009 and early 2010 as the official rate approached 10 percent. By December 2015, eight years after the start of the Great Recession, U-3 had declined to 5%, now considered 'full employment,' but U-6 was 9.9% (*The Economics Daily* 2015). Underemployment of nearly 10% may explain why the post-recession recovery has yet to pull up wages. Flat wages with rising demand is evidence of a highly elastic labor supply.

Net Income of the Community   In the geoclassical paradigm, rent is the income, not of persons or enterprises, but of the territorial state itself. Land value is produced by the whole community using the resource base open to it. It is the joint product of cultural and political institutions, government investment, natural resources, ecosystem services, and the unintended, uncompensated, incidental effects of people's actions on other people (externalities). Rent is concentrated in healthy cities, where households and enterprises cluster together for mutual benefit. Gaffney credits Henry George with recognizing the nature of urban synergy and the immensity of the values it produces:

> George saw cities as foci of communication, cooperation, socialization, and exchange, which he considered the basis of civilization. He saw cities as the new frontier, an endless series of new frontiers, because the city as a whole enjoys increasing returns. The presence of people with good mutual access associating on equal terms expedites cooperation and specialization through the market. Multivariate interactions in cities are synergistic... The whole is greater than the sum of its parts... This synergistic surplus, says George, lodges in urban land rents. Thus he explained an outstanding phenomenon of his times, which other economists were overlooking completely: the unparalleled rise of urban rents and land prices, and the wealth and power of the owners.
>
> (Gaffney 1988:6)

E.   A Disturbance in the Force

The significance of the rate of capital turnover was understood by classical economists. John Stuart Mill's *Principles of Political Economy* (1848) was the standard textbook for more than a generation. Mill wrote:

> If there were a tax on all commodities, exactly proportioned to their value, there would ... be a *'disturbance' of values* ... owing to ... the different dura-bility of the capital employed in different occupations... If a greater

proportion of one than of the other is fixed capital, or if that fixed capital
is more durable, there will be a less consumption of capital in the year,
and less will be required to replace it, so that the profit, if absolutely the
same, will form a greater proportion of the annual returns... If on these
two branches of industry a tax be imposed ... the one commodity must rise
in price, or the other must fall, or both: commodities made chiefly by
immediate labor must rise in value, as compared with those which are
chiefly made by machinery.
                                              (Mill 1848: Bk V, Ch IV: 504-05)

'With his philosophical bent,' says Gaffney, Mill 'looked deeper than
modern writers on sales taxation, and pointed out a systemic bias
inherent in the tax.'

> How memorable is Mill's word 'disturbance,' 150 years before Darth Vader
> in *Star Wars* sensed a 'Disturbance in The Force'! In Mill's and M'Culloch's
> usage, 'The Force' is value as determined in a market before or without
> taxes based on gross sales. Mill hid this light under a bushel, by offering
> just one example of a small difference, arithmetic only, and easy to over-
> look in passing, which is what later standard economists have done. We
> should, rather, set this light in a tower on a hilltop as a beacon sending
> its gleam across the wave to save the foundering ship of state.
>
>   (Gaffney 2011:5)

Many provisions of the US federal tax code contribute to the distur-
bance (Gaffney 2009, 1999, 1993). Most obviously, the personal income
tax treats wages and salaries as 'ordinary' income, taxed at the full rate,
while taxing other incomes less or not at all. The payroll tax earmarked
for social insurance falls exclusively on labor; it alone pushes a wedge of
about 15% (up to some cap) between what employers pay and what employees take home. Retail sales and excise taxes exempt many kinds of
property income, including the imputed income of one's house. Even a
uniform sales tax, as we have seen, is distortionary, because it falls on
gross income – turnover and exchange. Sales taxes are even more distortionary than income taxes, which deduct depreciation.

The Income Tax Treatment of Capital   The US federal tax code
'contains many loopholes and abatements for capital,' writes Gaffney,
'and these generally are geared to favor capital of longer life'. Tax
preferences 'move investors to prefer capital-using over labor-using techniques and combine more capital per worker in all processes' (Gaffney
1976:132). The treatment of flowing capital depends on how depreciation,

expenses and imputed income are handled. The imputed income of owner-occupied homes, for example, is exempt, even as mortgage interest and property taxes are deductible.

For tax neutrality, depreciation is a current cost that should be deductible. Depreciation allowances in the income tax do not slow turnover because annual depreciation is smaller for capital of longer life, making income taxes less distortionary than sales taxes. However, depreciation schedules often permit an enterprise to write off a depreciating asset, such as a building, faster than it actually declines in value, which does favor slow turnover. When a building is sold, if write-offs have been too generous, then a capital gains tax is due on the excess of the sale price over the depreciated book value. This recaptures just part of the lost tax revenue, however, because capital gains are taxed later and less than other income.

The US tax system is even more favorable to growing capital because of the preferential treatment of capital gains. While gains to capital that turns over within a year are taxed as ordinary income, long term gains are currently taxed at about half the recipient's marginal tax rate. Some capital gains are fully or partially exempt, including capital gains to homeowners selling one house to buy another, capital gains at death, and capital gains of nonprofits.

The primary benefit to growing capital is tax deferral. Just as depreciation is a current cost, appreciation is current income. Unrealized asset appreciation is hard to measure, so capital gains are not taxed until realized by sale, if at all – another source of institutional bias against turnover. Taxes deferred are taxes denied: the effective rate of a tax deferred ten years is 61.4% of the nominal tax rate if interest is 5% and just 39.6% if interest is 10%.[6] A tax on realized capital gains bears less heavily on growing capital than a tax on unrealized gains.[7] 'In effect,'

---

6 Compounded annually. The discount is $1/(1+r)t$.

7 Suppose, for example, that a stand of trees has an initial value of $100 at planting and grows in value by $10 per year. Ignoring land, taxes, and other costs, the stand should be harvested when its growth rate declines to the rate of interest. Letting y represent the year, the annual growth rate is $1/(y + 10)$, which equals 0.04 in year 15. If the stand is cut after 15 years, then the harvest value is $250 and the capital gain is $150. (This oversimplifies. Gaffney, following Faustmann, shows that the optimal harvest cycle maximizes the present value of the forest land. This result strengthens the conclusion that aggregate land value is the best measure of the social surplus. See Mary Cleveland, Chapter 3.) A 15% tax on realized capital gains yields $22.50 in revenue. If the interest rate is 4%, then the present value of the capital gain at planting time is $12.49, or 12.5% of planting cost. This means that if the owner sets aside, not $22.50, but $12.49

Continued on next page

writes Gaffney, 'by deferring taxes, the Treasury helps finance growing capital (except ordinary inventories of short life)' (Gaffney 1976:133).

A further consequence of tax bias is that corporations can help stockholders to avoid taxes by retaining profits, converting dividend income into capital gains. 'This puts more capital each year back in the control of corporate managers to reinvest, whether or not they have any good ideas,' says Gaffney. 'The net impact of the corporate tax system is to make internal capital artificially cheap to corporations and push them into ventures of deferred payoffs' (Gaffney 1976:135).

The Income Tax Treatment of Land 'When it comes to holding land,' writes Gaffney, 'the tax system is geared to make the burdens light and the rewards great' (Gaffney 1976:125). As noted, the imputed income of owner-occupied homes is tax-exempt; this includes the land under and around houses. Interest and property taxes are deductible for residential land as for owner-occupied houses. Appreciation is not taxed until realized by sale and is subject to the low 'capital' gains rate. For business real estate, landowners often borrow to buy land, paying out their rent income (which would be taxable at the ordinary rate) as interest (a deductible cost) in order to reap the land gains, which are taxed as capital gains (Hudson 1995).[8]

Not only land sites but also privately owned natural resources such as mines and oilfields qualify for various tax preferences as well as outright subsidies (Gaffney 2009, 1999). But the greatest benefit bestowed upon landowners by governments is the value that public investments and

---

7 *Continued from previous page:* in an interest-earning investment, it will grow to a value of $22.50 in 15 years, just in time to pay the tax. The effective tax rate is 8.3%, which is 56% of the statutory capital gains rate and just a third or so of the ordinary rate. A 15% tax on *unrealized* gains, paid at the end of each year, yields $1.50 in revenue each year for 15 years, the present value of which is $17.48, or 17.5% of planting cost. (We ignore the effect of the tax on optimal harvest date, but taxing gains upon realization slows turnover, reinforcing the point.) Taxing capital gains as they accrue collects 40% more revenue, in this example, that taxing realized gains at the same 15% rate. The longer is the harvest cycle, the greater is the revenue loss from taxing gains only as they are realized. Suppose that the trees grow in value by $100 per year. If the stand is cut after 24 years (when the growth rate is 4%), then the capital gain is $2,400. A 15% tax on realized gains yields $360 at harvest, the present value of which is 140% of planting cost. An annual tax on *unrealized* gains has a present value of 234% of planting cost. Taxing unrealized gains collects 40% more revenue than taxing realized gains when the rate of capital turnover is 1/15, but 67% more when turnover is 1/24.

8   Owners of real estate are also often able to impute part of the value of land to buildings and other improvements, allowing them to claim depreciation allowances for land which does not turn over and is not depreciable (Hudson 1995; Gaffney 1976:162).

institutions of all kinds, from the town water supply to law and order, give to land in the jurisdictions served. Gaffney writes:

> While keeping taxes low, government arranges high rewards for land-owners by building public works, as well as by the whole complex of allied policies to support and sustain land values. The result is a highly inflated incentive to buy more land than needed, sooner than needed, and to hang onto it longer than needed. This in turn results in spreading people and capital out thin over much more land than needed. And the last, finally, necessitates pumping billions of dollars of capital into stretched-out roads, pipes, lines, wires, and other linkages that tie the fragile web of society and economy together. None of this public capital is subject to any property tax, and he would be an eccentric public accountant who added a shadow tax to the capital to show its real social cost.
>
> (Gaffney 1976:127)

Property Taxes   A property tax targets possession, not activity. Its base is a stock of wealth, not a flow of income, so it does not penalize owners for using land and existing capital intensively and hiring labor to do it. It adds to the cost of holding assets, discouraging investment in those that turn over slowly and yield little gross income. Property taxes are applied unevenly, however, which offsets some of their advantages; most movable capital is exempt from property taxes except for business inventories, which turn over fast – reinforcing the pervasive bias. Furthermore, property taxes have different consequences for land than for manmade capital. A tax on capital discourages maintenance while deferring replacement, because investments that add to capital value provoke an increase in the tax assessment.

Real estate taxes fall partly on land value and partly on the value of capital goods affixed to land. Buildings are hit hard.[9] Gaffney argues that the property tax on buildings contributes mightily to urban blight, in which aging buildings are neither repaired nor replaced and each eyesore drags down the value of neighboring sites (Gaffney 1988). Land, however, requires no replacement. Its price is based not on cost of production, which is infinite, but on the value that market participants place on the amenities and access afforded by its location relative to the artifacts,

---

9   At rates of just 2% or 3% per year, a property tax amounts to a large fraction of construction cost, in terms of present value, over building life – about half, depending on interest rate, tax rate, and building life. Worse, it is heaviest in the early years, when a building is new and financing is tight (Gaffney 1965:273).

infrastructure, and interactions of the surrounding community. A tax on
land value captures social surplus directly.

Land income, N in the tables, is gross income minus non-land costs as
land is actually used. On a vacant lot it is zero, regardless of the land's
potential. Rent, by contrast, is potential income as judged by the market.
Rent varies, not with the owner's efforts, but with her opportunities. Land
income falls short of rent if the manager is less successful than what
might have been expected from competing. The present value of expected
future rents is land value, the selling price of land. Like any property
tax, an *ad valorem* tax on land throws up no obstacle to the efficient
employment of land, as it does not vary with intensity of use; but unlike
a tax on manmade capital, it cannot discourage turnover because land
does not turn over.

An advantage of taxing land value rather than rent is that, whereas
rent is often unobservable, land value is directly observable in selling
price. Another attractive feature of a land value tax is its treatment of
'capital' gains, that is, land gains. It is difficult to use the income tax to
capture invisible unrealized gains, but an *ad valorem* tax on land accomp-
lishes just that.[10] Appendix 3 shows that land value is a multiple of the
sum of rent and appreciation, so a land value tax falls equally on rent
and unrealized land gains. This feature alone recommends land value
taxation as an antidote to distortions imposed by the income tax.[11]

Tax Reform for Full Employment   The conventional macroeconomic prescription for unemployment is to subsidize capital in
order to raise the demand for labor. 'The argument is that investments
requiring heavy use of capital would not pay if taxed,' Gaffney explains.
'Yet when is the payroll tax or income tax abated because a labor-using
business cannot survive it?' (Gaffney 1976:128).

Gaffney's analysis leads directly to a number of reform proposals. First,
scrap sales and value added taxes. Next, correct the income tax provisions

---

10   The importance of taxing appreciation diminishes as the tax rate rises. As a land value tax
rate rises toward infinity (or a rent tax rate rises toward 100%), land value approaches zero, appreciation approaches zero, and the present value of taxes approaches the untaxed value of the land.
11   In imperfect, real-world capital markets, investors discount future returns at different rates.
Land buyers offering the highest prices may not be the most efficient producers; a low value of
prospective land income may be offset by low financing costs. As Gaffney has shown, the effects
of credit discrimination are neutralized by heavy land taxation. The tax is capitalized into a lower
purchase price, so buyers have less need for credit (Gaffney 1994a:71). This and other salutary
features of land value taxation arise in a dynamic world of uncertainty and market imperfections
(Feder 2003, Gaffney 1994a).

that favor land and capital over labor. Eliminate capital gains treatment and other preferences for capital that turns over slowly. Then, having plugged the loopholes for capital, lower the rates. This will be a heavy lift, so meanwhile, reduce income and payroll tax rates on earned income. Together, these amendments will convert the income tax to a tax primarily on property income.

To tax capital and land gains as they accrue, strengthen the property tax and get the assessments right. Align tax depreciation with real asset depreciation. To remove the bias for internalizing new capital, reduce the corporate tax rate and tax stockholders for undistributed profits at the rate applied to dividends. To capture surplus directly, focus the property tax on land values and raise the rates.

One source of excess burden can emerge if a small jurisdiction shifts its tax base to land value (and immigration is uncontrolled). Firms and workers will cluster there. Immigration will be a boon to aging cities in decline, but may continue until the advantages of the geoclassical tax regime are dissipated by crowding and congestion. The upshot is a spatial equilibrium in which the geographic distribution of economic activity is inefficient and the rent surplus is smaller than it might be (Gaffney 2004). From a geoclassical perspective, the problem is not the land tax but the tax regimes of surrounding communities that repel people and enterprise when they have a more attractive place to go. The obvious if ambitious remedy is a national land value tax, perhaps with international rent-sharing treaties along lines suggested by Nicolaus Tideman (Tideman 2009).

The total effect of a geoclassical regime depends of course on how the revenue is spent. As the Henry George Theorem (Box 2:2) suggests, public utilities should be priced at the marginal cost of service, promoting efficient use while adding to rents in the service area. To make government investment self-financing, tap rent to cover the resulting deficits. More generally, if land taxes finance government services and public works that are worth more than they cost, perhaps supplemented with cash dividends to citizens as shareholders in the commonwealth, then workers may supply less labor to the market, both because they have less need for extra income and because publicly provided goods substitute for market goods. Lower labor supply means higher wages and a reduced rent surplus. Moreover, as tax-induced disturbances are lifted and the economy rights itself, the marginal product of labor will rise and the demand for labor will grow.

Box 2.2 • Henry George Theorem

Henry George believed that as an economy develops and urbanizes; as people become more interdependent through division of labor and exchange, the need for collective governance must grow and the government budget must expand relative to the economy. Community development amplifies the synergistic surplus, so that rent will always be sufficient to finance the legitimate activities of government.

> The value of land is at the beginning of society nothing, but as society develops by the increase of population and the advance of the arts, it becomes greater and greater. In every civilized country, even the newest, the value of the land taken as a whole is sufficient to bear the entire expenses of government. In the better developed countries it is much more than sufficient.   (George 1879:406)

The Henry George theorem is one of a family of models developed by Joseph Stiglitz and others that formalize George's insight (Arnott & Stiglitz 1979, Vickrey 2001). In complex economies, enormous sums are invested in public goods and in distribution networks, such as water systems and other utilities that have large fixed costs but low or zero marginal costs. Marginal cost is less than average cost for decreasing-cost enterprises because of their high capital requirements, such as networks of pipes, roads, rails, or wires. For non-rival goods such as snow removal or watershed protection, the marginal cost to serve an additional user is zero. To exploit scale economies and the nonrival character of public goods, these services should be priced at marginal cost. A price above marginal cost inefficiently turns away some users who value the opportunity to use the system more than it costs society to permit them to use it.

Marginal cost pricing yields a fiscal deficit; however, the Henry George theorem indicates that efficient pricing of public services raises their net value to consumers – and the added value imputes to the lands served. The models suggest that under a range of circumstances, the rents generated by efficient provision of local public goods and decreasing-cost industries equal the amount of the public subsidy necessary to provide them. Failure to collect these rents to finance the associated expenditures causes excess burden.

If supply falls while demand rises, wages will rise sharply. The upshot is that the synergistic surplus may actually be somewhat lower while working families are much better off.[12]

---

12 Thanks to Mary Cleveland for this observation.

F. Turnover and Throughput

Recalling the fable of the three little pigs, we associate durability with quality and soundness. And we have come to see that, to achieve ecological sustainability on our crowded planet, the rate of throughput must be slowed. Throughput is the flow of material resources, energy, and ecosystem services extracted from the biosphere, cycled through the economy and, eventually, released back to the environment as waste (Daly 2013). Is it possible to slow throughput while at the same time accelerating capital turnover to raise the demand for labor?

The analysis thus far does not account for the environmental consequences of throughput. The energy and materials underlying production cost (C) and embodied in capital (K) were ignored, as were the flows of high-entropy waste that correspond to depreciation and consumption. If brick houses and straw houses are constructed using clean, renewable energy with abundant organic materials and are recycled or composted at end of life, then throughput is of little concern; more important is to economize on scarce sites by using less land for a given level of output and employment – exactly what is achieved by focusing taxes on land and promoting faster turnover in place. In today's industrial economies, however, few economic processes are free of negative environmental impacts.

There are three general answers. First, a durable capital good may by fully amortized before the end of its useful life so that capital consumption allowances may be reinvested elsewhere even as the old brick house still stands and serves.

Second, a major determinant of product life is the cost of labor skilled in craftsmanship and repair. We discard broken appliances not because they cannot be fixed, but because it is cheaper to replace them. But this is a predictable result of dysfunctional tax policy. The gap between the cost of labor to employers and the after-tax wage, the cost of education and training for skilled jobs, and a tax structure that persistently favors capital- and materials-intensive enterprises over labor-intensive enterprises all conspire toward the same result.

Third, though this chapter has focused on the location value of land, geoclassical principles pertain also to a community's rules of use for nature's gifts. Henry George regarded his tax plan as a way 'to make land common property' (George 1879:328). His intent was to use the tax system to effect an equal share-out of the rent of land, broadly defined to include all the 'materials and forces of nature,' while retaining private ownership and control of settled areas. It is a straightforward application of this idea to levy rent charges for the extraction of minerals, fossil fuels, and water. At minimum, subsidies for these activities should be eliminated. Not all the income from natural resources is net income; depletion, like appreciation, is a cost. 'User cost' is the present value of future net benefits foregone when non-reproducible resources are used today rather than saved for future use. User costs should be invested, not consumed, if the natural resource base is to remain unimpaired. Where feasible, geoclassical policy also charges polluters for invading the air, land, and water owned by private landholders and the public, inducing them to pollute less and search for cleaner technologies. A carbon tax, for example, is a fee for the use of the limited capacity of the atmosphere to safely absorb carbon.

> [These reforms] will help us find full employment on our present land base, permanently, freed from the compulsion to grow and expand that we inherited from generations of ancestors who had not yet learned the finite limits of the Earth. We can continue to create capital, and we can apply new ideas more quickly than now as faster replacement lets us embody new techniques in capital in a shorter time. Thus we can grow in every good sense by substituting real progress for the random lateral expansion of the past. We can find full employment in peaceful labor on our share of this small planet, and doing so, drop the burden of imperialism that may otherwise destroy us.
>
> (Gaffney 1976:153)

A consistent application of geoclassical principles slows throughput even while stimulating economic activity. It raises the prices of virgin materials, promoting reuse, recycling, and repurposing. It raises the relative cost of energy-intensive enterprises and those with large ecological footprints, while lowering the relative cost of labor-intensive enterprises with small ecological footprints. Incrementally and nonviolently, the whole system evolves toward low-throughput patterns of industry, infrastructure, agriculture, and trade.

G. Radical Simplicity

The question for public policy is not how to strike the balance between progressive goals of social justice and conservative goals of free and efficient markets. The notion that society must trade off equity for efficiency arises in the context of a mistaken paradigm. The question is not how much unemployment we must endure to choke off inflation, or how large government deficits must grow to keep the economy from drifting into decrepitude, or how aggressive we dare to be in the global competition for dwindling resource supplies, or how much redistribution is required to keep the peace.

The question is: Shall we share surpluses constructively or destructively (Gaffney 1988)?

The rule that would return rent to the community follows the same simple principle by which wages are paid to labor and interest is paid to suppliers of capital: markets work when productive factors are rewarded for their socially valuable efforts. The government and community of a territory together give value to land and should be compensated to motivate and sustain their contributions. If a nation's public sector were constitutionally structured to require that revenues be drawn from direct charges on land values and natural resource rents, with a portion of the proceeds to be invested for sustainability and intergenerational justice, then a budget-maximizing administration would be motivated to maximize the territory's sustainable surplus. To grow the surplus, a local, state, or national government would seek to offer a desirable mix of public services to attract residents and enterprise.

Geoclassical principles are relevant for any nation that aims to promote the general prosperity of its citizens, regardless of political structure. Governments prefer to avert destructive business cycles and avoid crashing unprepared into hard resource constraints. No one looks forward to the day when Too Big To Fail becomes Too Big To Bail. Even an authoritarian government unconcerned about winning the popular vote has an interest in families being able to maintain themselves 'in good working order' without public assistance. To deter challenges to its authority, it has an interest in preventing the accumulation of large stocks of private wealth. To promote civil order and patriotic pride, it has an interest in citizens' perceiving that the system is fair.

One way or another, all taxes tap into the economy's surplus. If we share surpluses destructively, 'to the victor go the ashes of the spoils' (Ochs 1968). Mason Gaffney shows how a properly designed public revenue system coaxes the surplus to grow, as grass grows thicker when grazed. By minimizing excess burdens and conserving scarce resources, the geoclassical system yields a larger synergistic surplus than any alternative. We can have both equity and efficiency, but we cannot have one without the other. 'In justice,' wrote George, 'lies the highest and truest expediency' (George 1879:367).

58   RENT UNMASKED

Appendix 1

Turnover, Interest Rates, and Factor Shares

Table A1 shows interest costs and the minimum required gross income
(sales revenue) for carrots and timber at three different interest rates. For
timber, at an interest rate of 2%, interest is 63% of cost; the harvest value
of timber must be 2.72 times planting cost to warrant sinking capital into
the tree farm (omitting rent). Because carrot-capital turns over 50 times
faster, the harvest value of carrots must be just 2% higher than planting
cost to warrant sinking capital into the carrot farm. The interest share
rises and the wage share falls as the interest rate rises – slightly for the
carrot farm; dramatically for the tree farm. For timber, at an interest rate
of 5%, interest is 92% of costs; the harvest value of timber must be over 12
times planting cost to warrant sinking capital into the timber enterprise.
At an interest rate of 10%, interest is 99% of costs; harvest value must be
over 147 times planting cost. Assuming for illustration that payroll com-
prises half of planting cost, the tree farm has a 50-year payroll of $50
while the carrot farm has a 50-year payroll of $2,500, fifty times larger.

Table A1 • Interest, Wages, and Turnover

Timber with Harvest at 50 Years and Planting Cost C = $100

Interest Rate	G ($100e^{50r}$)	Interest (50 years)	Interest/ G	Wage/G (if W = ½ cost)	50-year Payroll
.02	$271.83	$171.83	0.63	0.185	$50
.05	1,218.25	1,118.25	0.92	0.040	$50
.10	14,841.32	14,741.32	0.99	0.005	$50

Carrots with Harvest at One Year and Planting Cost C = $100

Interest Rate	G ($100e^{r}$)	Interest (1 year)	Interest/ G	Wage/G (if W = ½ cost)	50-year Payroll
.02	$102.02	$2.02	0.020	0.490	$2,500
.05	105.13	5.13	0.050	0.476	$2,500
.10	110.52	10.52	0.095	0.452	$2,500

Based on biological growth formula (continuous compounding): $G = 100e^{rt}$

Appendix 2

ATCOR and EBCOR with a Cobb-Douglas Production Function

To illustrate ATCOR/EBCOR we use an aggregate Cobb-Douglas production function with land and labor inputs. Labor supply is perfectly elastic. The stock of land in the jurisdiction is fixed.

Q = output
G = acres of land in the jurisdiction (fixed stock)
L = labor per month (flow)
g = real rent income of land (flow, per acre per month)
w = \$1 = after-tax real wage received by labor (per unit labor per month)
t = wage tax rate
$RENT = gG$ = aggregate rent of tax jurisdiction
$WAGE = (w + t)L$ = payroll including tax
$TAX = tL$ = total tax revenue
$\Delta Q, \Delta L, \Delta RENT$ = absolute values of tax-induced declines in Q, L, RENT
$EB = \Delta Q - w\Delta L$ = excess burden of a proportional wage tax

The Cobb-Douglas production function is: $Q = L^a G^{1-a}$ $(0 < a < 1)$

For a numerical example, take the case of $G = 144$ and $a = \frac{1}{2}$:

$$Q = L^{1/2} G^{1/2} = 12 L^{1/2}$$

The marginal productivity principle determines how much labor should be employed:

$$w + t = MP_L$$
$$1 + t = 6L^{-1/2}$$
$$L^* = 36/(1 + t2)$$

Use the marginal productivity principle again to find the equilibrium level of rent:

$$g = MP_G = (\tfrac{1}{2})L^{1/2}G^{-1/2} = (\tfrac{1}{2})|6/(1 + t)|/12 = (\tfrac{1}{4})/(1 + t)$$

With no tax, employment is $L^* = 36$, rent is 25¢ per acre, and output is \$72. The payroll and the aggregate rent are each \$36.

Table A2 shows solutions for various tax rates. In each case, from columns (8), (9), and (10), the wage tax reduces rent by the sum of the tax revenue and the excess burden: TAX + EB = ΔRENT.

Table A2

Cobb-Douglas Production Function: $G = 144$; $w = 1$; $Q = 12L^{\frac{1}{2}}$

(1)	(2)	(3)	(4)	(5)	(6)	(7)	(8)	(9)	(10)
t	L*	Q*	w + t	g	WAGE	RENT	ΔRENT	TAX	EB
0	36	72	1	1/4	36	36	—	0	0
0.2	25	60	1.2	1/4.8	30	30	6	5	1
0.5	16	48	1.5	1/6	24	24	12	8	4
1	9	36	2	1/8	18	18	18	9	9
2	4	24	3	1/12	12	12	24	8	16
5	1	12	6	1/24	6	6	30	5	25

The wage tax can yield at most $9, with t = $1 and L* = 9. At higher tax rates, efficiency is so compromised that employment falls faster than revenue per hour of labor rises. If, however, the wage tax were zero, then a rent tax up to g = 25¢ per acre, or $36 total – four times the maximum possible wage tax revenue and twice the rent when t = $1 – could be levied with no excess burden. A tax on rent yields more revenue than a tax on labor (or on labor and land incomes together).

This approach shows excess burden as a marginal effect only. It does not contemplate discrete changes in technology (production functions) in response to economic incentives. Because factor ratios are variable over a wide range and sensitive to relative factor prices, we expect a wage tax to motivate a search for labor-saving, land-using (and capital-using) technologies (Gaffney 2009:51).

Appendix 3

Rent, Appreciation, and Land Value

To show that a land value tax applies equally to rent and current appreciation, define:

V = Land value (selling price of land)
R = Current year's rent
A = Current year's appreciation
i = Annual rate of interest
t = *Ad valorem* annual tax rate on land

Land value depends on the flow of expected income (rent and appreciation) and the costs of holding land (interest and taxes). Prices adjust so that the annual cost of holding land equals the annual income. Cost is interest cost (iV) plus tax cost (tV); income is rent plus appreciation:

$$iV + tV = R + A \qquad \text{Solving for V: } V = [1/(i + t)](R + A)$$

Land value is a multiple $[1/(i + t)]$ of annual rent plus appreciation. The year's tax levy is a fraction (t) of land value. Therefore, a land value tax falls equally on rent and appreciation.

References

Arnott, Richard J., and Joseph E. Stiglitz (1979), Aggregate land rents, expenditure on public goods, and optimal city size, *Quarterly Journal of Economics* 93(4):471–500.

Daly, Herman (2013), Top 10 policies for a steady-state economy, *Countercurrents*. http://www.countercurrents.org/daly121113.htm.

Feder, Kris (2003), Clark: apostle of two-factor economics, in Robert V. Andelson, ed., *Critics of Henry George* Vol. I:353-394, Oxford: Blackwell.

Gaffney, Mason (2013), Europe's fatal affair with VAT, *Groundswell*, March-April.

Gaffney, Mason (2011), Sales tax bias against turnover and jobs, *Groundswell*, August-September.

Gaffney, Mason (2009), The hidden taxable capacity of land: enough and to spare, *International Journal of Social Economics* 36(4):328-411.

Gaffney, Mason (2005a), Defining 'consumption,' *GroundSwell*, September-October.

Gaffney, Mason (2005b), The sales tax: history of a dumb idea, *Groundswell*, March-April.

Gaffney, Mason (2004), A Cannan hits the mark, in Robert Andelson, ed., *Critics of Henry George* Vol. II:435-450, Oxford: Blackwell.

Gaffney, Mason (2003), Taxes, capital and jobs, *Geophilos* 3(1), Spring:62-74.

Gaffney, Mason (2001), Full employment, growth and progress on a small planet: relieving poverty while healing the Earth. Conference on Growth, Poverty and the Environment, sponsored by the Center for Process Studies of the Claremont School of Theology and the Claremont Graduate University, 18-21 October.

Gaffney, Mason (1999), Gains from untaxing work, trade and capital, by uptaxing land. Paper delivered at the Global Institute for Taxation (GIFT) conference of St. John's University, New York, 1 October.

Gaffney, Mason (1994a), Land as a distinctive factor of production, in Nicolaus Tideman, ed., *Land and Taxation*, London: Shepheard-Walwyn, 39-102.

Gaffney, Mason (1994b), 'Neo-classical economics as a stratagem against Henry George', in Mason Gaffney and Fred Harrison, *The Corruption of Economics*. London: Shepheard-Walwyn.

Gaffney, Mason (1993), The taxable capacity of land, in Patricia Salkin, ed., *Land Value Taxation*, Albany: Government Law Center of Albany Law School, 60-74.

Gaffney, Mason (1988), The role of ground rent in urban decay and revival, New York: Business Research Institute, St. John's University, The Henry George Lecture, October.

Gaffney, Mason (1980), Alternative ways of taxing forests, in Will Knedlick, ed., *State Taxation of Forest and Land Resources*, Cambridge: Lincoln Institute of Land Policy.

Gaffney, Mason (1976), Toward full employment with limited land and capital, in Arthur Lynn, Jr., ed., *Property Taxation, Land Use and Public Policy*, Madison: University of Wisconsin Press, 99-106.

Gaffney, Mason (1967), Tax-induced slow turnover of capital, *Western Economic Journal*, September: 308-323.

Gaffney, Mason (1965), Property taxes and the frequency of urban renewal,' *Proceedings*, National Tax Association, 57th Annual Conference, Pittsburgh, 272-85.

George, Henry (1879), *Progress and Poverty*. New York: Robert Schalkenbach Foundation (2008).

Hudson, Michael (1995), How rent gets buried in the national income accounts. Presented at the Council of Georgist Organizations Annual Meeting, Evanston, IL, 30 June.

Mill, John Stuart (1848), *Principles of Political Economy with some of their Applications to Social Philosophy*, 7th edition, Fairfield, NJ: Augustus M. Kelley (1987, 1909).

Ochs, Phil (1968), Tape from California, A&M Records.

Smith, Adam (1776), *An Inquiry into the Nature and Causes of the Wealth of Nations*, 5th ed., Edwin Cannan, ed., London: Methuen & Co. (1904).

The Economics Daily (2015), Unemployment rate 5.7 percent in January 2015; U-6 measure was 11.3 percent, http://www.bls.gov/opub/ted/2015/unemployment-rate-and-u-6-measure-in-january-2015.htm.

Tideman, Nicolaus (2009), The case for geoliberalism: a reply to Moellendo *International Journal of Social Economics* 36(4):489-506.

Vickrey, William S. (2001), Site value taxes and the optimal pricing of public services, *American Journal of Economics and Sociology*, December.

Wicksell, Knut (1954), *Value, Capital, and Rent*, trans. S. H. Frowein, London: G. Allen & Irwin.

Wicksell, Knut (1938), *Lectures on Political Economy*, London: George Routledge and Sons.

3

Time Travelling
Back to Space Age Economics

MARY CLEVELAND

HENRY GEORGE was the last of the classical economists, a 'school' first associated with Adam Smith, and later David Ricardo, Thomas Malthus and John Stuart Mill. In an era when the Enlightenment ideals of the American and French revolutions inspired increasing resistance to authority, George and his older contemporary, Karl Marx, both recognized the explosive revolutionary potential of the classical paradigm. So what was this paradigm? How did George interpret it in a way that changed the world? How did George misinterpret an important part of it? What other pieces of the story did he miss, notably in the work of contemporaries Martin Faustmann and Knut Wicksell? And how did the architects of neoclassical economics – notably John Bates Clark and Vilfredo Pareto – obliterate George and the classics to give us textbook Econ 101? In 70 prolific years, Mason Gaffney has addressed these important questions and more.

In his introduction to the *Wealth of Nations*, Adam Smith posed a key question: what determines how 'produce is naturally distributed among the different ranks and conditions of men in the society?' (Smith, [1776] 1904: I.1.5). This society fell quite visibly into three broad classes: the landlords, the capitalists, and the workers. They supplied the three basic 'factors of production': land, labor and capital. Landlords received 'rent', workers received 'wages' and the capitalists received 'profit' or 'interest'. There was some overlap between the classes and their incomes; the term 'profit' often conveyed a mixture of incomes. For example, a trader might own land, buildings and merchandise, and employ his own labor in the enterprise.

Classical economists used 'land' as shorthand for natural resources very broadly understood. 'Land' was not 'wealth', because it was not man-made. 'Land' included not just farmland but urban land, mines, rivers, ports, fisheries and any other kind of natural resource that could be made private under titles created and protected by the king. The Duke of Westminster owned (and still owns) much of the land under the posh West End of London! 'Land' also included various territorial rights, granted by the king, including patents, bank charters, rights-of-way, and commercial monopolies such as the exclusive Indian trade granted to the British East India Company.

Classical economists recognized that the landlords' 'rent', what we today call 'economic rent', is *unearned income*, arising from the privilege of holding titles to property under protection of the state. Adam Smith writes: 'As soon as the land of any country has all become private property, the landlords, like all other men, love to reap where they never sowed and demand a rent even for its natural produce' (Smith [1776] 1904: I.6.8). Unearned income did not carry the stigma it does today. On the contrary, it conveyed social superiority. Jane Austen's early 19th century landed gentry obsessed about inheriting or marrying property income of so many thousand pounds a year – heaven forbid anyone actually had to work!

The mathematically-minded financier David Ricardo figured out what determines the level of rents: the amount of rent a parcel of land commands depends on its degree of superiority to land just barely worth using (Ricardo, [1818] 1996). Superiority of land does not just depend on soil quality, but, much more important, on location. Land in the downtown of big cities commands the highest rents, due to its superior ability to facilitate the highest-value activities in an economy: the cooperation of highly skilled specialists like lawyers, bankers and brokers. Rent arises from simple 'arbitrage': for example, how much more would a developer pay for a good central lot than for one on the fringe of a city? Today economists still use the term 'Ricardian rent' in explaining the value of choice locations.

Therefore, the classical economists said, when population growth brings inferior land into cultivation, landlords' rents from superior lands are driven up. John Stuart Mill wrote:

The ordinary progress of a society which increases in wealth, is at all times tending to augment the incomes of landlords; to give them both a greater amount and a greater proportion of the wealth of the community, independently of any trouble or outlay incurred by themselves. They grow richer, as it were in their sleep, without working, risking, or economizing. What claim have they, on the general principle of social justice, to this accession of riches?   (Mill [1848] 1909: V.2.28)

Ricardo's explanation of landlords' rent left only wages for workers and interest (or profit) for capitalists to be explained.

Adam Smith was optimistic about workers' wages; he observed that their wages and conditions had already improved with population growth and new technology, and expected improvement to continue – as indeed would happen in the industrialized countries. But by the end of the 18th century the growing hordes of poor urban workers inspired more fear and hostility than sympathy. Writing in 1798, Thomas Malthus advanced a radical 'scientific' theory of wages: workers breed faster than new land can be opened for production. Hence, famine, disease and 'vice' will inevitably check their population, keeping their wages at 'subsistence' – just enough for them to feed their families and reproduce (Malthus, 1798). In language dripping with upper-class contempt for the lower orders, Malthus even opposed aid to the poor, on the grounds this would just encourage them to breed faster.

Malthus' subsistence wage theory seemed to solve the distribution problem. As Ricardo showed, with landlords' rent and workers' wages given, the balance of national income necessarily went to the capitalists – theoretically completing the entire distribution of income between the three classes of landlords, workers and capitalists! Based on subsistence wages, Ricardo also developed a crude 'labor theory of value,' explaining prices of goods by the amount of work it took to make them. Marx picked up this theory and ran with it.

The French Connection

Mason Gaffney reminds us that Adam Smith took many of his major ideas from the now little-remembered French 'Physiocrats' (Gaffney, 1982b). In 1764, confirmed homebody though he was, Smith could not resist the dazzling offer of £300 a year to tutor the young Duke of Buccleuch on a tour of Europe. They spent 1764 through 1766 in France. After a spell in Toulouse, Smith and his party visited French skeptic and iconoclast Voltaire in his hideout at Ferney on the Swiss border, whence he could easily escape periodic prosecution. Then they moved on to Paris.

The Paris salons teemed with Enlightenment intellectuals, including Benjamin Franklin, representing the British American colonies. Among the most influential were a group known as the 'Physiocrats' or '*Oeconomistes*', who argued for the 'rule of nature'. Their leader was physician to the king, François Quesnay. He developed the earliest macroeconomic model, the *Tableau Economique*, showing the multiplier effect of investment in agriculture. (The salon ladies referred to the *Tableau* as '*les Zig-Zags.*') Another influential Physiocrat was Anne Robert Jacques Turgot, at the time Intendant of the French province of Limoges. In 1766, Turgot wrote a short, sophisticated monograph, *Reflections on the Formation and Distribution of Wealth* (Turgot, [1766] 1793). The Physiocrats greatly impressed Adam Smith. Smith does not cite Turgot, but his economic ideas closely track those in Turgot's monograph.

The Physiocrats coined the motto *laissez faire*, short for '*Laissez faire et laissez passer, le monde va de lui même!*' ('Let do and let pass, the world goes by itself!'). To see where they were coming from, consider the pre-revolutionary French tax system. A small part of revenues came from taxes on land, exempting land belonging to the king, the church and the nobility. The bulk of revenues came from excise taxes on anything that moved, notably salt and tobacco. There were also poll taxes. These taxes were administered by the notoriously corrupt 'tax farmers' who paid the king for the privilege. In addition, the *corvee* required peasants to work for free on the roads. This corrupt and wasteful system no longer generated sufficient revenues; in short, the monarchy was broke.

The Physiocrats advocated abolishing this dog's dinner of imposts, and taxing land only – '*l'impôt unique*' – including royal, church and noble land! Why? Because, as Turgot makes clear, land alone generates a surplus that can be taxed without impeding work or investment. As Intendant of Limoges, Turgot managed to put some Physiocratic principles into effect, with such good results that the desperately-strapped new King Louis XVI appointed him Finance Minister in 1774. However Turgot's reforms did not go down well with the noble cronies of Queen Marie-Antoinette, who shortly had him fired. The king and queen may have blown their last chance to save the monarchy; in fewer than 20 years, they would meet Madame Guillotine.

The Classical Economists on Taxation

In classical times, most business was conducted in cash. Record-keeping was not adequate for our modern income taxes or sales taxes. That left two primary taxes: land taxes on the value of the landlords' land, and imposts and tariffs on bulk goods, collected mostly in ports and other trading centers.

Land taxes are the oldest form of tax, not only in Britain, but in all civilizations (Gaffney, 1994a). They were (and are) relatively easy to assess, because as grantor, a ruler could have a pretty good idea what the land was worth. In Britain, unlike France, the king had to rely on Parliament to impose the tax, giving Parliament increasing control over government. After 1688, during the reign of William and Mary, Britain's 'financial revolution' depended on an extraordinary land tax of four shillings to the pound, or 20% of assessed value (which was often much less than actual value [Heyck, 2002]). This high tax enabled Britain to develop a modern financial system: a permanent national debt consisting of bonds that paid regular interest; and a central bank, the Bank of England, founded in 1694, which loaned money to the government and issued currency. This system enabled Britain to fight several successful wars, especially against France's expansionist 'Sun King,' Louis XIV, and to extend its naval power around the world. With naval protection, Britain's merchant fleets prospered and its colonial empire expanded, bringing ever more tariff money into government coffers.

So what did Adam Smith propose? Following Physiocratic guidance, Smith set out four 'maxims of taxation'. They challenge our comfortable modern assumptions about taxation.

Smith's first maxim holds that:

> The subjects of every state ought to contribute towards the support of the government, as nearly as possible, in proportion to their respective abilities; that is, in proportion to the revenue which they respectively enjoy under the protection of the state.
>
> (Smith [1776] 1904: V.2.25)

Notice he is not just saying taxpayers should contribute in proportion to ability to pay, but effectively *in proportion to the benefits they receive from government*. As he makes clear, the greatest benefit is the security of property.

Smith's second and third maxims are just common sense: taxes should not be arbitrary, and they should be imposed at a time and place convenient to the taxpayer.

Smith's fourth maxim holds that 'Every tax ought to be so contrived as both to take out and to keep out of the pockets of the people as little as possible over and above what it brings into the public treasury of the state'. Taxes should cost as little as possible in expense and staff to collect. They should not 'obstruct the industry of the people'. The tax should not tempt people to evasion and then punish them severely for yielding to temptation. Finally, the tax should not subject people to 'the frequent visits and the odious examination of the tax-gatherer' (Smith, [1776] 1904: V.2.28).

What tax best meets these criteria? *The land tax!* Smith says it admirably meets the second, third and fourth criteria. It fails the first – the proportionate burden – because, while landlords had greatly increased in prosperity, assessments had not increased since William and Mary almost 100 years before! (Sound familiar?) That problem, says Smith, can be solved by following the recommendation of the French *Oeconomistes* to let the taxes rise and fall with the level of rents (Smith, [1776] 1904: V.2.36). That would make them 'the most equitable of all taxes'.

The Radical Classics, Marx and George

In the last third of the 19th century, the Gilded Age of the Rockefellers in the US, and the Rothschilds in London, two intellectual bomb-throwers came to prominence.

In London, Karl Marx beavered away on his masterwork, *Capital*, publishing Volume I in 1867 (Marx, [1867] 1906). A radical socialist scholar, Marx had escaped Europe during the crackdown following the publication of his *Communist Manifesto* in 1848. Building on Ricardo's labor theory, Marx argued that capitalists increasingly exploited workers by paying them less than the value of their labor. Eventually, inevitably, the workers would overthrow capitalism, ushering in a new era of proletarian harmony.

A far more unlikely bomb-thrower emerged in western United States: Henry George. An impoverished, self-educated San Francisco journalist, he recorded the spectacle of graft and violence as the Southern Pacific Railroad and other speculators grabbed vast chunks of land in advance of incoming settlers. In 1879 he published *Progress and Poverty: An Inquiry into the Cause of Industrial Depressions and of Increase of Want with Increase of Wealth ... the Remedy* (George, [1879] 1962). George accepted as self-evident the classical division of society into the three classes, though he quibbles with some of his predecessors' use of terms. He also accepted Ricardo's theory that the rent of a given parcel of land is determined by its superiority to land barely worth using. But – like Marx – he emphatically rejected the Malthusian 'subsistence' theory of wages, denouncing Malthus for blaming poverty on the improvidence of the poor rather than the exploitation of the rich. In fact, at the very time Malthus wrote, improving (though still awful) wages and conditions of workers in England already gave the lie to his model. George instead proposed a new and original marginal theory of wages, the mirror image of Ricardo's marginal theory of rent: wages are determined by what a man can earn working on freely-available land. (Since nominally all land is owned, at least by governments, in practice freely-available land means private or public land that is inadequately policed.)

George observed (as had Adam Smith before him (Smith, [1776] 1904: III.2.7) that large landholders often underused land, or withheld it from use altogether. He usually attributed the withholding during the land rush in California to 'land speculation'; but sometimes he recognized that wealthy owners withheld land simply because they could afford to. Combining the observation of withholding with his theory of wage determination on marginal land, George concluded that great inequality in land ownership directly created great inequality in wages. That is, the greater the proportion of land belonging to a wealthy minority, the lower the quality of land available to poor workers – and hence, by arbitrage, the lower the bottom tier of wages in a society.

George did not have to look far for a remedy; he simply lifted Adam Smith's case for land value taxation. Moreover, he pointed out, this remedy lies in the hands of every state and municipality: simply shift the general property tax onto land values only, and abolish any other taxes. The land tax would collect the unearned income of 'land monopolists', forcing them to sell or lease out underused holdings, thereby making land available to workers. The tax would effectively claim public ownership of natural resources by collecting the rent for public purposes, and distribute operating control of those resources to the most productive users.

While Adam Smith and the other classical economists had merely claimed the superiority of land taxation, George made it a worldwide crusade. He toured the English-speaking world – including Britain's oppressed Irish colony – stirring up huge crowds. He inspired leaders as diverse as John Dewey in the US, Winston Churchill in England, and Leo Tolstoy in Russia. In short, George became a threat to the *status quo*.

The Neoclassical Counter-revolution

The robber barons reacted. They, after all, the captains of oil, steel, coal and timber industries – such as John D. Rockefeller, Ezra Cornell, Henry Clay Frick and Andrew Carnegie – owned vast tracts of eminently taxable land and other natural resources. As Mason Gaffney has documented (Gaffney, 1994b), they hired experts to confuse and diffuse the opposition. So when Rockefeller set up the University of Chicago in 1890, the economics department understood its founder's needs. So did the economics department of Columbia University, recruited by its President (and later New York Mayor) Seth Low, an ally of J.P. Morgan, financier to the robber barons.

What did the robber-baron-friendly scholars do? Most influential was John Bates Clark of Columbia University, in whose honor is named the John Bates Clark Medal. Willfully misunderstanding the classical meaning of 'land,' he simply eliminated land altogether, by merging it into capital, because 'land and artificial goods are blended in an intimate mixture' (Clark, 1908: XIII.5). That's about as logical as saying if you spread a layer of jam on peanut butter, you might as well treat the result as a jam sandwich.[1] But it served a useful political purpose: it eliminated economic rent – unearned income – by merging it into profit. Thus Clark rendered George's – and Smith's – analysis and remedy meaningless. There was no longer any unearned income to tax! Without unearned income, it followed that all taxes were harmful, as, according Smith's fourth maxim, they discouraged both work and capital investment! Hence the modern maxim advocating 'broad-based' taxes: 'Tax everything a little bit to minimize the inevitable damage and make evasion less worthwhile by keeping rates low.'

Clark emphasized efficiency; laborers should be paid what they contributed at the margin. Thus, Clark writes:

> the share of wealth that falls to any producing agent tends, under natural law, to equal the amount that he creates. A man's pay tends to equal the value of the product or fraction of a product that can be specifically imputed to him.
>
> (Clark, 1898: 4)

---

1 Appraisers routinely separate land from buildings, because the value of land depends primarily on location, while the value of buildings depends on construction costs less depreciation. New York law requires assessors to report land and building values separately – a lingering effect of Henry George's influence.

So much for any claim that laborers were exploited!

Clark also eliminated time, and with it, history. Neoclassical economics became what it remains today, a flat world through which we flit for a moment like mayflies, a world of timeless truth like physics, good for showing that rent control creates a housing shortage, and a minimum wage creates unemployment, but helpless before phenomena like growing inequality or events like the 2008 crash. Clark's students, notably Frank Knight, shaped the Chicago School of neoclassical economics.

Let's recap what Clark accomplished. Clark merged land and capital into a timeless entity, 'Capital', designated 'K,' that mates with another timeless entity 'Labor', designated 'L', to produce time-less output, 'Q'. Wages depend solely on what the last bit of labor adds to Q. At a blow, Clark has eliminated inequality and unearned income, and reduced wages to a scientific formula determined by the inexorable operation of 'natural law'! Neoclassical economics in the USA

> *At a blow, Clark has eliminated inequality and unearned income, and reduced wages to a scientific formula determined by the inexorable operation of 'natural law'!*

followed Clark, to the extent that the future Clark medal and Swedish Bank 'Nobel' prize winner Robert Solow could joke in 1955 that '... if God had meant there to be more than two factors of production, He would have made it easier for us to draw three dimensional diagrams' (Solow, 1955: 101).

While Clark was reconstructing economics in America, European economists responded to the growing threat not only of George but also of Marx. One of these was Italian nobleman Vilfredo Pareto (1848-1923). Pareto contributed two major concepts. First, he estimated that 80% of the land in Italy belonged to 20% of the population, from which he concluded that inequality follows a natural law: the 80:20 rule, with which we should not tamper. More famously, he developed the policy rule known as 'Pareto optimality'. This rule holds that we should undertake no policy changes unless they make at least one person better off and no one worse off. Sounds fair and reasonable, doesn't it? By that logic the US should have paid the slaveholders in full after the Civil War! By that logic, once having cut taxes on the rich, we cannot raise them again! *The status quo rules, no matter how cruel or illogical the route that got us there.*

Box 3:1

Corporations as Unions of Landlords

In his *Financial Times* article, US economic editor Robin Harding glosses over the transition from classical to neoclassical economics by simply assuming that classical 'land' means only 'farmland.' He writes: 'As land became less important to the industrial economy, labor unions rose and European aristocracies were overthrown, the idea of economic rents died away' (Harding, 2012). How convenient! But I'm glad you mentioned unions, Mr. Harding, for after all, what is a corporation but a union of land-lords? And what is the modern 'industrial economy' but vast constellations of such unions, heavy in natural resources – think ExxonMobil. And that even includes Walmart. What is Walmart US, after all, but a collection of over 4,500 huge parking lots and one-story stores and distribution centers, occupying prime real estate at highway intersections across the country – not to mention extorting tax privileges from their local hosts?

The neoclassical revolution accomplished something more: it removed the taint of privilege and unearned income from corporations (Box 3:1).

How George Missed a Key Classical Concept

In the classical world, capital meant physical, man-made things, used in production of goods or more capital. Capital fell naturally into two classes: 'fixed', like buildings and machines, and 'circulating' like inventories of goods in process and consumption goods. A major part of circulating capital was the so-called 'wages-fund' – John Stuart Mill's term (Mill, [1848] 1909). The wages-fund was the stock of consumption goods that had to be stored up before the beginning of a production cycle, in order to compensate the workmen before the product was completed and sold, and a new stock of consumption goods purchased for the next cycle. The shorter the cycle, the more employment a given wages-fund stock could support. Thus because domestic trade necessarily operates on a shorter cycle than long-distance trade, Adam Smith could write that

> capital employed in the home-trade necessarily puts into motion a greater quantity of domestic industry, and gives revenue and employment to a greater number of the inhabitants of the country, than an equal capital employed in the foreign trade of consumption... (Smith, [1776] 1904) iv.2.6)

In his effort to model the distribution of income, David Ricardo created an elegant three-factor model with a fixed-length cycle, his 'corn model' (Ricardo, [1818] 1996). The corn model consists of a simple agricultural cycle with a single good, 'corn' (British for grain), that serves as both capital and consumption good. At the beginning of a cycle, the 'proprietor' holds a stock of corn, the 'wages-fund.' This serves to feed the workers until the new corn can be harvested. (If the proprietor does not own his own land, the fund also serves to advance the rent.) At harvest time, the proprietor receives back his original stock, plus a percentage profit. If the proprietor does not consume his entire profit, but uses it to expand his wages-fund and hire more workers, each harvest will exceed the prior – creating economic growth.

Unfortunately, Ricardo divided his wages-fund by the number of workers to come up with the Malthusian subsistence wage, thus apparently justifying the Malthusian hypothesis that due to workers' propensity to over-breed, wages always remained at subsistence. George reacted by dismissing the wages-fund as Malthusian ploy, together with the classical distinction between fixed and circulating capital. As noted above, he developed his own marginal theory of wages. As Gaffney has pointed out, George's dismissal of the wages fund deprives his case for land taxation of a powerful additional argument: liberating land will speed up the cycle of capital replacement, increasing productivity and employment (Gaffney, 1975).

Ironically, while George dismissed the wages fund for its Malthusian implications, John Bates Clark effectively dismissed it for a different reason: it was incompatible with his static model which makes no distinction between land and capital. Clark's model, carried over into modern macroeconomics, leaves us with an awkward series of monthly or annual snapshots, with no concept of a capital replacement cycle, let alone the possibility of creating more jobs by speeding up that cycle.

Gaffney Rediscovers Faustmann

Martin Faustmann, a German forester, worked out a formula for the proper length of time to let a tree grow before harvesting it, assuming a new crop of trees would immediately be planted. The answer is not obvious. Do we let a tree grow to 'maturity'? But trees like redwoods can grow for thousands of years, at an ever slower rate. So the proper time must be shorter. It is sometimes suggested we should cut a tree when it is no longer increasing in value faster than compound interest on the

planting cost. But that is not soon enough, because it does not account
for the value of clearing the land to start the next crop. We get the correct
answer by maximizing the present value of the forest land, solving for
the optimum cycle length. The answer depends both on the intrinsic
growth rates of different species of trees, on the interest rate applied and
on the cost of labor. The sooner a tree's growth rate slows, the higher
the interest rate, and the lower the labor cost, the sooner the tree should
be cut.

The Faustmann formula lay forgotten for many years, probably a victim
of the neoclassical elimination of time and rent. Gaffney resurrected the
Faustmann formula in *Concepts of Financial Maturity of Timber and Other Assets*
(1957). He received immediate acclaim, including from Paul Samuelson,
but the formula was soon forgotten again. However, as Gaffney elaborated
it, the formula extends way beyond trees, in fact to the whole economy.
It applies to any kind of output that is produced in a cycle using labor
and natural resources, although the more durable the output – as in trees
and buildings – the more important it becomes not to use too long a cycle.
The Faustmann formula solves the problem the early classical economists
grappled with: shorter cycles produce more output and employment, but
how much shorter?

The tree model applies at least roughly to any production process that
results in batches of goods which increase in value with time until sold
or used at the end of a cycle. The cycle may be intrinsically long, as for
trees, or intrinsically short, as for baked goods. Wine aging in a cellar is
a familiar long–cycle model, first constructed by Wicksell (Wicksell, [1905]
1971). The cellar owner maximizes the present value of land: space in his
cellar. Manufactured goods fit the model. In most cases, producing goods
on a longer cycle increases their quality and value, to a point. (Workers
are not so rushed; the first coat of paint can dry before the second is
applied, and so on.) The model also applies to groceries on a shelf: the
higher the price the grocer puts on the goods, the longer they will take
to sell. So he has to pick a price that gives him an optimal replacement
cycle.

A simple permutation of the Faustmann model serves to explain depreciating assets like buildings and machinery (and human capital, but we
won't go there). A building delivers a flow of services, from construction
or purchase time, until demolition or selling time. Usually, the service
flow declines steadily, at least as the building ages. Whether or not service
flow declines, the building depreciates, as it approaches the end of its

useful life. (It would depreciate even if its service flow remained constant, then suddenly ceased, like the 'one hoss shay'.) The amount of depreciation over the building's life just equals the cost of construction or purchase.

The building model applies at least roughly to any asset that yields a flow of services or income until replaced. Such assets include roads, machinery, reference books in a library, refrigerators, cars, clothing, paintings and 'durables' in general. In addition, such assets include things that produce a continuous flow of physical output over their lives, such as fruit trees or power plants. In fact, most production can be treated as a combination of the tree and building models, such as a factory whose plant and equipment produce batches of goods for sale. And note that the same asset may be appreciating or depreciating at different stages in its physical life. For example, a refrigerator appreciates on the manufacturer's assembly line; it then depreciates in the purchaser's kitchen.

In my own work, *Consequences and Causes of Unequal Distribution of Wealth* (1984), I applied Gaffney's work on the Faustmann formula to differences in the behavior of large and small firms (and rich and poor people). As I showed, large and small firms differ in that large firms have relatively low internal discount rates and high internal labor costs. This happens simply because large firms have easier access to cheap working capital, mostly internally generated, but face a labor bottleneck due to layers of supervision.

An immediate consequence of low internal discount rates is that large firms (or rich people) have a comparative advantage in acquiring and holding titles to high-rent natural resources. I define a high-rent natural resource as one that generates a high ratio of output to input of labor and materials, relative to other resources *in the same use category*. High-rent is usually but not always determined by location. For example, Wall Street land is high-rent for financial services compared to land in the same use in nearby central Newark. Well-watered, accessible forest land is high-rent compared to forest land on steep remote mountains. A broadcast license for the New York metropolitan area is high-rent compared to one for Pittsburgh. A patent for a heartburn drug is high-rent compared to one for a rare genetic disease, not due to location, but to number of customers. Under the same title-holders, the optimal cycle on a high-rent resource is shorter: buildings in Wall Street will be replaced more often than in Newark, trees on accessible land will be harvested more often, broadcast equipment and programs will be upgraded more often in New York, and more new patents will be developed for heartburn than for rare diseases. To casual observers, large firms' advantage in holding high-rent resources often makes them appear more modern and successful than small firms.

I constructed models both for appreciating assets like trees or wine in a cellar, and depreciating assets like buildings or machinery. For any kind of appreciating assets, large firms always generate more output *per man-hour*, leading to the false conclusion that they are more 'productive'. They also show a higher profit share of income, which is often taken to mean they are more 'efficient', when in fact they are merely more land- and capital-intensive. Large firms, however, provide less employment per dollar of sales or assets. For example, according to 2007 US Census data, comparing firms with over $100m in sales to those with under half-a-million, the big firms averaged three employees per $100m sales while the small ones averaged fifteen. Where large and small firms occupy the same quality land – as frequently occurs when sprawl places them side by side – large firms will use a longer cycle of production for both appreciating and depreciating assets. (However, if we compare large firms on high-rent with small firms on low-rent land, large firms may use a faster cycle.) There are some differences as to appreciating and depreciating assets between large and small firms. On the same quality land, large firms will operate with a higher ratio of appreciating assets to land, but a lower ratio of depreciating assets. That is, large firms may let their trees grow longer, but replace their buildings sooner. On much higher-rent land, large firms' ratio of improvements to land value is always lower, for trees or buildings.

As I showed, the more unequal an economy, the more it behaves like the dominant economic entities, so the Faustmann formula helps predict the effects of inequality on overall economic function. It fortifies George's case against inequality. The larger the proportion of an economy's land and other natural resources held by a wealthy minority, the more investments will be made on a longer, slower cycle, resulting in less output and employment than were those resources more widely held.

The Faustmann formula also makes it very easy to show how taxes on output, sales, or wages damage the economy: *they lengthen the cycle of production*. A tax on land has no effect at all when added to the formula. However, to the extent that a tax on land reduces inequality, it raises the discount rate applied in economic decisions, speeding up the production cycle, increasing output and employment.

George and Wicksell on the Boom/Bust Cycle

Progress and Poverty is subtitled *An Inquiry into the Cause of Industrial Depressions and of Increase of Want with Increase of Wealth ... the Remedy*. Yet George devotes only a very short chapter – 18 pages – to 'The Primary Cause of Recurring Paroxysms of Industrial Depression'. This is perhaps an acknowledgement that he is on shaky ground. In his final, unfinished book, *The Science of Political Economy* (1981), he does not address the issue at all.

George first reviews and dismisses as secondary other factors in the business cycle, notably

> the essential defect of currencies which contract when most needed, and the tremendous alternations in volume that occur in the simpler forms of commercial credit, which, to a much greater extent than currency in any form, constitute the medium or flux of exchanges ...' (George, 1879: 263)

He dismisses 'overproduction and overconsumption', blaming 'the speculative advance in rent' which he sees as equivalent to 'a lockout of labor and capital by landowners'. To summarize, George sees growth as setting off a speculative bubble which carries the seeds of its own destruction. That is, the bubble stimulates land withholding which eventually cuts off production, bursting the bubble. Then the cycle repeats.

George's remedy for the boom and bust cycle is the same: land value taxation. This eliminates the speculative value of land, bringing the 'speculative margin' back down to the 'productive margin' – raising wages to what a man can earn at the productive margin.

Swedish economist Knut Wicksell came of age during the 'marginalist revolution' set off by Stanley Jevons, Carl Menger and Leon Walras in the early 1870s. Like George, he was a rebel and social critic. Unlike George, he was an ardent Malthusian – a position which scandalized Swedish society and inhibited his career. Like George, he supported land value taxation, though without making it a crusade (Wicksell, Musgrave & Peacock, 1958:114-115).

Wicksell posits that there exists a 'natural' or 'real' rate of interest that, all else being equal, would bring desired saving into line with desired investment. This natural rate varies with conditions in the economy. A time of optimism, for example due to new technology, will raise the natural rate as investors compete for capital. However banks cannot easily identify the invisible natural rate; in the short run they may set their interest rates either higher or lower than the natural rate. If banks hold their rates lower than the natural rate, prices will rise. If higher, prices will fall (Wicksell, [1898] 1965: 69-72).

Wicksell's theory of interest and prices offers a potential explanation for the boom and bust cycle. Banks are conservative, he argues. They are slow to change their practices in the face of changing economic circumstances. So when the economy booms, banks may hold their rates too low for too long, fueling a bubble. Eventually the banks raise rates, and when the bubble bursts, hold them too high for too long, delaying recovery.

The excessively low bank rate during a boom 'may act as an incentive to increased business activity and thus to conversion on a large scale of liquid capital into fixed capital, which ... is the outstanding characteristic of good times...' Wicksell notes the implications for distribution:

> But if the formation of the real capital which is then absolutely essential is only based on the rise in prices itself, i.e. is due to diminished consumption on the part of those persons or classes of society with fixed money incomes, then the increased prosperity could scarcely be very great or enduring.   (Wicksell, [1906] 1967: 209)

Wicksell's theory resembles that of George in an important respect: he believes that real events in the underlying economy drive the boom and bust cycle. The interest rate and price effects follow and exaggerate the underlying population and technology cycle. At best policy can moderate the cycle by keeping the bank rate more in line with the natural rate.

George by contrast, sees a speculative cycle arising from the psychology of rapid economic growth, aggravated by inequality of landownership. The powerful single tax policy can simultaneously dampen speculation, reduce inequality and stimulate even more rapid economic growth. Where Wicksell is a pessimist, George is an optimist.

Gaffney on Speculation and the Boom/Bust Cycle

In *Land speculation as an Obstacle to Ideal Allocation of Land* (1956), Mason Gaffney develops a modern capital-theoretical explanation of what George called 'land speculation'.

As George describes them, land speculators are individuals who 'cannot or will not' put land to its best current use, because they are holding it for a rise in price. This definition needs clarification.

➤ All landholders 'speculate,' in the sense that they hold property only as long as the discounted value of expected future income (or other benefits) equals or exceeds the (net) market price.

➤ Some landholders withhold land even absent rising prices, because they have different priorities. Often they are wealthy enough not to need the income – think of the great lords of all civilizations who kept fertile land as hunting preserves.

➤ It is sometimes economically logical to withhold appreciating land from use lest the present use preempts a better use later. It would be a bad investment to plant an orange orchard in land that will be ripe for a subdivision in five years, or to build a two-story building on land soon ripe for six.

Gaffney disentangles these points. It is true that all landholders speculate. It is also true that – even absent rising prices – they may differ in their priorities. And given rising prices, they may vary in their optimism. More important, however, some land holders may use much lower internal discount rates than others in valuing land. In general, wealthier individuals and better-capitalized corporations use lower discount rates, for an obvious reason: having better collateral, they can borrow at lower rates, and having higher income, they have less urgent need for cash. This phenomenon is called 'capital market failure'. Wealthier individuals or organizations face their own internal structure of prices and incentives and respond accordingly. Within any category of use, low discount rate entities tend to use land less intensively. Land market failure and capital market failure are two sides of a coin. As Gaffney elaborates in 'The Unwieldy Time-Dimension of Space' (1961), they are an inescapable reality.

But while capital and land market failure are universal, they take a particularly pernicious form where land values are rising rapidly. On the western frontier, George observed tens of thousands of prime, well-located acres grabbed up and held out of use by eastern absentees, forcing settlers to spread out onto more remote and poorer quality land. He devoted his first book, Our Land and Land Policy ([1871] 1900) to describing this phenomenon. Dramatic widespread withholding happens because expectations of appreciation amplify the difference in offers for land between poor high-discount bidders and rich low-discount bidders.

Gaffney Combines George and Wicksell

In 'Causes of Downturns: An Austro-Georgist Synthesis' (1982a), Gaffney's working paper draws on his earlier work and on Wicksell to extend and clarify George's model. He identifies five major features of the boom and bust cycle.

1 Overpricing Land As George observed, a period of growth and prosperity sets land values to increasing, especially in transition areas between different uses: downtown-residential, residential-farmland, farmland-forest. Over-optimism about price increases gives large, low-discount buyers and holders an edge, driving more marginal buyers and users to less-suitable areas, aggravating sprawl. As George observed, excessive land prices and rents cut into wages and returns on investment.

2 Loss and Waste of Capital Excessive land prices distort and displace real investment. Owners of appreciating land, including US homeowners in the bubble before 2008, understandably begin to treat their appreciation as real income. They cash in by taking out new mortgages. They spend instead of saving. This 'wealth effect' causes net disinvestment. Owners of income property fail to reinvest. As Gaffney writes, 'It is as though grocers ate up part of their own wares, instead of selling and replacing them, leaving some shelves empty. Most of the flow of investing consists of refilling shelves as the goods go out. Now, that flow drops' (Gaffney, 1982a: 2). Low-discount buyers tend to hold rather than improve.

3 Over-conversion of Circulating Capital There is over-investment in fixed capital. George largely missed this point; Wicksell emphasized it, but only as a consequence of bank interest rates below the hidden 'natural' rate. Sprawl requires over-extended roads and utility lines. To save on expensive land, owners build overly tall buildings, or irrigate dry farmland to increase yields per acre. Gaffney identifies 'claim-staking', i.e. rent-seeking investments, like logging roads, some R&D, preemptive patenting, accepting losses to capture broadcast licenses, etc. He points out that 'This is the slowest-turning [capital] of all, because often the payoff is capturing land and its resources in perpetuity' (Gaffney, 1982a: 3). And then there is overinvestment in 'land-leading' capital, excess capacity in anticipation of further growth, for example platted land in swamps and deserts (Gaffney, 1982a: 4). Towards the end of a boom, such malinvestment creates a severe shortage of circulating capital, causing a brief spike in interest rates. Half-completed projects are abandoned, often never to resume. Existing capital loses real value, as more of its cash flow must now be imputed to interest. Gaffney calls this phenomenon a 'macro-economic glitch'.

4 Lower Marginal Rate of Return Overpricing land and rent leaves less for what Gaffney calls 'social investors', those who hire labor and build new capital. It lowers the return on real investment. This starts a vicious circle. Lower marginal rate of return on real investment makes land look even more attractive, further fueling the boom. The price rise becomes increasingly unstable, motivated more and more by expectations of further price increases. Once the rise even pauses, it must soon fall.

5 Collapse of Credit System There is a lacuna in both George and Wicksell: the role of collateral in credit extension. In fact, collateral and credit play an important role in a boom. Under any circumstances, banks extend more and cheaper credit to well-collateralized low-discount entities. In a boom, this increases these entities' ability to outbid poorly collateralized entities. However, as a boom progresses, lenders become increasingly ready to lend on inflated values to flaky projects – a further driver of prices and a further waste of capital. Loss of liquidity and unstable prices eventually burst the bubble. Land prices should drop like a rock when the expectation of growth disappears. In fact, the market freezes, as low-discount entities do what they do best – wait.

> *Gaffney has shown how the neoclassical revolution has created the barren and irrelevant textbook economics of today.*

In the credit system:

> ➤ After a few losses on bad collateral, banks tighten up their lending. In fact, they overreact, cutting off lending to all but their best collateralized customers.
> ➤ Government regulators overreact. As their equity shrinks, banks cut off lines of credit and stop rolling over loans to smaller customers. Businesses close, unemployment rises. The money supply dries up, possibly creating deflation.

As long as the market remains frozen, returns on investment remain preternaturally low. As banks ration credit, lending only to the best-collateralized, interest rates remain low as well. As Gaffney notes, this creates an illusion that there is an excess of liquid capital seeking investment. In reality, both supply and demand for new capital are low. And consequently production and employment remain low.

Much of the damage is invisible: infrastructure and buildings still stand, but lifeless as if hit by a neutron bomb. As prices and rents finally begin to fall, the economy slowly revives. Gaffney observes:

> Bank expansion and collapse add to the severity of boom and slump, so much so that the ordinary economist is likely to see the banking accordion as the original cause, rather than the effect of the cycle. Simple sequential observation, however, shows that land cycles have a life of their own, leading banking cycles.
>
> (Gaffney, 1982a: 6)

Gaffney's Contribution

Mason Gaffney has greatly enriched our understanding of the ideas of Henry George by showing their origin with the English classical economists and the French Physiocrats. He has also filled in serious gaps in George's understanding, notably of the cycle of production, and the cycle of boom and bust. Finally, he has shown how the neoclassical revolution, reacting against the radical implications of George and the classical economists, has created the barren and irrelevant textbook economics of today.

References

Clark, J.B. (1898), 'The Future of Economic Theory', *The Quarterly Journal of Economics*, 13(1).

Clark, J.B. (1908), *The Distribution of Wealth: A Theory of Wages, Interest and Profits* (1908 ed.), New York, The MacMillan Company.

Cleveland, M.M. (1984), 'Consequences and Causes of Unequal Distribution of Wealth', Ph.D., University of California, Berkeley.

Gaffney, M. (1956), *Land Speculation as an Obstacle to Ideal Allocation of Land*, University of California, Berkeley Retrieved from http://www.masongaffney.org/dissertation.html

Gaffney, M. (1957), *Concepts of Financial Maturity of Timber and Other Assets*, Raleigh, North Carolina State College.

Gaffney, M. (1961), 'The Unwieldy Time – Dimension of Space', *American Journal of Economics and Sociology*, 20(5).

Gaffney, M. (1975), 'Toward Full Employment with Limited Land and Capital' in J. Arthur Lynn (ed.), *Property Taxes, Land Use and Public Policy*, Madison, University of Wisconsin Press.

Gaffney, M. (1982a), 'Causes of Downturns: An Austro-Georgist Synthesis'.

Gaffney, M. (1982b), 'Two Centuries of Economic Thought on Taxation of Land Rents' in R. Lindholm & J. Arthur Lynn (eds.), *Land Value Taxation in Thought and Practice*. Madison: University of Wisconsin Press.

Gaffney, M. (1994a), 'Land as a Distinctive Factor of Production' in N. Tideman (ed.), *Land and Taxation*, London, Shepheard-Walwyn.

Gaffney, M. (1994b). 'Neo-Classical Economics as a Stratagem Against Henry George', in F. Harrison (ed.), *The Corruption of Economics*, London, Shepheard-Walwyn.

George, H. ([1871] 1900), *Our Land and Land Policy: Speeches, Lectures and Miscellaneous Writings*, New York, Doubleday, Page & Co.

George, H. ([1879] 1962), *Progress and Poverty: An Inquiry into the Cause of Industrial Depressions and of Increase of Want with Increase of Wealth ... the Remedy*, New York, Robert Schalkenbach Foundation.

Harding, R. (2012), 'Economics and society: Barrier to a breakthrough', *Financial Times*, February 22. Retrieved from http://www.ft.com/intl/cms/s/0/7e316f80-5c80-11e1-911f-00144feabdc0.html#axzz2Jrm2D3yP

Heyck, T.W. (2002), *The Peoples of the British Isles: A New History : From 1688 to 1870, Volume 2*, Chicago, Lyceum Books.

Malthus, T.R. (1798), *An Essay on the Principle of Population*, Retrieved from www.econlib.org database. Retrieved from http://econlib.org/library/Malthus/malPop.html

Marx, K. ([1867] 1906), *Capital: a Critique of Political Economy, Vol. I, The Process of Capitalist Production* (S. Moore & E. Aveling, Trans.), Library of Economics and Liberty.

Mill, J.S. ([1848] 1909), 'Principles of Political Economy with some of their Applications to Social Philosophy' in W.J. Ashley (Series ed.) Retrieved from www.econlib.org database. Retrieved from http://www.econlib.org/library/Mill/mlP.html

Ricardo, D. ([1818] 1996), *Principles of Political Economy and Taxation*, Amherst, Prometheus Books.

Smith, A. ([1776] 1904), *An Inquiry into the Nature and Causes of the Wealth of Nations* in E. Cannan (Series ed.), Retrieved from www.econlib.org database. Retrieved from http://econlib.org/library/Smith/smWN.html

Solow, R.M. (1955), 'The Production Function and the Theory of Capital', *Review of Economic Studies, 23* (2).

Wicksell, K. ([1898] 1965), *Interest and Prices: A Study of the Causes Regulating the Value of Money*, New York, Augustus M. Kelley, Bookseller.

Wicksell, K. ([1905] 1971), *Lectures on Political Economy, Volume One: General Theory*, New York, Augustus M. Kelley.

Wicksell, K. ([1906] 1967), *Lectures on Political Economy, Volume Two: Money [1906]*, New York: Augustus M. Kelley.

Wicksell, K., Musgrave, R.A., & Peacock, A.T. (1958), 'A New Principle of Just Taxation' in *Classics in the Theory of Public Finance*, London, Macmillan.

4

Shifting the Landscape: Mason Gaffney as Ultimate Heterodox

FRED E. FOLDVARY

ECONOMICS is not a unified science, but is divided into schools of thought. The mainstream dominant school is called 'neoclassical'. It evolved from the classical school that was dominant in the United Kingdom and the United States from the late 1700s to the late 1800s. The other schools are referred to as 'heterodox.'

In economics, orthodox economics is the theory presented in most textbooks. Classes and textbooks divide economic theory into two divisions, microeconomics and macroeconomics. Microeconomics, also called 'price theory,' concerns the parts of the economy, such as consumption, production, exchange, and market structures such as competition and monopoly. Macroeconomics examines the economy as a whole, including national income and output, economic growth, money, interest rates, and economic fluctuations.

While neoclassical microeconomics is a unified theory, mainstream macroeconomics is split into various neoclassical sub-schools, including Keynesian (named after John Maynard Keynes), New Classical, and Monetarist. These are included in economics textbooks and dominate scholarly thought.

Contemporary heterodox schools of thought include Institutional, Marxist, Austrian, Georgist, Evolutionary, and post-Keynesian theories. There are also schools that use the theories of other schools and apply them in special ways, such as the feminist and humanist schools.

Mason Gaffney has been a leading economist in the Georgist school of economic thought. This economic landscape derives from the theory developed by Henry George during the latter 1800s. George expanded on the theory of the classical school, and integrated economics with ethics. While the current Georgist school uses classical and neoclassical theory, it places much greater emphasis on the role of land in the economy than the usual treatment by those schools. The land-centric Georgist theory of the business cycle, for example, is unique to that school of thought. In Georgist thought, land is central to issues such as economic inequality, growth, and poverty, which qualifies Georgism as a distinct school of economic thought.

Nevertheless, the basic economics of land, rent, and rent-based public finance can be explained using the neoclassical microeconomic concepts of supply, demand, consumer and producer surplus, elasticity, and deadweight loss. For example, the 20th-century Georgist economist Harry G. Brown 'was a neoclassically trained economist who used neoclassical tools to plead the Georgist case before other NCEists' (Gaffney, 1994b: 123).

The basic problem with the neoclassical school is not so much that its theory is incorrect, but that it is incomplete, and its practitioners act as though that incomplete doctrine is sufficient to explain the economy, resulting in harmful policies. As stated by Warren Samuels (1996:x), neoclassical economics 'does have much to offer by way of deep insights into how economies operate. But there is much which neoclassical economics omits or on which it presents arguably myopic and/or stylized versions.'

The main argument of the critics of neoclassical economics is that the mainstream has failed to, as young folks say, 'keep it real'. The main task of economics is to understand the implicit reality beneath superficial appearances. Neoclassical economics recognizes the distinction between nominal gross domestic product (measured in current prices) and real GDP (adjusted for inflation). The theory distinguishes between nominal interest rates and real rates, the latter adjusted for inflation. Neoclassical texts teach the difference between accounting profit and the real gain, economic profit, which is net of implicit costs. But when it comes to land, neoclassical economics does not keep it real. It counts only explicit rent, not the implicit rent that hides in interest, profits, taxes, and bids suppressed by lower profits due to taxation.

The Georgist school of thought includes ethics as well as economics. Henry George added a moral dimension to the theory of land, which differentiates him from classical predecessors such as Ricardo, and also aligns himself philosophically with Proudhon (1840), who had rejected the homesteading doctrine of land ownership. The ethics of land carries human equality to the benefits of nature, an economic equality that is not based on outcomes but on natural rights. In Georgist ethics, human beings are equal self-owners, and therefore the proper owners of their labor, products, and wages. The benefits of land are measured by rent, and so the rent properly belongs to the members of relevant communities in equal shares (Foldvary, 1999).

Many neoclassical economists do not disagree with the basic ideas of Georgist theory, but do not use it in their publication and teaching. We can classify the economists of the Georgist heterodox school – 'geoclassical economics' – as those who have published Georgist theory and included it in their teaching. There are also economists who have agreed with and written on Georgist theory, but have not made the school of thought dominant in their publications and policy advocacy.

Mason did include geoclassical economics in his courses. Geoclassical instructors typically include land and rent in their classes on principles and public finance. For example, Kris Feder has a Seminar in Geoclassical Economics. Mary Cleveland uses *Progress and Poverty* in her course on Poverty, Inequality & the Environment. I include land and rent within public finance and other courses. Gaffney's publications have been used in courses taught by others, including his work on natural resources.

The web site 'Rate My Professor', where students rate their instructors, grades the teaching by Mason Gaffney as A+. One student stated that Gaffney was 'One of the most brilliant economics professors around.' Another student says, 'Professor Gaffney has been one of the most insightful person I have ever met. He is full of economic knowledge and is willing to explain a concept to you in great detail if you ask for it. For me, he is one of the greatest teachers I have had and one of the most interesting person I've met too.' Of course a professor cannot please everyone; one student commented, 'he is too stuck on George'.

Mase, as we call him, has contributed chapters to collections of Georgist writing, and has written whole books on Georgist economics, and thus shall be recorded in economic history as one of the major Georgist

economists, with the same prominent stature as his predecessors Henry
George and Harry Gunnison Brown.

Gaffney is a complete economist, meaning that he has done work in
all three aspects of economics: theory, history, and economic thought.
He has contributed to economic analysis, the history of the economy, and
the history of economic thought. For example, Gaffney wrote on the
history of sales taxes, showing how they often resulted in political or
military defeat, and has written on the history of economic thought, the
ideas of Henry George, the Physiocrats of France, and economists of
various schools of thought.

The main purpose of heterodox economics should be to provide alternative explanations of economic reality in order to prescribe effective
remedies for economic problems. The neoclassical mainstream theories
have failed to eliminate the causes of social problems, and they present
false choices. For example, neoclassical economics tells us that there is
an inevitable trade-off between equity and efficiency. The textbooks say
that if we seek a greater equality of income, that implies redistribution
from the rich to the poor, which results in less production and less
growth, since the taxes reduce investment and growth. Gaffney points
out that this is a false choice, as we can have both greater equality and
greater efficiency with a tax shift, the replacement of market-hampering
income and sales taxes with the collection of land rent.

Another heterodox idea of Gaffney is what he calls the 'quantum leap
effect' (Foldvary, 2008). Neoclassical theory recognizes that taxes impose
a deadweight loss or excess burden, as they raise the purchase price and
reduce the quantity. Gaffney applies Georgist economics to show that the
damage done by taxes can be much greater than what conventional theory
implies. Taxing the gross receipts of a company that cannot pass on its
costs will deplete the profit and make the firm shut down. It is replaced
by a firm that can more easily pass on the tax, but employs fewer workers.
Think of a book store replaced by a gas station. This large reduction in
employment and output is a quantum leap down of employment and
output. Moreover, by reducing output, government gets less revenue from
taxing gross receipts than if it tapped the rent.

A major contribution for economic history is Gaffney's calculation of
the taxable capacity of land. He found that about half of the value of real
estate is land value. Neoclassical economists do not deny that taxing land,
as an inelastic factor, has a lower deadweight loss than taxing more elastic
sources such as capital. But they dismiss so-called 'land value taxation'

as unimportant because they believe that land rent constitutes only around two percent of national income. Gaffney showed that there is enough rent to pay for public goods, consistent with the 'Henry George' theorem of public finance developed by Joseph Stiglitz and others.

The greatest heterodox contribution of Gaffney was his delving into the history of economic thought to uncover the dark side of the history of neoclassical economics. *The Corruption of Economics* revealed the deliberate and successful endeavor by landed interests in the USA to deflect the land-tax movement sparked by Henry George. The best way to stop the movement to tax land value was to change economics itself, so that LVT would lack an academic imprimatur.

The evolution of neoclassical from classical theory is usually thought of as involving marginal analysis, basing value and prices on marginal or additional utility, costs, and revenues. But, as Gaffney exposed, neoclassical theory also eliminated land from the central place it had with classical theory. Neoclassical economics is now a two-factor school, based on the mathematical treatment of labor and capital. On the production side, neoclassical economics treats output as a function of capital and labor: $Q=f(K,L)$. On the income side, neoclassical economics merges land rent with capital yields, labeling it only as income from capital. Thus major issues such as income inequality become a matter of capital versus labor, while land ownership remains hidden, suppressed, and forgotten. As Gaffney puts it, when land is mentioned, it is compartmentalized into its own box, out of sight and mind from the living room of the economic mansion.

Rebellion Against Orthodoxy

Students in universities throughout the world have rebelled against the neoclassical curriculum, especially since the crisis of 2008. An article by John Cassidy in *The New Yorker*, 'Rebellious Economics Students Have a Point', states that 'the student rebellion is calling for a more pluralistic and diverse approach, rejecting the textbook methodology that all too often reduces economics to a set of mathematical exercises.' The International Student Initiative for Pluralism in Economics has called in an open letter for more of the real world in economics courses. Businesses that hire economists have also observed that economics graduates can solve differential equations but have little understanding about how economies actually work.

The Student Initiative (International, 2015) calls for 'a variety of theoretical perspectives, from the commonly taught neoclassically-based approaches to the largely excluded classical, post-Keynesian, institutional, ecological, feminist, Marxist and Austrian traditions.' Also, 'students should be systematically exposed to the history of economic thought and to the classical literature on economics as well as to economic history.' As this organization is open to classical and other schools of thought, they surely are open to Georgist heterodoxy.

Another student organization is The Post-crash Economics Society at The University of Manchester. They seek to broaden the range of perspectives. The Society promotes self-education and book-club readings. Such student initiatives offer an opening for geoclassical economists.

The biggest error made by students protesting the neoclassical paradigm is the mistaken idea that neoclassical economics is a 'free market' school of thought. This is illustrated by the headline in an article (Inman, 2014), 'Economics students aim to tear up free-market syllabus.' It is good that undergraduates at Manchester University seek to include alternative theories. But the economics mainstream believes in central banking, the current tax structure, and regulations that 'correct market failure.' The genuine free-market economists are mostly in the Austrian school.

Academic economists have also protested neoclassical orthodoxy. The Association for Heterodox Economics was founded in 1999 by Frederic Lee. It holds an annual conference in which all heterodox economists are welcome. Lee was editor of the *American Journal of Economics and Sociology* during 2009-13. Clearly this is an organization that Georgist economists can participate in to make the 'geoclassical' paradigm more prominent.

Heterodox professors criticize a state-funded 'intellectual monoculture' based on journal rankings 'that are heavily biased in favour of orthodoxy and against intellectual diversity' (Inman, 2013). But they badly mix together a critique of neoclassical doctrines and the concept of a free market. The neoclassical orthodoxy is not that of a pure free market, since the orthodox view includes the doctrine of market failure.

The failure of most of heterodox economics to 'keep it real' with an understanding of land and rent is illustrated by the book by John Mueller, *Redeeming Economics*. The book reflects the widely held viewpoint that the field of economics has gone astray. But the index has no entries for land, rent, or George, and its prescription for tax reform is a reform of the income tax. The sad part is that the book was published by the Intercollegiate Studies Institute, founded by Frank Chodorov, who had been the head of the Henry George School of New York.

Post-Keynesian Heterodoxy

The followers of John Maynard Keynes established several schools of thought, including neo-Keynesian, New Keynesian, and Post-Keynesian economics. The first two are macroeconomic schools within the neo-classical framework.

The post-Keynesian Economics school has been a prominent heterodox doctrine. Post-Keynesian concepts include aggregate demand, financial instability, the impact of inequality, and the effect of uncertainty on expectations. PKs are organized in a Post-Keynesian Economics Study Group. Georgist economists have not had such organizations, despite a few attempts to establish a scholarly association. Several heterodox associations have been created including the European Association for Evolutionary Economics (1988), International Association for Feminist Economics (1992), Progressive Economics Forum (1998), Association for Heterodox Economics (1999), and Society of Heterodox Economists (2002)' (Lee, 2009). The Austrian school has a Society for the Development of Austrian Economics and the Mises Institute.

Post-Keynesians combine the theories of Keynes and Ricardo and take them into new directions. The key variable in Post-Keynesianism is effective aggregate demand. If demand is lacking, a market economy will not achieve full employment, and so they advocate that government put the unemployed to work. Post-Keynesians such as Hyman Minsky also emphasize the fragility of the financial system, and advocate tighter regulations. They believe that since money is created by governmental agencies, taxes use up currency and spending generates currency. Also, the amount of money can affect employment.

Rejecting the efficiency and equity of market economies, Post-Keynesians rely on a wise and benevolent government to generate demand, eliminate unemployment, and guide the financial system. Unfortunately, governments have failed to do these tasks well, and the deeper problem is that Post-Keynesians have not investigated the iatrogenic effect, that economic problems are caused by bad policy rather than the market itself. Post-Keynesians suffer from the same myopia as the neoclassicals they criticize, overlooking the role that land ownership plays.

While post-Keynesian concepts are important, they are not unique to that school, nor do they confront the root causes of phenomena such as inequality. Inequality due to privilege does create social problems, but among the heterodox schools, only the Georgists understand the inequality

of land tenure, and the implicit subsidy to land ownership, as the key
cause of unearned inequality along with macroeconomic instability.

Institutional Economics   Institutional economics posits that the key
variables of an economy are not abstractions such as supply and demand,
but institutions such as government, labor unions, corporations, and
money. The school was influenced by pragmatist ideas and the views of
Thorstein Veblen, the best known institutionalist. The school emphasizes
evolutionary economics. Recent contributors include John Kenneth
Galbraith. 'The institutionalist conception of society is holistic in nature'
(Whalen, 1996, p.87). They believe that market economies neither self-
regulate nor self-destruct.

Gaffney (1994a:72) drew on Veblen's (1923) last book *Absentee Ownership*,
to discuss Veblen's treatment of land acquisition. As a form of 'conspicuous
consumption,' some rich persons seek to own land for the prestige and
status of the sheer holding. This desire for land has no saturation limit,

While economists should study institutions, the school of thought lacks
an analysis of the causes of social problems, and therefore also does not
provide effective remedies.

Institute for New Economic Thinking   Another organization of
heterodox yearnings is the Institute for New Economic Thinking, founded
in 2009 with initial funds from George Soros. INET is a nonprofit institute that examines theory and policy to provoke new economic thinking.
But its advisor board of prominent economists almost guarantees that
INET will be dominated by old thinking. The research topics featured
on its web site are on topics, such as tax breaks for foreign profits, peripheral to the basic causes of poverty, excessive inequality, and depressions.

INET initiated the Curriculum Open-Access Resources in Economics
(CORE) project to transform economics. But members of the Association
for Heterodox Economics concluded that an INET-sponsored curriculum
'did little if anything to foster the critical thinking about economics and
policy that AHE espouses. Inclusion of heterodox economics in the
curriculum has been explicitly ruled out.'

The Austrian School   The Austrian school of economic thought has
perhaps had the most popular success of the heterodox schools. Founded
by Carl Menger in 1871, the main topics of the school include subjective
values, methodological individualism, entrepreneurship, a time-preference

theory of interest, heterogenous capital goods, the Austrian theory of the business cycle, and critiques of socialism and governmental intervention. The critiques attracted free-marketeers to the school, and while its theories are not based on free-market ideology, its conclusions – that markets coordinate well, while intervention typically fails – has made Austrian economics a free-market school. The most prominent Austrians have been Ludwig von Mises, Friedrich Hayek, and Joseph Schumpeter.

Austrian capital theory remains heterodox, as it has not been adopted by the neoclassical mainstream. Menger theorized a structure of capital goods based on their turnover or period of production, from lower-order goods with short periods to the highest order goods of long duration. Lower interest rates make the structure taller, as they induce more investment in capital goods of highest order. In a free market, all is well, as high savings result in low interest rates, and thus more investment, and that offsets the reduced consumption implied by more savings.

But with central banking, the monetary authority manipulates interest rates, making them depart from what the Swedish economist Wicksell called the 'natural rate,' based on the people's preference for present-day goods over future goods. When interest rates are pushed down, as they were after 2001, there is excessive investment in higher order capital goods, such as real estate construction. Austrian economics emphasizes that an artificially low interest rate, as has occurred also since 2008, creates unsustainable assert bubbles. At the peak of the boom, interest rates and other costs have risen, and the investments turn out to have been wasted. The crash of the market in capital goods, such as real estate improvements, brings down with it the financial counterparts.

The Austrian remedy is to let the market set the rate of interest and the money supply. That stops the 'malinvestment' in higher-order goods. While the Austrian theory fits the economic history, it is incomplete. The usual presentation of the Austrian cycle overlooks the role of land. Cheap credit buys land together with the buildings, and the expansionary monetary policy fuels 'malspeculation' along with 'malinvestment' (Foldvary, 2012). The integration of land into Austrian theory creates a synthesis that explains all past major US depressions (Foldvary, 1997). The land aspect fits well in the Austrian cycle, and indeed, one Austrian, Karl Pribam (1940) did include real estate in his analysis of the business cycle. Moreover, as noted above, Mason Gaffney incorporated Austrian capital theory into his Georgist cycle theory, and Georgist students of business cycles can benefit from the Austrian critique of central banking.

Steve Keen, Heterodox Economist   Steve Keen has been a leading economist in the dissatisfaction with neoclassical economics. In a 2009 article, 'The Creative Destruction of G8 Economics,' Keen states 'that neoclassical economics is not only wrong – it's dangerous.' But from a Georgist perspective, Keen himself has misunderstood the economy. He disagrees with the neoclassical proposition that 'all instability in the system can be traced to market interventions rather than the market itself.' Gaffney, following Henry George, identified the real estate cycle as the primary mover in the boom-bust cycle. The problem is not the non-existing free market but government's fiscal and monetary subsidies to land value, which fuels the unsustainable speculative boom. The remedy, what Gaffney calls 'geofiscalism,' is not a governmental interference but a market-based paying back of value received from government, preventing what Fred Harrison (2006) has called the 'clawback' of taxes paid by the wealthy.

Keen provides no remedy for neoclassical failures. He (2009) states, 'the development of an alternative is still a long way off...' Alternative schools of thought are 'not yet developed to the point of providing a fully fledged alternative to neoclassical economics.' Evidently Keen has not read Gaffney and other Georgist economists. This illustrates the typical heterodox literature, which criticizes neoclassical thought without fully considering alternatives. As Georgist economic thought is also heterodox, it can be considered a heterodoxy within the heterodox complex, thus Gaffney is a 'heterodox heterodox' economist, or the ultimate in heterodoxy.

Keen's remedies are basically more of the same. He writes, 'Economics also has to become a fundamentally monetary discipline' which emphasizes the 'dangers of excessive debt and deflation.' Neoclassical economists already write about excessive debt, and the financial press has had many articles on deflation. Keen adds, 'The discipline must also become fundamentally empirical.' Nobody can dispute that, but the question is, what do we do with the data? The problem is that Keen and his fellow heterodox economists were too focused on the financial side of the land-value boom, and thus were not able to see the effective fiscal remedy, the collection of the rent that was capitalizing the land values.

Keen's list of 'names that are conspicuously absent from modern economics courses – Karl Marx, Thorstein Veblen, John Maynard Keynes, Irving Fisher, Michal Kalecki, Joseph Schumpeter, Hyman Minsky, Piero Sraffa and Richard Goodwin' does not include Henry George and his modern followers such as Mason Gaffney. As a heterodox economist, one would think that he has read the heterodox literature, but evidently not *Beyond Neoclassical Economics* (Foldvary, 1996). Kris Feder's chapter in that book, 'Geo-economics,' summarizes the Georgist approach.

Universalist Economics   Regarding the Georgist school, Warren Samuels (1996, xiv) wrote that Kris Feder's chapter 'introduces the reader to what may be both the most dramatic and the most venerable school – indeed movement – of heterodox economics, that following Henry George.' Indeed the Georgist school is 'dramatic' in providing a practical program and a vision of prosperity for all, and the social harmony that would follow.

What is needed is an integration of all schools of thought and method into a universal theory. A 'pan-theoretic of universalist economist does not confine himself to one approach of school of thought, but seeks to integrate several paradigms' (Foldvary, 1996b:19). Ideally, the theories of heterodox schools should be included in courses and textbooks. Short of that, there should be classes on comparative economic theory, and courses on a variety of schools including the Georgist.

Marxist Economics   Karl Marx based his theory on the classical school, extending it by claiming that the surplus from production is wages taken by capitalists from worker. Therefore labor is exploited, and there is a class struggle as workers fight back with strikes, unions, and revolution.

There are several Marxist subschools. One of them is nondeterminist Marxism, which rejects economic determinism, such as, for example, the proposition that market economies inevitably self-destruct. Nondeterminist Marxism rejects Marx's labor theory of value (Ameriglio et al, 1996). But neither the old overdetermined nor the new nondetereministic Marxim have provided effective remedies for social problems.

Georgist Economics   The Georgist school, in which Mason Gaffney is affiliated, has included several economists who were strongly aligned with it, including Harry Gunnison Brown, William Vickrey, and contemporaries such as Nicolaus Tideman, Kris Feder, Fred Foldvary, Fred Harrison, Mary Cleveland, Joseph Stiglitz, and Michael Hudson. Michael Hudson's (2012) book *The bubble and beyond* examines the role of land as well as financial aspects, much like the real estate cycle works of Foldvary (1997, 2007), Gaffney (2009), Anderson (2008), and Harrison (2005). Hudson especially criticizes national income accounts for not including the amount of land rent, as land rent gets masked as interest, profits, and tax payments, and he emphasizes the negative effects of the debt leveraging and rent-extraction of the FIRE sector: finance, insurance, and real estate.

Gaffney's Heterodox Publications

After the Crash: Designing a Depression-Free Economy
The greatest contribution that heterodox economics can make is to explain the boom-bust cycle and its remedy. Gaffney's contribution in this book, and elsewhere, is deep, comprehensive, and clear. As Cliff Cobb (Gaffney 2009:2) noted in his introduction, 'Gaffney unites diverse economic traditions (institutionalist, Austrian, Georgist, and others)'.

Gaffney draws on Austrian economics to integrate its time structure of capital goods into the land-based Georgist theory. The period of production, or rate of turnover of capital goods, is a key element of Austrian theory, which Gaffney applies.

Gaffney is able to present a comprehensive theory by applying the history of economic thought. From Knut Wicksell (1934), a Swedish economist who wrote favorably on land-value taxation while also advancing Austrian theory, Gaffney took the concept of economic valence. Taken from the chemical meaning, the valence of a factor such as capital goods is the degree to which it combines with and thus promotes another factor, such as labor or land.

In emphasizing the role of economic investment, an increase in the stock of capital goods, Gaffney harks back to the French economists of the 1700s. Their school of thought, called Physiocracy (the rule of natural law), proposed a single tax on land value a century prior to its popularization by Henry George.

Like Harrison (2005) and myself, Gaffney draws on the economic history of land values presented by Homer Hoyt (1933) to analyze the timing of the cycles. Gaffney's explanation of the boom and bust is a 'real assets' model that integrates land prices, economic investment, the time-structure of capital goods, bank leverage, and fiscal and policies (Gaffney, 2015). As stated by Gaffney (2009, p.55), 'the theories of Keynes and other schools of economic thought have focused too much attention on questions of money and finance as if an economy could be well-managed on the basis of correct monetary policies alone. What I hope I have begun to make clear is that monetary policy is a refinement. It will fail if the basics, involving land and capital, are not attended to.'

The Mason Gaffney Reader
In the introduction, Lindy Davies (2013b:xiii) points out that Gaffney 'is not shy about pointing out – and constructively building on – the errors

he finds in George's work.' Economic science differs from a religious cult in learning from but not worshiping its leading figures.

Gaffney's heterodox rejection of the neoclassical false trade-offs is seen comprehensively in his 'Eighteen Answers to Futilitarians' (Gaffney, 2013a). The dismal choices of orthodoxy include equity vs. efficiency, environmental preservation vs. consumption, inflation vs. unemployment, and free choice vs. urban sprawl. As stated by Gaffney (p.5), 'those allegedly hard choices are false, calculated to unman us and make resolute action seem futile.' Gaffney shows how Georgist policy reconciles these alternatives. We can have it all.

The neoclassical policy to provide greater equality is efficiency-hampering redistribution. But the Georgist tax shift (called geofiscalism by Gaffney), replacing taxes on labor, profits, and goods, with public revenue from land rent, creates both greater equality and efficiency. Likewise, the green tax shift, replacing destructive taxes with pollution levies, generates both greater efficiency and economic growth. The 'Phillips Curve' tradeoff between inflation and unemployment has been discredited by history. And land-value taxation induces compact cities, avoiding subsidy-based choice.

Gaffney's had previously waxed poetic on the false trade-off of tastes vs. sprawl (Gaffney, 1964:132):

> O, Thou, who didst with windfall and with waste
> Beset the streets where buildings may be placed.
> Thou wilt not with predestined choice propel
> Me outwards, then impute my sprawl to 'taste!'!

One of the themes of Gaffney's research on economic history is that there is, in fact, ample rent for the provision of public goods. This research is presented in 'The Unplumbed Revenue Potential of Land' (Gaffney, 2013b). Land value is underestimated in several ways, including under-assessment, rent from tax-exempt land, tax methodology such as excessive depreciation, mistaken and incomplete national-income accounting, rent hidden in mortgages interest and profit, and the suppressed rent due to taxation that reduces locational gains.

One of the French economists admired by Gaffney was A.R. Jacques Turgot. Gaffney's article on Turgot applies this history of thought to US economic history. As intendant or governor of Limousin, France, Turgot applied the Physiocratic policies of taxing land, free trade, and investing in infrastructure. In 1774, impressed with the results, King Louis XVI made Turgot his comptroller general. The aristocrats opposed such 'geocracy' and Turgot was dismissed. Influenced by the free-trade ideas of Turgot and Adam Smith, the founders of the US Constitution included the Commerce Clause, which prevented the states from erecting trade barriers among themselves.

The Corruption of Economics

Perhaps the most heterodox of all economics works has been *The Corruption of Economics* (1994). The book not only presents Georgism as a heterodox view, but digs into the economic history of neoclassical economics to uncover its pernicious origin. The literature on the history of economic thought usually presents the neoclassical turn as taking place in the latter 1800s. The history of thought orthodoxy explains that the change was towards marginalism, especially marginal utility. The 'marginal revolution' was crafted by William Stanley Jevons of Great Britain, Carl Menger of Austria, and Leon Walras of Switzerland. The neoclassical story relates that classical theory had a labor theory of value, as did Marxist economics. The three marginalists independently discovered that prices originate, not on labor and other costs of production, but on the marginal utility of goods, the extra value to the buyer from getting one more unit. Menger, founder of the Austrian school, emphasized that values are completely subjective, and not intrinsic to any goods.

But there was another aspect of the neoclassical revolution that is omitted from the neoclassical literature. Classical economics was a three-factor school, recognizing the three input categories or factors of production: land, labor, and capital goods. The neoclassical revolution eliminated land, making it a two-factor school.

Part of the reason for dropping land is that as economics became ever more mathematical during the 1900s, output as a function of two variables is much more tractable than if there are three interacting variables. But the major reason for dropping land was a deliberate plan to stop the movement to tax land sparked by Henry George. Thus land was removed from the theory of production, but the income from land, rent, could not simply be dropped, since it is part of national income. Neoclassical economics merges land rent into income from capital, and so it also disappears on the income side. Moreover, in dropping land from economics, the neoclassical turn relegated George to minor player, at most briefly mentioned in textbooks on the history of economic thought.

We then get critics on the left who decry the increasing share of income from capital, while wages have been stagnant. Thomas Piketty (2014) claims that there has been a greater rise in capital's share of income relative to wages, as the rate of growth of capital is greater than the rate of economic growth. The policy prescription of Piketty and other critics of markets is on taxing financial assets and transactions, as they too fail to understand that it is land rent that captures the gains from economic growth. Much of this gain takes the form of shares of stock, corporate profits, mortgage interest, and derivatives such as mortgage-backed securities, masking the ultimate source, the land rent.

Piketty's empirical claims have been rebutted by, among others, Matthew Rognlie (2015), who finds that the increase in financial wealth has been in land value, especially in housing, as 'the non-housing capital share shows no clear trend' (p.17). He adds, 'since the higher cost of housing is mainly due to higher residential land values, rather than elevated construction costs for the structures themselves, it has made a particularly large contribution to net capital income' (p.18).

Gaffney's chapter is titled 'Neoclassical Economics as a Stratagem against Henry George.' The main actor in this drama is John B. Clark. According to Gaffney, Clark wrote at least 24 works directed against George and land value taxation. Another critic was the prominent public finance economist Edwin Seligman, the dominant academic voice advocating a progressive income tax.

Another important character in overturning classical theory was Alvin Johnson of Cornell University. The school was named after Ezra Cornell, who held and speculated on western lands. Johnson was a student of Clark. The neoclassical stratagem was to change not just the theory but also the language, the meaning of economic terms. As stated by Gaffney (1994b, p.75), 'Formerly, rent was simply the return to land. NCEists redefined it as the surplus over opportunity cost of any resources at any time, thus removing any difference of land from labor or capital ... The idea was to remove from land the dangerous stigma of yielding unearned values, targetable as taxable surpluses.' For example, a movie star paid $1 million to act in a movie, whose next best opportunity is being a salesman earning $100,000, has an economic rent of $900,000.

In 1914 Johnson published 'The Case against the Single Tax.' He wrongly stated that the Georgist policy was for the state to manage the land. Johnson wrote, without providing any data, that much of the financial wealth of the middle class is in land value, and that the full taxation of land value would take more value from them than they would regain in the removal of other taxes. Of course in 1914, the 16th

Amendment had just been enacted, in 1913, and the middle class did not yet suffer from the income tax. At any rate, if the collection of rent replaces all other taxes, the total and average tax burden is no greater. Also, what Johnson left out was that after the tax transition, the reduced price of land would offset the payment of the tax; a land value tax replaces what would otherwise be paid in mortgage interest, or, if the land is paid for in full, the tax on the rent is offset by the interest yield of the money saved from the lower purchase price of land.

Gaffney regards Frank Knight of the Chicago School as another pivotal figure. Frank Knight (1924:591) wrote that land yields no unearned surplus, and is 'produced' by discovery and by conquest: 'The original 'appropriation' of such opportunities by private owners involves investment in exploration, in detailed investigation and appraisal by trial and error of the findings, in development work of many kinds necessary to secure and market a product – besides the cost of buying off or killing or driving off previous claimants.'

The antipathy of such economists to land-value taxation is not based on the pure neoclassical theory, but stems from an ideological bias that accompanied the rise of neoclassical doctrine, a bias that comes partly from ignorance and partly from an emotional attachment to the status quo. The task of Georgist economists is therefore to inform scholars and journalists that land rent is in fact sufficient to pay for public goods, and that the public collection of rent is not a mere fiscal reform but has profound beneficial consequences.

Skousen on Gaffney

Mason Gaffney deserves to be included in books on the history of economic thought, and indeed, financial writer Mark Skousen (2009:233) features him among the pages on Henry George in his history of economic thought book, with the heading, 'By George, It's a Conspiracy!' Skousen quotes from the back cover of the book, 'To stop Henry George the fortune hunters hired professors to corrupt economics and halt democratic dialogue. The use of that corrupted economics continues to this day.'

Skousen then writes that Gaffney and Harrison (co-editors and chapter authors) 'made the unbelievable claim that the world's 'power elites' schemed to silence this popular social reformer.' Skousen points out, as an apparent contradiction, that 'Georgists claim that Henry George's *Progress and Poverty* is the most influential economics book ever written.' Skousen concludes by saying, 'Conspiracy theories have abounded throughout history, advocated by tight-knit political or religious groups filled with true believers. Followers of Henry George fit this category in economics.'

Evidently Mark Skousen has not thoroughly read the ample historic evidence provided by Mason Gaffney. On the one hand, it is good that some people are paying attention, but on the other hand, such a brief and superficial review unfortunately furthers the view of Henry George and Georgist economics as a cult not to be taken seriously. Readers of Skousen and other critics will mostly read such second-half reviews and not bother to read *Corruption of Economics* or *Progress and Poverty*.

Gaffney's Chapters in Books

Land and Taxation
There have been several books that explain geofiscal policy, but they have not penetrated into both the mainstream and the prevailing heterodox spheres. *Land and Taxation* (1994a) has chapters on land economics, history, and comparative analysis. Gaffney's chapter is 'Land as a Distinctive Factor of Production.' Where it mentions land, neoclassical economics treats the resource as just another factor, nothing special. The Georgist heterodox view says otherwise. Economic concepts such as supply and demand are the same for land as for other inputs, but the classical economists treated land as distinct for good reasons. Among other characteristics, land is not produced (and thus has no economic cost), is permanent, and spatial land has a fixed supply.

As a consequence, land rent is a surplus. Neoclassical economics misleadingly labels this a 'producer surplus,' as though the workers and firm owners create it. The classical economists knew, and the geoclassical economists still know, that the 'producer surplus' is land rent, and since landowners produce neither the land nor the products of the land, it should be called a 'nonproducer surplus.' Gaffney concludes the chapter with an explanation of land-driven booms and busts.

Land-Value Taxation: The Equitable and Efficient Source of Public Finance
Gaffney's chapter is 'Tax Reform to Release Land.' He writes that real estate taxes influence land use. Sprawl is caused by subsidies to land value, generating an excess use of land. He also speaks of low-density zoning as inducing forced land consumption. Property taxes applied to buildings induce less vertical use of land and greater horizontal expansion. Gaffney points out that mortgage interest is the largest cost of a building. The next greatest typical cost is the property tax on improvements. Levies

on land value release land held for speculation and to obtain implicit subsidies.

Another benefit of geofiscalism pointed out by Gaffney is that the lower purchase price of land makes land available to people with less income. As Gaffney states, levies on land value would be neutral if credit markets were perfect, if a lender could accurately know the likelihood that the borrower would pay the interest and pay back the principal. But since credit markets are uncertain, that prevents loans to worthy lower-income buyers. By reducing the need for credit, rent-based public revenue makes land more available to them. Nicolaus Tideman adds that the elimination of speculation near the peak of a real estate bubble eliminates the winner's curse of bidding too high, thus also making land-value taxation better than neutral. The 'better than neutral' theme is unique to Georgist economics, as other schools either regard levies on land rent as either neutral, or, misunderstanding it, worse than neutral.

Henry George: Political Ideologue, Social Philosopher, and Economic Theorist
Adapting some ideas from the Austrian school, Gaffney credits the Austrian economists with the concept of the 'period of production.' Capital goods have a duration during which they are produced, provide a return, and depreciate down to zero value. That provides a distinction from land, which is eternal, having no period of production. The opponents of land-value taxation thus also opposed the Austrian theory of capital goods. Chicago school economists such as J.B. Clark and Frank Knight 'aimed to wipe out any bright line, or any line at all, between land and capital.

Conclusion

Mason Gaffney will have a place in history as the ultimate heterodox economist. His teaching, writing, and presentations will have a lasting legacy as an eloquent heterodox heterodox economist.

References

Ameriglio, Jack, Antonio Callari, Stephen Resnick, David Ruccio, Richard Wolf (1996), 'Nondeterminist Marxism', in Fred E. Foldvary, ed., *Beyond Neoclassical Economics: Heterodox Approaches to Economic Theory*, London, Edward Elgar.

Anderson, Phillip. (2008). *The Secret Life of Real Estate and Banking*, London, Shepheard-Walwyn.

Association for Heterodox Economics (2013), 'Pluralism, Heterodoxy, and the Prospects for a New Economics Curriculum: Assessing the potential of INET', *What's the Use of Economics*, and the CORE Project. http://hetecon.net/documents/The_prospects_for_a_new_economic_curriculum.pdf

Cassidy, John (2014), 'Rebellious Economics Students Have a Point', *The New Yorker* (May 13). http://www.newyorker.com/news/john-cassidy/rebellious-economics-students-have-a-point

Cobb, Clifford W (2009), 'Editor's Introduction', in *After the Crash: Designing a Depression-Free Economy,* ed., Clifford Cobb, Malden, MA: Wiley-Blackwell.

Davies, Lindy, ed. (2013a), *The Mason Gaffney Reader,* New York, Henry George Institute.

Davies, Lindy. (2013b). 'Mason Gaffney: The Great Elucidator', in Lindy Davies, ed., *The Mason Gaffney Reader,* New York, Henry George Institute.

Feder, Kris (1996), 'Geo-economics', in Fred E. Foldvary, ed., *Beyond Neoclassical Economics: Heterodox Approaches to Economic Theory,* London, Edward Elgar.

Foldvary, Fred E., ed. (1996a), *Beyond Neoclassical Economics: Heterodox Approaches to Economic Theory,* London, Edward Elgar.

Foldvary, Fred E. (1996b). 'Comparative Economic Theory', in *Beyond Neoclassical Economics: Heterodox Approaches to Economic Theory,* London: Edward Elgar Publishing.

Foldvary, Fred E. (1997), 'The Business Cycle: A Georgist-Austrian Synthesis', *American Journal of Economics and Sociology,* 56(40), (October).

Foldvary, Fred E. (1999), 'The Ethics of Rent,' in Kenneth Wenzer, ed., *Land-Value Taxation: The Equitable and Efficient Source of Public Finance,* New York, M.E. Sharpe and London, Shepheard-Walwyn.

Foldvary, Fred E. (2007). *The Depression of 2008,* Berkeley: Gutenberg Press. http://www.foldvary. net/works/dep08.pdf

Foldvary, Fred E. (2008), 'The Gaffney Quantum Leap Effect', Prosper Australia. https://www. prosper.org.au/2008/07/02/the-gaffney-quantum-leap-effect/

Foldvary, Fred E. (2012), 'An Austrian Theory of Spatial Land', in David Emanuel Andersson, ed., *The Spatial Market Process,* (Advances in Austrian Economics, Volume 16) Emerald Group Publishing.

Gaffney, Mason (1964), 'Containment Policies for Urban Sprawl', in Richard Stauber, ed., *Approaches to the Study of Urbanization,* Governmental Research Center, The University of Kansas.

Gaffney, Mason (1994a), 'Land as a Distinctive Factor of Production', in Nicolaus Tideman, ed., *Land and Taxation,* London, Shepheard-Walwyn.

Gaffney, Mason (1994b), 'Neoclassical Economics as a Stratagem against Henry George', in Mason Gaffney and Fred Harrison, eds., *The Corruption of Economics.* London, Shepheard Walwyn.

Gaffney, Mason (1999), 'Tax Reform to Release Land', in Kenneth Wenzer, ed., *Land-Value Taxation: The Equitable and Efficient Source of Public Finance,* New York, M.E. Sharpe and London, Shepheard-Walwyn.

Gaffney, Mason. (2009). *After the Crash: Designing a Depression-Free Economy,* ed., Clifford Cobb, Malden, MA: Wiley-Blackwell.

Gaffney, (Mason. 2013a). 'Eighteen Answers to Futilitarians', in Davies, Lindy, ed., *The Mason Gaffney Reader,* NY: Henry George Institute.

Gaffney, Mason (2013b) 'The Unplumbed Revenue Potential of Land', in Lindy Davies, ed., *The Mason Gaffney Reader,* New York, Henry George Institute.

Gaffney, Mason (2013c), 'Turgot's Legacy: Our Commerce Clause', in Lindy Davies, ed., *The Mason Gaffney Reader,* New York, Henry George Institute.

Gaffney, Mason (2015), 'A Real-Assets Model of Economic Crises: Will China Crash in 2015?', *American Journal of Economics and Sociology,* 74(2) (March).

Gaffney, Mason and Fred Harrison (1994). *The Corruption of Economics,* London, Shepheard-Walwyn.

Harrison, Fred (2005). *Boom Bust: House Prices, Banking, and the Depression of 2010,* London, Shepheard-Walwyn.

Harrison, Fred (2006), *Ricardo's Law: House Prices and the Great Tax Clawback Scam,* London, Shepheard-Walwyn.

Hoyt, Homer (1933), *100 Years of Land Values in Chicago,* Chicago, University of Chicago Press.

Hudson, Michael (2012), *The Bubble and Beyond: Fictitious Capital, debt Deflation and Global Crisis*, Dresden, Islet.

Inman, Phillip (2013), 'Academics back students in protests against economics teaching', *The Guardian*, (18 November). http://www.theguardian.com/education/2013/nov/18/academics-back-student-protests-neoclassical-economics-teaching

Inman, Phillip (2014), 'Economics students aim to tear up free-market syllabus', *The Guardian*, (24 October). http://www.theguardian.com/business/2013/oct/24/students-post-crash-economics

International Student Initiative for Pluralism in Economics (2014), *An international student call for pluralism in economics*, (Open Letter). http://www.isipe.net/open-letter/

Johnson, Alvin S. 1914, 'The Case against the Single Tax', *The Atlantic Monthly* 113.

Keen, Steve (2009), 'The Creative Destruction of G8 Economics', *Adbusters Magazine*, (July 8). https://www.adbusters.org/magazine/84/creative-destruction-neoclassical-economics.html

Lee, Frederic S. (2009), 'The Emergence of Heterodox Economics, 1990-2006', in *A History of Heterodox Economics: Challenging the mainstream in the twentieth century*, Routledge.

Knight, Frank (1924), 'Some fallacies in the interpretation of social cost', *Quarterly Journal of Economics* 38.

Moss, Laurence S. (2008), 'Keeping Land in Capital Theory: Ricardo, Faustmann, Wicksell, and George', in *Henry George: Political Ideologue, Social Philosopher, and Economic Theorist*, Malden, MA, Blackwell.

Mueller, John D. (2010), '*Redeeming Economics*', Wilmington, Delaware.

Piketty, Thomas (2014), *Capital in the Twenty-First Century*, Cambridge, MA Belknap Press of Harvard University Press.

Pribram, Karl (1940), 'Residual, Differential, and Absolute Urban Ground Rents and Their Cyclical Fluctuations', *Econometrica* 8, (January).

Proudhon, Pierre-Joseph ([1840] 1994), *What is Property? An Inquiry into the Principle of Right and of Government*, ed., and trans. Donald Kelley and Bonnie Smith. Cambridge University Press.

Rate My Professor (2015), http://www.ratemyprofessors.com/ShowRatings.jsp?tid=266430

Rognlie, Matthew (2015), *Deciphering the fall and rise in the net capital share*, Brookings Papers on Economic Activity. http://www.brookings.edu/about/projects/bpea/papers/2015/land-prices-evolution-capitals-share

Samuels, Warren J. (1996), 'Foreword', in Fred E. Foldvary, ed., *Beyond Neoclassical Economics: Heterodox Approaches to Economic Theory*, London, Edward Elgar.

Skousen, Mark (2009), *The Making of Modern Economics*, 2nd edn, Armonk, New York and London, M.E. Sharpe.

The Post-Crash Economic Society (2013), 'Post-Crash Economics: The world has changed, the syllabus hasn't – is it time to do something about it?', *Real-World Economics Review Blog*. https://rwer.wordpress.com/2013/10/25/post-crash-economics-the-world-has-changed-the-syllabus-hasnt-is-it-time-to-do-something-about-it-2/

Tideman, Nicolaus, ed. (1994), *Land and Taxation*, London, Shepheard-Walwyn.

Tideman, Nicolaus (1999), 'Taxing Land is Better than Neutral: Land Taxes, Land Speculation and the Timing of Development', in Kenneth Wenzer, ed., *Land-Value Taxation: The Equitable and Efficient Source of Public Finance*, New York, M.E. Sharpe and London, Shepheard-Walwyn.

Veblen, Thorstein (1923), *Absentee Ownership and Business Enterprise in Recent Times – The Case of America*, New York, B.W. Huebsch, Inc.

Wenzer, Kenneth, ed. (1999), *Land-Value Taxation: The Equitable and Efficient Source of Public Finance*, New York, M.E. Sharpe and London, Shepheard-Walwyn.

Whalen, Charles J. (1996). 'The institutional approach to political economy', in Foldvary, Fred, ed., *Beyond Neoclassical Economics: Heterodox Approaches to Economic Theory*, London: Edward Elgar Publishing.

Wicksell, Knut (1934), *Lectures on Political Economy*, Vol. I, trans. E. Classen, New York, Macmillan.

5

Accounting for the Common Good: Mason Gaffney's Philosophy of Reconciliation

FRANCIS K. PEDDLE

C ITIZENS of the modern polity are to be forgiven if they seem perplexed by the decisions and financial guidance routinely served up by their governments and institutions. Everyone wants higher wages, while lamenting their stagnation in recent decades. Central bankers wag their fingers and remind us that if the fantasy of higher wages actually comes to fruition then the punishment will be higher interest rates. The consequence is obvious in our debt saturated society: you then pay more for everything, from houses to cars and education. Governments, like people, also want more revenue. They can achieve that in only two ways: either through taxation or debt financing. Nobody really knows the limits of either approach, but limits do definitely exist. The more in debt governments go, the more scarce credit becomes. This is also a truism despite the printing of money in such beguiling forms as quantitative easing or negative interest rates. Currency devaluation is also another way to financially repress most of the population. Today, many of the world's free floating fiat currencies are in a downward death spiral.

Taxation reduces the base upon which it is levied. Economists call this deadweight loss. When governments tax labour income, or business net income or individual consumption, the less you will have of these things. What less means takes many forms, including distorted business decisions, inefficient allocation of resources, and the lawlessness of underground economies. Promotion of the common good is integral to the definition of society. The irony is that much of what society does subsidizes and encourages the bad, like inequality, urban sprawl, and the oversized financialization of the economy. For example, while real estate bubbles and unaffordable housing are good for some individuals, they are bad for society. Yet the most tax subsidized and tax-favored sector of the economy is residential and commercial real estate.

Decisions today about public policy with respect to fiscal and monetary matters are never made in a complete vacuum. Falling unemployment rates may not automatically lead to an increase in interest rates because overall wages may not have increased or labour force participation may be flat or declining. House price inflation, well above the general inflation rate, is often attributed only to easy credit or foreign buyers. Infrastructure spending by governments may actually reduce employment in the medium term by inflating rents around, for instance, transit hubs and thus unduly burdening nearby businesses.

How one accounts for the common good not only shapes public policy, both economically and legally, but it also determines individual perceptions of whether society is achieving its social and political goals. This teleological approach to the common good has been a constant in Western philosophy even from ancient and medieval times (Aristotle, Aquinas). Through a lifetime of reflection and writing on the nature of economics, Mason Gaffney has provided us with a startling roadmap for how we can better account for the common good that goes far beyond the narrow confines of current economic thinking. Mainstream economics today only serves up a bitter diet of trade-offs. The ensuing contradictions leave one comatose. They leave one angry. They force false choices. Or we can try to think them through to a philosophy of reconciliation. This is the principal feature of Mason Gaffney's economic philosophy. Therein he challenges the central tenets of contemporary mainstream economics. His economic philosophy highlights a deep web of false assumptions in modern economic thinking that give rise to an intransigent set of illusory choices which in turn have widespread negative outcomes for the advancement of the common good. Mason Gaffney's philosophy of reconciliation is a revolutionary challenge to the current economics of trade-offs, instability, financial repression, and gross inequality.

The Common Good:
Definitions, Perceptions and Realities

Philosophers and economists have different approaches to what constitutes the common good. For philosophers it is any identifiable or specific good that is universally shared and beneficial for all members of the community. The rule of law and personal safety would, for instance, be a common good for all members of society as would be equality in association or equality of opportunity. The promulgation or derogation of such common goods are *indicia* of whether a society is progressing or failing. These indicators are often difficult to quantify. They tend to cluster around broad cultural and social criteria such as quality of life and happiness indices (Bruni, 2006).

Economists, on the other hand, more narrowly define common goods (tangible and intangible) as public goods. They are characterized in the economic literature as non-rivalrous and non-excludable. The classic definition was supplied by Paul Samuelson back in the 1950s. He labelled public goods 'collective consumption goods', all of which have the universal characteristic 'that each individual's consumption of such a good leads to no subtraction from any other individual's consumption of that good' (Samuelson, 1954: 387). This characteristic of 'no subtraction' is now usually described in terms of the *non-rivalry* and *non-excludability* of public goods. Conversely, private goods are rivalrous and excludable. Rivalrous private goods preclude their consumption by someone else. If you catch a fish or extract a mineral, then someone else cannot consume these things. Excludability means that someone can prevent another from consuming a good if they have paid for it, or have a legal right that guarantees exclusion, such as a lease, a license, or a patent.

Public goods are non-excludable. No exclusion or pre-emption is possible with regard to them. Examples of tangible, non-excludable public goods are water and air. Intangible public goods are such things as cultural products like literature and music, or the knowledge commons. The consumption of these public goods does not reduce the possibility of another individual's consumption unless a temporary monopoly is granted through intellectual property laws. Social capital generally gives rise to various forms of public goods such as labour force participation rates, ducation, or social safety nets. Economists like to put numbers on public goods by aggregating demand curves for them. Some public goods are obviously natural, i.e. not produced at all or have no production cost, such as locational values and advantages, while others are provided by governments and have a cost of production such as transportation infrastructure.

Access to tangible *common-pool resources* has the potential to become rivalrous on account of resource scarcity, enforceability problems, or legal restrictions, all of which can give rise to the 'tragedy of the commons'. Rivalry is associated with non-optionality in relation to consumption, while excludability can exist without exhaustive rivalrous consumption for it can pre-empt all successive users or consumers. One might consume, for instance, a parking lot for a given period of time, after which the pre-emption of the time slot passes to a subsequent user or 'consumer'. It should be pointed out that a failure to finely delineate and comprehensively define 'consumption' often gives rise to highly distortionary and regressive tax regimes, such as the value-added sales taxes that are predominant in many countries, though they often exempt pre-emptive consumption. Gaffney's critique of modern sales tax regimes focuses on their limited and perverse definition of consumption as well as their negative impact on the turnover of capital (Gaffney, 1970, 2013b). Today, public finance economics almost universally advocates value added sales taxes over income taxes. Apart from arguments about investment and savings, this prevalent view among tax economists stems from a narrow view of the tax base as being possible only on the basis of income *or* consumption, *or* some combination of both.

Gaffney, as one of the foremost land economics of our time, prefers to understand the concepts of non-rivalry and non-excludability in terms of the pre-emption of time slots as well as the pre-emptive occupation of space. Pre-emption of our space/time dictions by rent-seeking actors is the principal and most corrosive form of monopolistic practice in our society, especially with respect to urban ground rents. To some degree everyone wishes to engage in this practice. The appreciation of residential real estate, *via* land price inflation, is now universally viewed as the most important vehicle of individual savings, even for retirement. Boom and bust cycles which periodically and relentlessly threaten the whole financial system do not seem to deter people from their devotion to this economic myth, which is widely encouraged by government tax policies. This is why meaningful tax reform is so difficult within current political culture. There can be no significant redress of the problems associated with income and wealth inequality until governments retool their tax systems to focus on the public capture of economic rent.

For Gaffney there are moral and economic grounds for taking this approach. The creation of a new tax regime that challenges the privatization of the commons and public goods must be based both on the moral principle that no human being has a pre-existing right to monopolize any part of nature or the external, non-human world. Conversely, there should be more general recognition of the principle that the product of human effort is sacrosanct and should be disturbed or interfered with as little as possible by government. The co-operative interaction of these two principles makes for a more productive and efficient economy, while at the same time providing a super-neutral, enforceable, and fair regime for the raising of public revenue.

Philosophers of economics, especially those interested in classical economics, tend to view the issues of monopoly, rent-seeking, and non-rivalrous and non-excludable goods in terms of economic justice, inequality, poverty, wealth creation, and social conflict. The principal writers in this tradition are Adam Smith, David Ricardo, John Stuart Mill, and Henry George. These classical political economists, although they differ considerably on numerous issues, engage in the careful analysis of the definition of key terms in economics like wealth, value, and the different sources of income. They also do it by trying to avoid mixing apples and oranges, which is a pervasive problem in 20th century neoclassical economics. Ever since John Bates Clark, and his disciples like E.R.A. Seligman and Richard Ely in the late 19th century, economists generally viewed all three factors of production, i.e. land, labour, and capital, as the same in certain fundamental respects. So, for instance, neoclassical economists take all forms of monopoly as homogenous, and furthermore they see no differentiation in the sources of income or profit (Clark, 1899). In modern parlance, 'a buck is a buck is a buck,' with no concern about where the various bucks may have come from. Economic rents are in this view the return to any factor of production in excess of what would be needed to keep it in the market (Furman and Orszag, 2015). To the horror of classical political economists rents would thus be seen as accruing to any of the factors of production. The conflation of land or nature or raw materials into the residual factor of capital facilitates the perception of a sanitized and unfocused view of economic rent (Gaffney, 1994). One of Gaffney's most important contributions to a resurgent philosophy of economics is his critique of neoclassical conceptualization of the nature of capital.

Apart from the more narrow economic portrayals of public goods, there are longstanding philosophical variants on the nature of the common good which are traditionally framed in such terms as utilitarian, naturalistic, deontological, or value-theory approaches. Materialist views of social progress tend towards utility measures of human wellbeing. The advancement of the common good can also be understood in terms of the greater maximization of intangibles like freedom, equality, human rights, dignity and decency, and any subsidiary set of universally accepted principles. Value-theory plays a powerful role in a society's perception of what constitutes the common weal. This tends towards the culturally relative. Shifting values cannot be discounted. Within any given society or historical period the highest goods often clash or find little common ground. Religious adherence and stricture may, for instance, be a greater public good than gender equality, or *laissez-faire* economics a lesser good when the environment plays havoc on people's lives.

More particularly, we wish to maintain within the context of Mason Gaffney's work, and without specific reference to any generalized theory of ethics, that the common good of any society is advanced if an economics of trade-offs and either-or choices is set aside and replaced with a more functional distribution of the return to the three factors of production within the economic system. Furthermore, a far greater reliance on the capture of economic rent, classically defined, for public purposes, would do more than anything else in the current economic milieu to advance not only equity and efficiency, but much broader common goods such as liberty, equality, and human dignity. In Gaffney's view the economic rent, or surplus value, that inevitably grows and accumulates through natural advantages, public spending, or any form of collective effort, ought to be the principal, if not almost exclusive, source of government revenue.

The severing of economic rent from land (nature) is for Gaffney one of the greatest mistakes of twentieth century economics (Dwyer, 2014:906 and Gaffney, 1994b). Focusing indiscriminately on costless *and* productive income as a source of taxation across all labour and capital factors of production has led to significant welfare losses and distorted capital formation, such as the currently destabilizing allocation of capital to the real estate sector. Ironically, and counter-intuitively, economics ought to be the destruction of market value.

> *The seemingly unassailable imperatives of modern day global finance capital are perhaps the most economically disruptive forces ever unleashed in history.*

The seemingly unassailable imperatives of modern day global finance capital are perhaps the most economically disruptive forces ever unleashed in history.

Gaffney's detailed development and modern amplification of Henry George's fiscal economics of land value taxation would restrain the power of global finance capital by focusing on the taxation primarily of locally generated urban ground rents. As Terence Dwyer nicely puts it:

There are no more pernicious sayings in economics than 'there is no such thing as a free lunch,' 'economics is about the allocation of scarce resources,' or 'economics is about profit maximization.' The history of the theory of land value taxation gives the lie to all of these. The history of land value taxation shows that economic theory need not be a dismal science or confined to a coarse study of vulgar money-making. It can display a harmony of theory, policy, and justice as elegant and beautiful as any theorem in mathematics (Dwyer, 2014: 669).

Gaffney, unlike Piketty, Shiller, Akerlof, and many others, does not see our economic system fundamentally as a creature of individual behavior, or political fiat, or, on the other hand, ineluctably subject to industrial fluctuations and nasty business cycles. His is an economic philosophy with a practical remedy that promotes intra- and inter-generational equity. Thomas Piketty, for instance, sees economics not as a 'science' but as 'political economy' (Piketty, 2014). Economics, for him, is a sub-discipline of the social sciences, much like the imponderables of history or political science. To view economics as a science is, in Piketty's view, to arrogantly set it above the other social sciences and thus to undermine its political, normative, and moral purposes. This is a fair enough criticism as long as it is aimed at the ahistorical, uncritical, and calculative rationalism of neoclassical economics. Like Piketty, Gaffney would undoubtedly want to see the adoption of those public policies and institutions which would most advance the common good and realize the ideal republic. Gaffney, however, would strongly disagree with Piketty about which tax regimes would further the public good. He would certainly not endorse Piketty's definition of capital. For Gaffney the ideal manifesto for our time would be *Rent in the Twenty-First Century*, much like he would rename Adam Smith's magnum opus *The Rent of Nations*.

For Gaffney, all economic systems are governed by certain ineluctable laws. The articulation of these laws is the object of economics (Young, 1996). The science of economics deals with the community as a whole, not the individual. This is what sets economics apart from social sciences, if one indeed wishes to define such soft sciences in terms of the various behaviours and pathologies of individuals. In this regard Gaffney's economics is the contemporary adoption and expansion of the vision of *The Science of Political Economy*, which is Henry George's systematic reconstruction of its principles. There is no place in this reconstruction for mapping the varied topographies of individual foibles, or the history of the vicissitudes of political and legal institutions, or irrationality, and its accompanying social pathologies. In this sense both Gaffney and George are economic purists, modern day Platonists, who wish to carve out the contours of the discipline and then judge society's perennial penchant for throwing up obstacles to its own advancement.

The policy platforms of governments and allied institutions can conform to economic laws or disrupt them. The degree to which they have done so is the historical tapestry of civilization. There is no doubt such a thing as 'political' economy, or the historically relative and dynamic give and take of self-interest, group conflict, and entrenched self-legitimizing wealth. To say economics is a science in the non-mathematical sense of a pattern of inescapable laws is a position not normally found today in mainstream or heterodox economics. Gaffney is viewed as 'heterodox' even in the heterodox economic community. His economic philosophy speaks more to a more powerful normative economics, i.e. how economies and their associated public revenue systems *ought* to function and when they do so how utility outcomes will be maximized.

A general philosophy of economics advances equality of opportunity, minimal state interference in economic life, and base line insurance against individual catastrophic failure. The common good is often referred to in these terms. Contemporary societies, however, decidedly and deliberately, do not advance these principles in their systems of public finance. Rather they encourage the privatization of economic rent or the surplus value created by the community as a whole and by doing so necessarily place terrible taxation burdens on the income and consumption of the less well off in order to fund government expenditures. This is the inverted world of contemporary tax economics with its mirages, sleights of hand, and piecemeal efforts to avoid deadweight and unfair taxation. Gaffney's philosophy of economics has been a lifelong endeavor to put this inverted world aright.

Accounting for the Common Good as Reconciliation

If one looks at Gaffney's scholarly and popular writings as a whole the theme of reconciliation lies behind both his technical economic analyses as well as his more philosophical reflections. His main source of inspiration is Henry George, the late nineteenth century economic and social philosopher, who took the reformist world by storm in the 1880s with his *Progress and Poverty* (O'Donnell, 2015). Commencing with a rigorous critique of the grim outcomes portrayed by Malthusian economics and population theory as well as the conceptual incoherence of the wages fund doctrine, George was able to forge a philosophy of abundance which tackled head on the ravages of industrial depressions with an economic remedy that uplifted the wages of labour and confronted the scourge of extreme inequality in the Gilded Age. Gaffney's reformist economics is a redrafting of the Georgist curative for the twenty first century.

In order to understand Gaffney's basic assumptions, it is necessary to look critically at the dichotomous philosophies that are redolent in modern economic thinking and convert their underlying either-or logic into an economic philosophy of reconciliation. The first dichotomy to be challenged is the trade-off between equity and efficiency.

> *Gaffney's position is that both equity and efficiency are fundamentally rational and consistent.*

Gaffney's position is that both equity and efficiency are fundamentally rational and consistent. They can thus be harmonized. To treat distributional equity as human and efficiency as a natural economic principle (J.S. Mill, 1886) is to set up a false dichotomy which leads to an illusory division between ethics and economics.

Secondly, the never-ending, mostly squalid, political stand-off between demand side and supply side economics needs to be buried in the mists of history. A social order which avoids the privatization of economic rent and the socialization of income from labour and capital would, for Gaffney, stimulate both the demand side and the supply side, thus avoiding the perpetual rift in modern economics between Keynesian style manipulation of aggregate effective demand and those who follow Say's Law, which says that supply creates its own demand (or in other words there can be no long-run glut of goods). Gaffney, following George, rejects the theory that overproduction or under-consumption are the causes of industrial depressions (George, 1987: 266).

Thirdly, Gaffney would down-tax both labour and capital This is a claim that is usually met with incredulity from the dichotomous economic philosophers because in their world there is *only* capital *or* labour. Down-tax *both* and you would starve the 'beast' as some like to pejoratively refer to government. They view all taxes as bad and see the contest of taxes through the bipolarity of the net income of capital or wages and consumption. By shifting the general burden of public revenue generation to the recapture of economic rent Gaffney is able to advocate a multi-faceted attack on the current system, or a broad-based and radical tax reform, by simultaneously down-taxing income from labour and capital, and up-taxing inert property. Large scale reductions can therefore be effected on income, consumption and capital taxes without reducing public revenues.

A fourth economic advance toward the common good would be to adopt a fiscal regime that stimulates both investing and saving. In the either-or world of mainstream economics stimulating investing is usually given as the rationale for un-taxing businesses, while stimulating savings and capital formation is generally the rationale for consumption taxes. Both approaches from the Gaffney perspective are inherently contradictory. They also violate the Georgist first principle of taxation, i.e. that taxes should bear as little as possible upon production. Ultimately, the bias in modern public finance, that you can only tax wages or consumption, is rooted in the neoclassical two-factor theory of economics. The stimulation of production through land value taxation means in effect that it is a super-neutral tax since it stimulates productivity and thus expands the base upon which it is levied.

Modern taxation systems are generally viewed as vehicles for social engineering. There is very little evidence, however, that these tax measures, or tax expenditures as they are sometimes called, actually advance in any significant way the common good. For example, urban sprawl, poor land development planning, and land use regulation have made many cities, especially in North America, incur high costs with respect to the provision of municipal services because of very inefficient land allocation. Higher carrying charges on land, with lower taxation of capital improvements would encourage better land use, primarily through moderate densification in cities. Land value taxation promotes the better use of urban land resources without interfering with the market.

Most people in the world now live in an urban setting. However, municipalities in many places do not have inherent or plenary taxation powers. Their power to tax property, for instance, is often granted by national or sub-national governments. Land value taxation would reverse this anomaly by allowing municipalities to access economic rent, which is primarily present in urban centers or the centers of exchange. This would significantly reduce the gamesmanship between various levels of government in a federation, and in unitary states as well. It would make government more accountable to those who are directly financing its operations and receiving its benefits.

Greater reliance on the capture of urban ground rents would restrain urban deterioration while stimulating urban renewal (Gaffney, 1988, 2007; Peddle,1994). The current system of property taxation discourages capital improvements thus fostering urban deterioration and decay. It essentially taxes (i.e. penalizes) what is good for the community while subsidizing that which is bad. Land value taxation removes these disincentives to urban renewal and it does this without requiring additional expenditures or revenue loss through tax abatements.

There is considerable use today of tax abatements and special enterprise zones to little overall effect. These measures are highly selective and often give rise to widespread corrupt practices in the real estate industry. They do little to discourage the hollowing out of cities, which can take many forms, such as speculative vacancies and widespread under-utilization of urban properties. The latter often gives the false impression that there is a scarcity of serviceable land in cities. The generic down-taxing of capital improvements and concomitant up-taxing of land or locational values has the effect of advancing urban renewal without undermining the tax base through abatements, exemptions or the creation of special enterprise zones. Such abatements shift the tax burden to other property owners and create greater inequities in the tax base. Land value taxation advances fairness in taxation because there is less differentiation in land values in urban centers than there is in capital improvements. Fairness in taxation is an essential component of the common good. Land value taxation prevents a tax system from becoming a 'surrealistic pagoda of pestilent greed'.

An additional issue with respect to the common good concerns public infrastructure. The chief dichotomy here arises in the frequent attempts by government to stimulate the economy through infrastructure spending while at the same time ignoring the rise in land prices and the all-important issue of capturing of these unearned increments to help fund the infrastructure spending that gave rise to the higher land prices in the first place. The trade-off is in either public transport deficits or excessively high user costs, which affects the poor the most. Most public transportation systems are deficit-financed because they rely on debt for the initial capital outlay and then user charges to service that debt and operate the system. The public capture of the increase in land values that invariably accompanies the provision of transportation infrastructure would eliminate the requirement for user fees to sustain the operation of the system and would be sufficient to service the debt of the initial capital outlay.

An economic philosophy of reconciliation, as opposed to creative destruction or catagenesis, also advances the aims of ecological economics. Industrially induced climate change is today at the epicenter of the crisis of the Anthropocene. By redirecting our economic consciousness to land as a distinctive factor of production, and to putting in place a tax regime that does not encourage the wasteful use of precious land and other environmental resources, much can be done to reduce green emissions, especially non-point pollution, which is the most difficult area in getting international agreements to combat climate change (Gaffney, 1988/89).

Finally, in debates over what constitutes the common good there is often a heated philosophical exchange between those who advocate communal rights as opposed to those who focus more on individual, private rights. The taxation of labour income and the return from capital is the socialization of private property rights. The community, or the socially conjoined effect, is the originator of economic rent, or the 'unearned increment' as J.S. Mill and others have called it. It is the unearned increment that the current system of public finance allows principally to stay in private hands. Perversely, the political economy of most governments in the world privatizes what ought not to be privatized and socializes what ought not to be socialized. Gaffney's philosophy of reconciliation reverses this inversion of collective and individual rights. By reinforcing property rights, while at the same time restoring to government what properly lies in its sphere, the close relationship between private property and communal rights is rebalanced.

Conclusion: Gaffney's Economic Philosophy of Reconciliation

The measures and initiatives outlined here in Gaffney's economic philosophy are guideposts to a large scale reformist agenda. That agenda has both a research component with respect to quantifying the widest gap in economic intelligence today, namely, the role of economic rent, and privilege-seeking in relation to it, in our society (World Bank, 2006). It also provides the theoretical template for practical initiatives in tax and fiscal reform generally at both the municipal and higher levels of government. Gaffney uniquely combines an aspirational philosophy of abundance with an innovative land and natural resource economics. As long as the profession of economics remains trapped in a perverse logic of either-or choice and dismal trade-offs, it will continue to advocate policies that undermine the common good. Gaffney's work retools an economic philosophy of reconciliation for the 21st century. In his vision the dismal science once again becomes a Rubenesque tableau of 'Abundance Suppressing Avarice' rather than avarice subduing abundance.

References

Aquinas, Thomas (1964), *Commentary on Aristotle's Nicomachean Ethics*, trans. C.I. Litzinger, O.P., Notre Dame, Indiana, Dumb Ox Books.

Aristotle, (1915), 'Ethica Nicomachea', trans. W.D. Ross, in *The Complete Works of Aristotle*, Oxford University Press.

Bruni, Luigino (2006), *Civil Happiness, Economics and Human Flourishing in Historical Perspective*, New York, Routledge.

Clark, John Bates ([1899] 1965), *The Distribution of Wealth: A Theory of Wages, Interest and Profit*, New York: Augustus Kelly.

Dwyer, Terence (2014), 'Taxation: The Lost History', *The American Journal of Economics and Sociology*, 73(4) (October), pp.627-998.

Furman, Jason, Orszag, Peter (2015), 'A Firm-Level Perspective on the Role of Rents in the Rise of Inequality', *A Presentation at 'A Just Society' Centennial Event in Honor of Joseph Stiglitz*, Columbia University. https://www.whitehouse.gov/sites/default/files/page/files/20151016_firm_level_perspective_on_role_of_rents_in_inequality.pdf.

Gaffney, Mason (1970/71), 'Tax-Induced Slow Turnover of Capital', *American Journal of Economics and Sociology*, 29(1), 29(2), 29(3), 29(4), 30(1). http://www.masongaffney.org/publications/I11-TaxInducedSlowTurnoverofCapital.CV.CV.pdf.

Gaffney, Mason, (1988), 'The Role of Ground Rent in Urban Decay and Development', *The Henry George Lecture, St. John's University*, Distributed by the Robert Schalkenbach Foundation, New York, 2nd edn, 'How to Revitalize a Failing City'.

Gaffney, Mason (1988/89), 'Non-Point Pollution', *Journal of Business Administration*. Special Issue, Future Directions for Economics, 18(1 & 2), pp.133-154.

Gaffney, Mason, (1944), *The Corruption of Economics*, London, Shepheard-Walwyn.

Gaffney, Mason, (1994), 'Land as a Distinctive Factor of Production', in Nic Tideman ed., *Land and Taxation*, London, Shepheard-Walwyn, pp.39-102.

Gaffney, Mason (2007), *New Life in Old Cities*, New York, Robert Schalkenbach Foundation.

Gaffney, Mason (2009), 'The Hidden Taxable Capacity of Land: Enough and to Spare', in Henry George as Social Economist and Radical Reformer, *International Journal of Social Economics*, ed., Francis K. Peddle, 36(4), pp.328-411. Contains an extensive bibliography of Gaffney's works as does www.masongaffney.org.

Gaffney, Mason (2009), '*After the Crash: Designing a Depression-Free Economy*', Clifford W. Cobb, ed., London, Wiley-Blackwell.

Gaffney, Mason (2013), *The Mason Gaffney Reader: Essays on Solving the 'Unsolvable'*, New York, Henry George Institute.

Gaffney, Mason (2013), 'Europe's Fatal Affair with Value Added Taxation', *Groundswell*. www.mason gaffney.org.

George, Henry (2016) ' Our Land and Land Policy and Other Works' in *The Annotated Works of Henry George*, Vol I, Francis K. Peddle and William S. Peirce, series eds., Maryland, Fairleigh Dickinson University Press.

George, Henry (1981), *The Science of Political Econom'*, New York, Robert Schalkenbach Foundation.

George, Henry (1987), *Progress and Poverty*, New York, Robert Schalkenbach Foundation.

George, Henry (1981), *Social Problem'*, New York, Robert Schalkenbach Foundation.

Mill, John Stuart (1886), *The Principles of Political Economy*, London, Longmans.

O'Donnell, Edward T. (2015) *Henry George and the Crisis of Inequality*, New York, Columbia University Press.

Peddle, Francis K. (1993), 'Henry George and Albert Schweitzer: Economic Justice and Reverence for Life', *Good Government*.

Peddle, Francis K. (1994) *Cities and Greed: Taxes, Inflation and Land Speculation*, Ottawa, Canadian Research Committee on Taxation.

Peddle, Francis K. (1995) *Henry George and the End of Tax Commissions*, Ottawa, Canadian Research Committee on Taxation.

Piketty, Thomas (2014), *Capital in the Twenty-First Century*, trans. Arthur Goldhammer, Cambridge, Harvard University Press.

Rubens, Peter Paul, 'Abundance Suppressing Avarice, 1632 -1634', Whitehall Palace.

Samuelson, Paul A. (1954), 'The Pure Theory of Public Expenditure', *Review of Economics and Statistics*, 36(4), pp.387-389.

Seligman, E.R.A. (1919), *Essays in Taxation*, New York, Macmillan.

Shiller, Robert, and George Akerlof (2015), *Phishing for Phools: The Economics of Manipulation and Deception*, Princeton University Press.

Shiller, Robert, and George Akerlof (2009), *Animal Spirits*, Princeton University Press.

Smith, Adam (1937), *The Wealth of Nations*, New York, Modern Library.

Stiglitz, Joseph E. (2012), *The Price of Inequality*, London, Allen Lane.

Stiglitz, Joseph E. (2012), *The Great Divide: Unequal Societies and What We Can Do About Them*, New York, Norton.

World Bank. (2006). *Where is the Wealth of Nations? Measuring Capital for the 21st Century*, Washington, D.C.

Young, John (1996), *The Natural Economy*, London, Shepheard-Walwyn.

PART II

The Clean Slate

The western frontier was not closed. It was foreclosed. Many more people could have earned decent livelihoods if the land had been used for the good of all, the original settlers, the late-comers and nature itself. But that was then. What about now? From his hilltop home in the midst of orange groves an hour's drive east of downtown Los Angeles, Mason Gaffney reflected on the drama of a continental edge that remained rich in untapped resources. Land all the way from Alaska down through Canada to the Mexican border is being willfully abused. And so are the citizens whose grandfathers had come too late to stake a claim in territories rich in minerals and nutrients.

We can no longer avoid a fresh start.

A multi-disciplinary diagnostic approach is needed to fathom out the depth of the pathological disturbances being registered around the world. A rehabilitated science of political economy needs to play a leading role in formulating therapeutic strategies. One of the challenges is the 50-year decline in the global economy as forecast by the Organization for Economic Cooperation and Development. A new approach to production and the distribution of income is needed. The Clean Slate, an ancient device for restoring stability to disturbed communities, has its modern variant in the philosophy of taxation. Correctly redesigned, the two pricing mechanisms that operate in the private and public sectors could cohere to emancipate people's full potential.

Growth guided by humane values rather than savage exploitation can be restarted. Nature would play its part, revealing yet more layers of services. Both the environment and humanity would be enriched, a prospect that is beyond the capacity of the growth model based on crude materialism. In Part II, the authors explain how a responsible form of governance could fulfil the needs of all citizens.

6

The $14 trillion Lift-off
from the Great Stagnation

FRED HARRISON

T HE SCLEROTIC financial arteries seized up in 2008. What remained of the vitality of the capitalist order was finally dissolved. Gone, too, were the delusions that had sustained this model of economics. As governments floundered, the dysfunctional doctrines on which their policies were constructed were exposed. But public analysts, with few exceptions, were reluctant to classify the downturn as a depression. They feared the comparison with the 1930s. Their notion of a Great Recession was yet another linguistic device to evaded reality – and to avoid responsibility for allowing a foreseeable event to occur (Box 6:1).

The global economy was locked in a downward spiral. Economies continued to haemorrhage their capacity to add the value that was needed to pay down sovereign debts. Most of the new jobs were of the low-productivity kind, insufficient to generate the consumption needed to soak up the millions of unemployed people who had been marooned by the land-led boom that peaked in 2007.

The deterioration in the long-term capacity of once dynamic economies is not a secret. The Organisation for Economic Cooperation and Development (OECD) broadcast its forecast in 2014. The global growth rate peaked at 3.5% in the decade running up to 2020, below the long-run

Box 6:1

Short-changing Society

The 2008 crisis originated with the reckless advance of mortgages to people who could not afford them. This happened, notably, in the US and UK. The initial dishonesty by financiers was compounded when banks packaged those 'toxic' mortgages and sold them to gullible investors in Germany and Iceland. A tiny number of financial speculators in America worked out what was going on (documented by Michael Lewis in *The Big Short* [2011]), and they went 'short' on those sub-prime deals. In essence, they bet that the deals would cause the financial system to collapse. But when would it collapse? They calculated that this would occur when home-owners defaulted on their second and third mortgages.

Wall Street's bankers did not understand that they had laid a trap for themselves. Low-income home-owners would default. *How* that would happen, and *when*, was predictable. In his undergraduate degree thesis, Mason Gaffney analysed the process which was at work in the run-up to the Depression of the 1930s:

> The divergence of speculative value and capitalized yield must eventually become clear. In 1928 in Chicago nominal owners of much real estate started to fail to meet second mortgage payments. Such conditions will make investors aware of their errors and cause them to refuse to continue subsidizing the high holdout prices of other factors and a crash will ensue if holdout prices are sticky.
>
> (Gaffney 1948: 213)

Wall Street's Masters of the Universe turn blind eyes to history, when the lessons touch on real estate. In 2008, shareholder wealth measured in billions of dollars was destroyed by an event that need not have happened.

average of about 3.7%. Then it was *downhill over the following 50 years, declining to an annual 2.4% in 2060 if existing policies continued to operate* (Braconier *et al* 2014: 15).

The OECD's analysts in Paris proposed a menu of reforms to head off the stagnation. The need for structural change was obvious: the projected growth rates were insufficient to make up for the lost ground, let alone fund the measures needed to meet the ecological and demographic crises. But governments were in the grip of institutional paralysis. Their ambivalence was illustrated by political vacillation in France: politicians talked of the need for change (especially in labour laws) but they lacked the will to implement the legislation (Colin 2016). The OECD reported that half of the countries it surveyed were effectively taking no action at all (Figure 6:1).

Figure 6:1

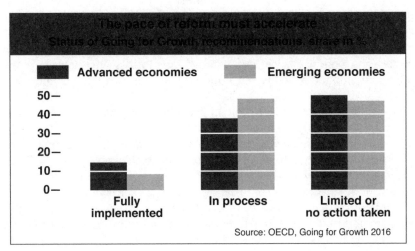

The pace of reform must accelerate
Status of Going for Growth recommendations, share in %

Source: OECD, Going for Growth 2016

The crises now challenging every nation on earth cannot be attributed to cyclical or random causes. They are *logical* features of the system itself. The current trend in the impoverishment of working people, and the deepening problem of inequality, could be traced back to the Reagan/Thatcher era. But this 40-year period was the continuation of a trend going back two centuries and more. At the same time, while the purchasing power of wages and salaries were in steady relative decline, the fortunes of corporations grew increasingly buoyant. The Washington-based McKinsey Global Institute revealed that global corporate earnings before taxes and interest more than tripled from $2 trillion in 1980 to $7.2 trillion in 2013 (Dobbs 2015). This was a rise from 7.6% of world gross domestic product to almost 10%. Revealingly, corporate net earnings after taxes rose even more sharply.

In part, the growth in profits could be explained by the fall in borrowing costs and the weakening of the price of labour. Digital technology reduced the need for people to carry out traditional functions. The character of corporations was shifting from value-adding to value capturing: many had become classic rent-seeking operations (see Ch. 8). In this,

Box 6:2

Fiscal Haemorrhage

The Republic of Ireland sought growth by cutting the rate of corporation tax. Multi-national corporations responded by locating their headquarters in Dublin. Their cut in tax liabilities contributed to the upward twist in residential property prices and weakening of the fiscal system. The exercise ended with one of the severest housing crises in the western hemisphere. The lessons were not learnt. After savage cuts to its welfare programmes, Ireland re-embarked on its old course in the years following the 2008 crisis.

The spillover effects were felt in the UK. The Cameron government empowered the Northern Ireland assembly to cut the corporation tax in the hope of stemming the flow of resources southwards into the Republic. And in his budget in March 2016, Chancellor of the Exchequer George Osborne announced that he was reducing the UK corporation tax and Capital Gains Tax – with the loss of revenue offset by a cut in welfare benefits.

The financial consequences of Corporate Tax avoidance were roughly guesstimated by the OECD. Annual losses suffered by governments were anywhere between $100bn and $240bn. Zucman (2015: 53) puts the loss in tax revenue at $190bn. The loss to the US government was particularly grievous because American multinationals hoarded $2 trillion of their earnings abroad to avoid paying tax. There is one solution only to this tax-dodging tragedy (see Ch. 9).

they were aided by governments that deployed fiscal policies which damaged their budgets. Tax competition drove down the rates of corporation tax, injuring the capacity to generate sufficient revenue to fund social services. Sovereign indebtedness climbed to dangerous levels (Box 6:2).

How did the global economy manage to drive itself into The Great Stagnation?

Capitalism had proved sufficiently resilient to out-manoeuvre the socialist model that Karl Marx had dreamed up during his endless hours of reflection in the Reading Room of the British Museum. His thesis on the inevitable stages of history (moving from primitive communism through feudalism to capitalism and the final triumph of communism) was put to shame by the test that Marx himself invoked: history. Communism reverted to capitalism.

As the Soviet empire imploded, around the world the hit-men operating on behalf of the Washington Consensus drew all the blood (Perkins 2004; Hiatt 2007). No politically acceptable alternative model of society existed. The Western model was proclaimed 'the end of history' (Fukuyama 1992). The fall of communism vindicated 'liberal' society. Complacency carpeted the corridors of power. Globalised society had reached its systemic apotheosis. The International Monetary Fund was the arch enforcer of the faith. Economic fundamentalists were licenced to dismantle the safety barriers which had been erected around the financial system in response to the Depression of the 1930s. Self-discipline and social regulation were abandoned as the guardians of the world's financial networks, led by Alan Greenspan at the US Federal Reserve, proclaimed the New Normal. In that climate of self-congratulation, Francis Fukuyama, who had served as a member of the Policy Planning Staff at the US Department of State in Washington DC, appointed himself the arbiter of trust (Fukuyama 1995).

The cumulative effect of the trends that came to a head in 2008 was bankruptcy on an epoch destroying scale.

According to the OECD, there is little prospect of a rescue operation from within the prevailing economic paradigm. The reasons are many.

> *Innovation* is now largely confined to digital technology and robotics, a trend that replaces labour and maximises rents.
> *Wages* continue downwards as a proportion of total income. In the US, average real income in the bottom 90% was lower in 2013 than it was in 1972 (Gordon 2016: 610).
> *The 'savings glut'*: corporations hoarding cash rather than risk investments in an era of historically low interest rates.

There was an exquisite irony to this outcome, a twist of history that Marx had failed to anticipate as he idealised the future of the revolutionary proletariat. In contributing to the demise of the muscular capitalist order that had spawned them, the revisionist communist states adopted the very practises that were corrupting capitalism. As a consequence, the post-communist authorities undermined the capacity of their societies to rebalance and raise the living standards of their populations on a sustainable basis.

The world needs a new economic paradigm, one that can deliver the win-win outcomes that do not exclude anyone.

ATCOR: the $14 trillion Growth Plan

Sufficient growth momentum is being thwarted because there is

❖ *insufficient demand from consumers*: confidence has been savaged by decades of declining real wages. Growth over the 1992-2010 cycle was funded by sovereign and household debt. And

❖ *the decline in productivity,* in part resulting from the unwillingness of entrepreneurs to risk their cash in new investments. Huge political and economic uncertainties afflict the global economy.

The outlook is dismal, especially so if we rely on the doctrines of the rent-seeking culture. And yet, sufficient latent demand exists *here and now* to raise productivity and lay the foundations for long-term steady-state growth. Mainstream public commentators are not able to see beyond the nostrums of conventional wisdom to alert people to the possibility of releasing that potential. A rare exception is Martin Wolf, chief economic commentator on the *Financial Times*. In reviewing the declining trend in UK growth rates, he identified 'the obvious candidates' for policy reforms. These included higher taxes on 'public bads (congestion and pollution) and heavier taxation of rents, particularly of land' (Wolf 2016). That general prescription can be made tangible by calculating the order of magnitude of the gains that are available to us *today*, worldwide, to pull the global economy out of its freefall.

The latent increase in spending power is at least $14 trillion. My estimate is a conservative calculation, taking into account the current endowments of land, labour and capital, and the scale of the tax-take within OECD member countries. If their governments were to correctly rebalance fiscal policy, $14 trillion would be added to world GDP. That sum could be created and shared between private consumption, corporate investment and social expenditure.

My $14 trillion added value rests on the claim that public services pay for themselves in the form of the rents which they produce. There is enough taxable net income – rent – to fund all the services we need (Gaffney 1998). That net income, however, was long ago privatised; so governments now collect it covertly, indirectly. Unwrapping the arithmetic begins with the recognititon that *existing taxes disguise the rents that we all help to generate as we go about our business.*

✔ When we pay 'income tax', governments extract what would other-wise surface as economic rent in a society that had not alienated its net income.
✔ When we pay corporation tax or most of the other taxes, similar distortions are sanctioned by government. Revenue that could have been collected *directly* as an annual ground rent is collected *indirectly* as taxes on the incomes of labour and capital.

The theory that explains this convoluted process was outlined long ago by John Locke in *Some Considerations on the Consequences of the Lowering of Interest and the Raising of the Value of Money* (1691), and by philosophers of the Enlightenment, including the French Physiocrats. They offered a comprehensive account of the interaction between land, labour and capital in the market economy. This understanding was erased in the 20th century by the neoclassical economists. It is retrieved in the acronym coined by Mason Gaffney: ATCOR – All Taxes Come Out of Rent. The seeds of the ATCOR thesis appear in Gaffney (1970); the acronym came later, in Class Notes that included *The Great Economists*. There are marginal qualifications to the rule that all taxes come out of rent; but as a practical guide to policy-making, it is robust (Box 6:3).

In 2015, the total tax revenue of OECD member countries was about 35% of GDP (US $48 trillion). If we subtract from this sum that part of revenue that is collected in the form of rent charges (as with the revenue from property taxes) we are left with a sum of about $14 trillion. If taxes currently used to raise that revenue (such as the income tax) were abolished, and the same sum was collected as an annual ground rent (a revenue neutral approach), the impact would be electrifying. The way in which people work, save and invest would be transformed. Productivity would immediately be raised above historical trends. As people go about their business with renewed optimism

✔ *land* hoarded or under-used would be brought into use as owners responded to the payment of the annual ground rent for the services they received;
✔ *labour* would find new ways to deliver value-for-money services; personal rewards would not be penalised with taxes on how much they earned; and
✔ *capital* that is invested in 'tax-efficient' schemes would be reallocated to achieve optimum satisfaction for customers and investors.

Box 6:3

Converting Golden Rents into Base Metal

Politicians engage in the process of reversing the magical art of alchemy. Instead of converting base metal into gold, they manage to achieve the opposite result. A case study was provided in the budget delivered to the UK Parliament by Chancellor of the Exchequer George Osborne in March 2016. He announced that, in 2017, 600,000 small businesses would be exempt from the property tax (the Business Rate) on their commercial premises. A further 250,000 enterprises would pay reduced rates. This, claimed Osborne, was evidence of the Conservative Government helping enterprises to build the economy.

The Institute for Fiscal Policy (IFS), an independent London think-tank, rained on the chancellor's parade. It announced that 'in the long run, we can expect a lot of that [change] to be capitalised into the value of the underlying properties. It is pretty clear that the primary beneficiaries of this tax cut in the long run will be landlords, and not small businesses'.

The incidence of taxation – who shoulders the final cost? – is well established in classical theory. But thanks to the intervention of neoclassical revisionists, we have the situation described by Ryan Bourne, head of public policy at the IFS: the Business Rate is 'one of those classic examples where people confuse who ultimately signs the cheque, and where the real incidence of the tax falls'. The IFS noted how economic distortions arise when Business Rates are levied on buildings as well as the value of land. This 'distorts investment decisions because it's based on property values'. A charge exclusively on land, however, is 'non-distortionary' (Spence and Chan 2016).

As Chancellor Osborne congratulated himself on his financial alchemy, turning golden rents into deadweight losses, the government's official forecaster, the Office of Budget Responsibility, downgraded its forecast for growth and productivity in the UK economy.

National income and growth rates would rise as people anticipated the benign changes that were underway. But by how much would they rise? Economists differ on their measures of what they call the 'excess burden' of taxes that distort economic activity. Some have concluded that the losses are of the order of $2 for every $1 raised by the taxes that damage people's economic behaviour (Box 6:4).

I base my assessment on Mason Gaffney's judgement, which rests on a lifetime's study of how real estate markets affect the economy. He lived

Box 6:4

Top-end Losses

Martin Feldstein is a professor of economics at Harvard who chaired the President's Council of Economic Advisers in the 1980s. Using the marginal impact of taxes, he concluded that the damage to the US economy exceeded the ratio of 2:1 – that is, over $2 of losses in wealth and welfare were incurred for every $1 raised in taxes. His estimates began with a minimum of $0.78 per $1, assuming that a 10% increase in the tax rate increased tax revenues by 10% (Feldstein (1999: 678).

But on the more realistic assumption that a 10% increase in the income tax rate will produce significantly less than 10% extra tax revenue (the fall in income will reduce tax revenue), he estimated the deadweight loss at $44/$26, or $1.7 loss per $1 raised. And if the effect on social security revenues is also taken into account, the ratio was $44/$21.4 or $2.06 loss per $1 of revenue.

through, and personally observed the fallout from, five 18-year business cycles. In his view, the appropriate starting point for the reassessment of an economy's productive potential is a tax-induced loss of wealth and welfare as measured by a 1:1 ratio (Box 6:5). This means that, if the OECD countries transformed their tax regimes to collect *existing* revenue directly from rent, people would respond by generating $14 trillion on top of what is currently being produced. That value would be channelled into the arteries of the global economy to fuel the factories, stock-pile the retail shelves, satisfy the demands of consumers, enrich cultures and fund the public services that people desperately need.

Why is this financial reform not on the political agenda? According to the neoclassical economists who monopolise public debate with their 'evidence based' arguments, policy options are limited by sovereign indebtedness. This favours the austerity programmes which, in Italy, created 'corporate asphyxia' (Sanderson 2015). Their reasoning was grounded in false theories. Correctly understood and weighed, *the meaning, mechanism and metrics of rent transform the intellectual imagination.* Immediate progress could be achieved through judicious capital formation within a fiscal framework that recycled the ensuing rents to fund the investments. The USA illustrates the economic drama that is waiting to be played out (Box 6:6).

Box 6.5

The Gold Standard

By basing estimates on average deadweight losses, what is sacrificed in statistical precision is gained in public comprehension. Taxpayers are intuitively aware that there is an unaudited loss associated with the taxes they pay, but governments decline to measure the losses which they inflict on their societies. Politicians bombard taxpayers with value judgements, such as the claim that they favour 'fair' taxes, but such notions are plastic. They mean whatever conforms to the politician's ideology.

The gold standard against which the damage caused by taxes must be judged is not controversial. When revenue is directly collected from economic rent, no damage is inflicted. In fact, rent-charging tools are 'better than neutral' (Tideman 1999; similar insights are in Feldstein 1977). That is because they positively reinforce behaviour that increases people's wealth and welfare. This is how one textbook explains the point:

> Land will not be forced out of use, because land that is very unprofitable will command little rent and so pay little tax. Thus there will be no change in the supply of goods that are produced with the aid of land, and, since there is no change in supply, there can be no change in prices. *The tax cannot be passed to the consumers* (Lipsey 1979:370: emphasis in original).

The public charge on ground rents falls (as Adam Smith insisted it would) on people who benefit from the use of services provided by nature and/or society.

The transition to the reforms which I have outlined would need to be carefully planned. They would begin with reductions in whichever tax was deemed to yield the quickest benefits under prevailing conditions. If the urgent need was to create employment – reduce the income tax. If the immediate need was to increase consumption – reduce VAT ... and so on, until the damaging taxes were replaced by the collection of rent.

Realistically, we could not expect politicians of all the OECD countries to display the statesmanship needed to synchronise these reforms. But if just one leading nation took the initiative, the synergy they would unleash in their economy and communities would alert the others to the wisdom of following suit. If they failed to respond, they would pay a heavy price: loss of competitiveness in the global economy.

Box 6.6

Self-funding Infrastructure

The scope for expanding economic activity through the public sector is dramatically highlighted by the scale of one of the challenges facing the USA – the shortfall of investment in infrastructure. The American Society of Civil Engineers (2013) warns that $3.6 trillion needed to be spent between 2016 and 2020 on upgrading amenities ranging from roads and bridges to schools and public parks; from drinking water to railway networks.

Conventional economic thinking assumes that the funds for those upgrades in the social infrastructure need to be sitting in the bank before the investments can take place (the 'Can we afford it?' argument). In fact, those services would pay for themselves out of the new value which they would create. By raising productivity, additional revenue is generated out of which to fund the investments. The quality of people's lives would rise by leaps and bounds, and they would be able and willing to pay for the additional benefits they received. All that is needed is the fiscal mechanism that transmits the added rents back into the public purse to cover the cost of the infrastructure.

Epochal change is already underway. The choice is between change driven by out-of-control events, or change that is democratically determined by the will of the people. The starting point is the renegotiation of the social contract.

A New Social Contract

The Welfare State was an experiment that has been well tried and tested. The test, however, was rigged. The financial settlement imposed on it meant that, sooner or later, the Welfare State would implode. The weight of the demands imposed upon it would exceed the capacity of the economy to fund it. The goals were humane, but the architects of the Welfare State were prevented by the rent-seekers from establishing a sustainable funding formula (Box 6:7).

The nature and capacity of the Welfare State will be evaluated in terms of one of its own tenets: equality. The evidence for the UK shows that, contrary to the authorised narrative, Britain does not honour the right of people to be treated as equals. Similar evidence could be compiled for any of the other comparably affluent OECD countries.

Box 6:7 • Financing the Welfare State

The embryonic model was imported from Germany into the UK. The original intention, mandated by the British electorate, was to fund the Welfare State out of the nation's stream of rents. At the beginning of the 20th century, politicians formulated safety nets for the aged and the unemployed. The strategy was initiated by Liberal Chancellor of the Exchequer David Lloyd George. His taxes on land and natural resources were set out in the 1909 Budget. Landlords in the House of Lords blocked the funding reform, so old age pensions and unemployment benefits had to be funded out of taxes on the incomes of working people.

The next initiative was by a Labour Chancellor. Philip Snowden introduced a land value tax bill in 1931. The bill was enacted, but a reactionary Conservative Party played for time until it could delete the law from the statute book in 1934.

A third attempt was made immediately after the Second World War. The prospects were better, this time, for two reasons: (1) the aristocratic underpinning of the rent-seeking culture was debilitated by events of the previous 50 years, and (2) Winston S. Churchill was leader of the Conservative Party – and he had played a major role in the Liberal campaign leading up to the 1909 Budget. The Labour Government's land-and-tax policies, however, were framed to accommodate socialist principles. They could not integrate efficiently with the grain of the market economy. Initiatives were repeatedly made between 1947 and 1975. Predictably, they all failed (Blundell 1994).

The fully-fledged Welfare State was doomed from the outset. One day it would have to be deconstructed for want of funds.

➤ Taxes on labour and enterprises constrained the economy from achieving its full potential.
➤ The rent-seeking culture would systematically increase the proportion of the population dependent on welfare benefits, both those in-work and out-of-work.

It was just a matter of time before the safety nets would have to be unpicked on the back of the claim that they were unaffordable. That became the mantra of the two Cameron Governments following the Crash of 2008. Aside from spending on education and health, the 'benefits' paid in the form of housing subsidies and tax 'credits' paid to those in work and pensions, amounted to 12.5% of GDP in 2015.

➤ A large part of those benefits were direct transfers to landlords – raising the cost of housing for everyone else.
➤ In-work tax 'credits' were a Kafkaesque device that allowed people to keep their wages, as if their governments were doing them a favour.
➤ Funding the costs of state-sponsored poverty entailed an ever-increasing sovereign debt.

According to the Institute for Fiscal Studies (Hood and Johnson, 2016), the tax-and-benefits changes instituted by the Cameron government would fall proportionately most heavily on the poorest members of the population.

At the two points in time when humans are most vulnerble – at birth and death – some people are more equal than others. Inequality flows logically from the culture of rent-seeking, which is the primary driving force in society today. How the rent-seeking culture has embedded corruption as a routine feature of mainstream institutions and collective behaviour has been described in the case of the UK (Harrison 2015). Here, we focus on a singularly tragic indicator: the gap in life expectancy. In a population that has shared the same health and welfare services for 70 years, some babies are born more equal than others.

The National Health Service (NHS) is regarded by the people of Britain as the crowning glory of the Welfare State. The reverence indicates an almost sacred status. From birth to death, people are entitled to free medical treatment at the point of need. The Accident & Emergency wards are available to everyone at no cost. Life-saving operations are undertaken free of charge. And yet ...

❖ Average life expectancy for boys born in Kensington and Chelsea in 2014 was 83.3 years compared to 74.7 years for boys born in Blackpool (gap: 8.6 years). For new-born girls, life expectancy was highest in Chiltern (86.7 years) and lowest in Middlesbrough (79.8 years).

When we drill down to the level of municipal wards, the gaps are found to be even more startling. The *Strategic Review of Health Inequalities in England post-2010* (Marmot, 2010) reports that, in one area in the borough of Kensington and Chelsea, a man could expect to live to 88 years. A few miles away in Tottenham Green, one of London's poorer wards, male life expectancy is 71 years. That is a gap of 17 years.

❖ The discrimination is intensifying over time. Between 1993 and 2014, male life expectancy at birth increased by an average of 3.1 years in Blackpool compared with 10.3 years in Kensington and Chelsea. Female life expectancy at birth increased by 7.9 years in Camden (London); in Stevenage it remained at the 1993 level.

In Scotland, the gap in life expectancy between low-income Drumchapel, a suburb of Glasgow, and neighbouring high-income East Dunbartonshire, is 13 years. In England, life expectancy divides the north from the south. Life expectancy at birth is generally lower in the north than in the south. In 2014, life expectancy for new-born girls was highest in

Chiltern (86.7 years) and lowest in Middlesbrough (79.8 years). In the north-eastern town of Stockton-on-Tees, life expectancy is 17.3 years lower for men and 11.4years lower for women in the most deprived areas compared to the most prosperous neighbourhoods in the town.

❖ Discrimination exists between countries. Life expectancy is not only higher in England than in Wales: the gap between them is increasing. The increase for men was 4.4 years in England compared with 4.1 years in Wales. Women in Wales also lagged behind England (2.7 years compared to 3 years).

A number of factors are offered as plausible accounts for the lower life expectancy in England's northern regions. These include socio-economic, environmental (including working conditions), educational and lifestyle factors, which may act throughout one's lifetime, and possibly over generations. Attempts to explain the spatial discrepancies include higher deprivation in certain areas among older people, higher unemployment and housing deprivation, and higher prevalence of binge drinking and smoking. Griffiths and Fitzpatrick (2001) used an employment and income-based measure to explain geographical variations.

There is beyond doubt a strong statistical association between life expectancy and deprivation at local authority level: *decreasing life expectancy was associated with increasing deprivation*. But none of the scholarly studies cited by the Office for National Statistics (ONS 2015) provides a scientifically robust *explanation* for the spatial variations. The statistics merely describe variations in life chances.

The geography of premature deaths conforms to the profile of the spatial variations in the distribution of rents as described by David Ricardo, the 19th classical economist (Harrison 2006: 119-131). The variation in the spatial distribution of premature deaths fits the distribution of privately appropriated rents. This is not a random or coincidental outcome. It is the result of cultural causation. To a life-determining extent, people's prospects are shaped by the way in which rent is allocated through government revenue-and-expenditure policies. Those policies are grounded in a culture of greed, which results in variable life chances underpinned by privilege or poverty (Harrison 2015). Because tax policy does not equalise the distribution of those rents, poverty persists in the fifth richest nation on earth. Unequal life chances are determined by generalised deprivation: premature deaths are the institutionalised result of a socially-sanctioned killing cult (Harrison 2016, Ch.6).

Box 6:8

Education: Victimised by House Prices

Tens of thousands of lives are prematurely terminated in the UK alone by the transmission mechanisms that exclude parts of the population from their nation's net income. The estimate for the NATO countries alone is about 500,000 people every year (Harrison 2012: 55-56). Education serves as one of those transmission mechanisms.

Education is deemed to be the single most important way to advance in life. It affects the whole range of desirable social and economic outcomes, including health. In the Welfare State, schooling is free at the point of need. But educational opportunities are not evenly distributed. Discrimination is made visible through the real estate market.

Because the net gains from a good educational system are not ploughed back into the funding of schools, they are captured as higher prices for houses that are located near the best schools. This creates a vicious circle. People who can capture rents are financially able to purchase dwellings near the best schools. This gives their offspring a better chance in life compared to children whose parents do not have access to rents. First choice access to the best schools is determined by one's capacity to afford the best located houses.

A self-reinforcing, two-way process of discrimination operates. When the education authorities award a high rating to a school, the price of houses in the neighbourhood is bumped up (Pickford 2016). That rise in house prices then excludes lower-income families from the neighbourhood, obliging their children to accept schooling in less well-endowed locations. Inter-generational effects come into play as the dynamics of economic apartheid play themselves out.

The fatal tragedy in the midst of the Welfare State is not mitigated by taxes that purport to redistribute income in favour of the poor. The number of households in England unable to afford an acceptable standard of living rose steadily in the five years up to 2015, from 19% to 24%. But policy-makers are unwilling to face the fact that, 70 years after the inauguration of the Welfare State, individuals do not control their destinies. Politicians refuse to face this reality, because to do so would oblige them to explain why they permit the rent-seeking culture to discriminate against, and kill, so many people in the silent civil war in the midst of what is called civilised society (Box 6:8).

Towards a Clean Slate

Healthy lifespans are also curtailed in the Welfare State.

❖ In the wealthy UK southern town of Wokingham, a boy born in 2014 can expect over 70 years of good health, compared to 55 years for a male born in the northern town of Blackpool. Girls born in the wealthy London borough of Richmond upon Thames can expect 72 years of good health, compared to the 54.4 years for women in the northern metropolis of Manchester.

The Marmot Indicators for health inequalities, published in 2015 by the UCL Institute of Health Equity, documents the cost in lost productivity as a result of health inequalities. The sum was between £31 and £33 billion a year; £20-32 billion/year in lost taxes and higher welfare payments, and £5.5 billion/year in additional NHS healthcare costs. These costs oblige government to fund public services out of borrowed money, creating debt, higher taxes, social instability and yet further political pressure to downgrade the welfare benefits of people living on the breadline.

But the statistics should not be treated as evidence that the spirit of the Welfare State itself is flawed. The Welfare State was forced to employ arbitrary taxes to redistribute people's earned incomes. That fiscal strategy failed because it targetted high incomes with marginal tax rates that did not take into account *how* those incomes were received. Wealth taxes were similarly self-defeating: they ignored the composition of wealth. Political visionaries of the early 20th century like Winston Churchill intended to employ a justice-based revenue system to support people who were vulnerable at the point of birth and death. They knew it was vital to distinguish between

✔ earned income and the 'unearned increments' which (J.S. Mill wrote) land owners reaped even as they slept; and
✔ property created by labour power, distinguished from rent-generating assets that provided owners with revenue which they did not create.

A fiscal system that recognised those distinctions would automatically transfer power away from rent-seekers and back to working people acting through their democratically accountable governments. Families, and their hamlets, towns and cities, would be richly endowed every year if

Box 6:9 • Death, Debt and the Distribution of Rent

Benjamin Franklin wrote (in 1789), that 'In this world nothing can be said to be certain, except death and taxes'. He did not draw a causal link between death and taxes. Rent is that link. The UK illuminates the fatal process at work.

Death. Mortal inequality is determined by the nature of tax policies that discriminate in favour of people who own land in high-value locations.

Debt. In 2015, the UK government reduced spending on social benefits because its net worth had grown to minus £1.5 trillion.

Rent. The Cameron government ignored how it wilfully distributed publicly-generated rent – a sum sufficient to fund all public services – to privileged citizens.

One measure of the maldistribution is offered by the value of household dwellings and 'other buildings and structures' owned by non-financial corporations and government. This is estimated at £7 trillion by the Office for National Statistics (2015: 5-6). If we conservatively assume that land is 50% of that value, and convert the market price into its annual stream of income (using an interest rate of 5%), the income that is fossilised in real estate is about £175bn. That value is locked up in family homes and buried beneath factories and office blocks, instead of flowing back into the communities that create it. Not included is the rent of farmland, or the fabulous rents generated by assets like minerals, the electro-magnetic spectrum, rights of way, water, wind power, pollution easements, aircraft time-slots…a list of rentable assets comprehensively documented by Mason Gaffney (1998: 221-233).

When the impact of the Welfare State's fiscal policies are assessed over a lifetime (rather than 1-year snapshots), the fatal character of the tax regime is exposed. According to the Institute for Fiscal Studies, the distributional impact of progressive taxes appears to work well in targeting the rich. Over the adult lifespan, 93% of individuals pay more in taxes than they receive in social security (Levell et al., 2015). This supports the authorised view that progressive taxes favour the poor. But the IFS, in auditing the impact of tax policies, fails to quantify the value that governments quietly distribute to land owners.

➤ From a life chances perspective, the highest income tax payers receive back from government far more than they pay into the public purse, when we take into account the lifetime rise in residential land values (Harrison 2006: 21-24, 297).
➤ Low-income tenants reap no capital gains to offset their tax liabilities. They are net losers, measured in terms of the years they spend on earth, the years spent in good health, or in their spending power.

The Welfare State has been exceptionally generous to the owners of land.

public policy conformed to the pricing principles to which people adhere in their everyday lives – *paying for the goods and services they consume*. That would make it possible to eliminate the Treadmill Taxes which depress productivity. By restructuring their public finances, people would organically redesign their communities and social systems along sustainable lines. Societies would be launched into a new phase of social evolution.

The Welfare State has ill-served the poor (Box 6:9). Les Mayhew, a professor at London's City University Cass Business School, reports that the richest 5% of men in Britain are living on average to 96.2 years, which is 33.3 years longer than the poorest 10%. The gap has grown by 1.7 years since 1993 (Mayhew and Smith 2016). If there is a democratic wish to retain the Welfare State, tax policy needs to be fine-tuned to reflect people's personal needs and endowments. Central to this fiscal agenda is the empowerment of people to allocate their labour and capital, and their society's land, to achieve their full potential. This necessarily entails the transformation of High Finance, which will not occur without a democratic renegotiation of the social contract.

A clean slate renewal becomes possible once we perceive the fatal short-comings of the economic models used by 'experts' to guide governments. That those models are flawed is confirmed in technicolour charts published by oversight organisations like Britain's Office of Budget Responsibility. Constant revisions to data that was supposed to trace the recovery of the economy (such as GDP growth rates and productivity increases: Chote 2016) expose the unreliability of the models grounded in neoclassical doctrines. Economic stagnation is due solely to the failure of those who serve as the guardians of society to fulfil their duty of care. They decline to apply lessons learned from their past failures. Confessions are few. One hint of such a confession came from one of Britain's top civil servants, Sir Nicholas Macpherson, just before he stepped down as permanent secretary at HM Treasury. He observed:

> I became very struck in the last decade about how little history people know. History does repeat itself, not in exactly the same way, but you do have booms, you do have busts, you do have banking crises, you do have fiscal crises. These things come around with depressing regularity and so by understanding the past you can better deal with the present. (Viña 2016)

Ultimately, the profound crisis in western society does not stem from an inability to *understand* the past. It resides in the willingness of the community of 'experts' to self-censor themselves, and therefore the rest of us (Harrison 2016). They fail to put to good use the evidence that is beneath their feet and in front of their eyes. As a consequence, the simple truths – and the corresponding reforms – are not spelt out for the benefit of the people whom they presume to instruct.

References

American Society of Civil Engineers (2013), *Report Card for America's Infrastructure*, http://www.infrastructurereportcard.org/

Blundell, V.H. (1994), 'Flawed Land Acts 1947-1976', in *Land and Taxation*, Nicolaus Tideman, ed., London, Shepheard-Walwyn.

Braconier, Henrik, G. Nicoletti and Ben Westmore (2014), *Policy Challenges for the Next 50 Years*, Paris, OECD.

Chote, Robert (2016), *Economic and Fiscal Outlook*, London, Office for Budget Responsibility, March. http://budgetresponsibility.org.uk/

Colin, Nicolas (2015), 'France is backing away from much-needed labour reforms', *Financial Times*, March 17.

Dobbs, Richard, *et al.* (2015), *Debt and (not much) deleveraging*, Washington, DC, McKinsey Global Institute.

Dobbs, Richard, *et al* (2015), *The New Global Competition for Corporate Profits*, Washington, DC, McKinsey Global Institute. http://www.mckinsey.com/business-functions/strategy-and-corporate-finance/our-insights/the-new-global-competition-for-corporate-profits

Evans-Pritchard, Ambrose (2015), 'Debts in every part of the world have become potent cause for mischief, says OECD chief', *Daily Telegraph*, January 20.

Feldstein, Martin (1977), 'The Surprising Incidence of a Tax on Pure Rent: A New Answer to an Old Question', *Journal of Political Economy*, Vol. 85, No. 2 (April).

— (1999), 'Tax Avoidance and the Deadweight Loss of Income Tax', *Review of Economics and Statistics*, Vol. 81(4), pp.674-680.

Foley, Stephen (2015), 'Philanthropy', *Financial Times*, December 24.

Fukuyama, Francis (1992), *The End of History and The Last Man*, London, Hamish Hamilton.

— (1995), *Trust: The Social Virtues and the Creation of Prosperity*, London, Hamish Hamilton.

Gaffney, Mason (1948), 'A Study of the Causes of Unemployment', Reed College, OR (June).

— (1970), 'Adequacy of Land as a Tax Base', in Daniel Holland (ed.), *The Assessment of Land Value*, Madison, University of Wisconsin Press.

— (1994), 'Neoclassical Economics as a Stratagem against Henry George', in Mason Gaffney and Fred Harrison, *The Corruption of Economics*, London, Shepheard-Walwyn.

— (1998), 'An Inventory of Rent-yielding Resources', in *The Losses of Nations*, Fred Harrison, ed., London, Othila Press.

— (2009), *After the Crash: Designing a Depression-Free Economy*, Cliff Cobb, ed., Chichester, Wiley-Blackwell.

— (2009), 'The hidden taxable capacity of land: Enough and to spare.' *International Journal of Social Economics*, 36:4, pp.328-411.

— (2009), 'George's Economics of Abundance: Replacing dismal choices with practical resolutions and synergies', http://www.usbig.net/papers/195-Gaffney—George's%20Economics%20of%20Abundance—Apr09.pdf

Gordon, Robert J. (2016), *The Rise and Fall of American Growth*, Princeton, Princeton University Press.

Griffiths, C., and J. Fitzpatrick, eds (2001), *Geographic Variations in Health* (DS No.16), Office for National Statistics, www.ons.gov.uk/ons/rel/subnational-health3/geographic-variations-in-health—ds-no- 16-/2001/index.html

Harrison, Fred (2006), *Ricardo's Law*, London, Shepheard-Walwyn.

— (2010), *2010 The Inquest*, London, DA Horizons.

— (2012), *The Traumatised Society*, London, Shepheard-Walwyn.

— (2015), *As Evil Does*, London, Geophilos.

— '(2016), *The Economic Consequences of Kate Barker*, London, Geophilos.

Hiatt, Steven, ed. (2007), *A Game As Old As Empire*, San Francisco, Berrett-Koehler Publishers.

Hoffman, John (1988), *State, Power and Democracy*, Sussex, Wheatsheaf Books.

Hood, Andrew, and Paul Johonson (2016), 'Are we "all in this together"?' London, Institute for Fiscal Studies. http://www.ifs.org.uk/publications/8210

Levell, Peter, Barra Roantree and Jonathan Shaw (2015), 'Redistribution from a Lifetime Perspective', London: Institute for Fiscal Studies.

Lewis, Michael (2011), *The Big Short*, London, Penguin.

Lipsey, Richard G. (1979), *Positive Economics*, 5th edn., London. Weidenfeld and Nicolson.

Marmot, Michael (2010), *Fair Society, Healthy Lives – The Marmot Review. Strategic Review of Health Inequalities in England post-2010*. (http://www.instituteofhealthequity.org/projects/fair-society-healthy-lives-the-marmotreview/fair-society-healthy-lives-full-report)

Mayhew, Les, and David Smith (2016), *An Investigation into Inequalities in Adult Lifespan*, London: Cass Business School, City University.

Office for National Statistics (2015), *National Balance Sheet, 2015 Estimates*, London.

— (2015), 'Life Expectancy at Birth and at Age 65 by Local Areas in England and Wales: 2012 to 2014', *Statistical Bulletin*. https://www.ons.gov.uk/peoplepopulationandcommunity/births deathsandmarriages/lifeexpectancies/bulletins/lifeexpectancyatbirthandatage65bylocalareasin englandandwales/2015-11-04

Perkins, John (2004), *Confessions of an Economic Hit Man*, San Francisco, Berrett-Koehler Publishers.

Pickford, James (2016), Improvement in school rating boosts house prices in local area', *Financial Times*, March 21.

Sanderson, Rachel (2016), 'Italian tycoon warns of corporate 'asphyxia'', *Financial Times*, March 17. http://www.telegraph.co.uk/business/2016/03/18/landlords-not-businesses-to-benefit-from-osbornes-rates-relief/

Spence, Peter, and Szu Ping Chan (2016), 'Landlords not businesses to benefit from Osborne's rates relief', *Daily Telegraph*, March 18.

Viña, Gonzalo (2016), 'Student unearths nuggets from political h istory for Whitehall', *Financial Times*, March 17.

Wolf, Martin (2016), 'The age of uncertainty is upon us', *Financial Times*, March 18.

Zucman, Gabriel (2015), *The Hidden Wealth of Nations*, Chicago, University of Chicago Press.

7

The Potential of Public Value: Assessing the Dynamics of Real Estate

TED GWARTNEY

AXES ARE IMPOSED on 'anything that moves'. That is the principle behind the doctrine that fiscal policy should be 'broad based'. And yet, the easiest, cheapest and fairest way to raise the public's revenue is from the one source which, in its urban form, does not move.

Land cannot be concealed in tax havens. Identifying those who are liable to a public charge on the rent of land is easy: they are the people who benefit from the occupation of land. In principle, this does not require knowledge of the identity of the owner of property, so concealing property rights in complex corporate entities registered in tax havens becomes pointless. And yet, with a few exceptions, fiscal authorities worldwide employ the most convoluted way of going about their business raising revenue to fund public services. That paradox has engaged me during my 50 years as a professional assessor of real estate.

My curiosity about the anomaly in public finance began in 1963. I was a student majoring in real estate at San Diego State University. My college courses included real estate appraisal, a subject that attracted me because my father was a real estate broker. One day, an announcement appeared on the bulletin board for an off-campus course given by the

---

Box 7:1

On Separating Land from Building Values

Friedrich Hayek is one of the distinguished – but grudging – endorsers of a public charge on the rent of land. In *The Constitution of Liberty* he acknowledged that 'the argument for its adoption would be very strong'. On what did he rest his reservations? He claimed that it was difficult to distinguish between the value created by nature and society, from the value created by individuals (such as developers) who invest capital in and on the land (1960:352-353).

In the UK, land and buildings are not valued separately for property tax purposes. But in the property market, developers buy land for redevelopment on the basis of values which assume that the sites are clear of improvements. In the US, the majority of assessors are required to show land and building values separately. The professional textbook published by the International Association of Assessing Officers (Property Appraisal and Assessment Administration, 1990), has a section on how to value land, and a portion on 'Land Valuation with Insufficient Sales.' The value of buildings is a residual value obtained by subtracting land value from total value.

Henry George School in San Diego. The school advocated the replacement of all taxes with a single charge on the rent of land. I attended their meetings with the intention of proving that this theory was wrong.

Until then, I had found economics difficult to understand. That changed, once I had completed the free 10-week course. At the conclusion of that course I was handed a copy of *House and Home* magazine (August 1960). Contributors to that magazine explained why land value (rent) was the best source for public revenue. Mason Gaffney was the guest editor who compiled the numerous empirical studies which, for the first time, made me realise that, while land was static, the market for real estate was dynamic. Property rights are the interface between public policy and private activity, and the interplay between the two turned the rent of land into a moving target.

And so I embarked on a career as a property appraiser, a skill that I put to use on behalf of Bank of America to appraise commercial properties for mortgage applications.

Early in my career in real estate appraisal I realized that it was possible to achieve some of the benefits of the principles advocated by Henry

George. By working in municipal tax departments, I could help communities to raise more revenue from land rather than from buildings. This brought me into contact with assessors and commercial real estate appraisers who were fascinated with the techniques for valuing land. Many of them promoted the need to raise the greater proportion of public revenue from land values, despite the claims by apologists for the current tax regime that it is difficult to separate the value of land – for tax purposes – from the value of buildings (Box 7:1).

It then became clear to me that land was a moveable feast for the public that wanted both fairness and efficiency from their governments.

Mason Gaffney's ATCOR Thesis

Henry George had advocated the rent of land as the exclusive source of revenue to fund public services. This became known as the Single Tax. But while the theory was robust, economists claimed that it was not possible to abolish those taxes that distorted activity in the private markets. They asserted, without evidence, that the revenue from land was insufficient. Among them were two distinguished British professors, one of whom (Mervyn King) was to become Governor of the Bank of England. They wrote in a manual that is used to teach the economics of public finance:

> [I]t is apparent that the total of economic rents, of all kinds, is not now a sufficiently large proportion of national income for this to be a practicable means of obtaining the resources needed to finance a modern State.
>
> (Kay and King 1990: 179).

Such statements color the minds of students, since they come from seemingly authoritative sources. And yet, practitioners in the field of property economics know that the statistics in official databases are totally unreliable. Economists trained in the theories of post-classical economics are unable to diagnose the dynamics of property values. The interaction between market prices and the kinds of taxes employed by governments elude them.

As a practical example, we may note what property assessors have observed when they lowered building assessments. This resulted in a lower tax-take. Who gained? The reciprocal of lower assessments is a rise in the value of land. In other words, the revenue base was not lost. It shifted to land rents and values, which can then be taxed. So when we reduce building assessments, and raise tax rates on the land under them, we are still taxing the same real estate; we are just taxing it in a different and more progressive manner. On the basis of that evidence, from over 50 years as a property professional, I was able to conclude that higher revenue could be generated out of land.

Mason Gaffney formalized this process in economic theory. He retrieved the insights of the early philosophers who had noted this phenomenon. He coined the acronym ATCOR: All Taxes Come Out of Rents. This offers a vitally important insight into the history of tax policy. The late medieval aristocrats, who appropriated the lands of the commons, so that they could turn the commoners into tenants, thought they were being smart: they thought they could reduce the Land Tax and replace the revenue by inventing new taxes on earnings and consumption. In reality, they were merely turning the public revenue system into a bizarrely complex business, because the net income produced by their tenants – the sum that was left which they could pay as rent to the landlords – went down in proportion to the new taxes for which they became liable.

The proposition that taxes are ultimately shifted upwards, to fall on those who claim to own the rent of land, follows from three major premises.

1   The supply of land is fixed inside each tax jurisdiction.
2   After-tax interest rates are determined by world markets, so the local supply of capital remains perfectly elastic at a fixed, after-tax rate.
3   Labor is quite mobile.

This process was described by Joseph Stiglitz in these terms:

> The burden of the tax on capital is not felt, in the long run, by the owners of capital. It is felt by land and labor ... in the long run, workers will emigrate ... this leaves land as the only factor that cannot emigrate ... the full burden of the tax is borne by land owners in the long run... While a direct tax on land is non-distortionary, all the other ways of raising revenue induce distortions.
>
> (Stiglitz 1986:567-68)

And so, it makes sense, economically and ethically, to frame the revenue system to take account of what works naturally. This can be achieved, in part, under existing property tax legislation by:

➤ Improving assessment procedures: land is usually under assessed
➤ Increasing the frequency of assessment: best when done annually
➤ Assessing property at the selling prices: as revealed in the market-place
➤ Showing land and building assessments separately: to enhance public understanding
➤ Depreciating buildings and improvements: that's what happens in real estate markets
➤ Shifting assessment off of buildings and onto land: to shift closer to optimum outcomes

Each property has a land value and if improved it also has a building value. Buildings are capital improvements that are created by man's labor and incur a cost to produce. They wear out over time and must be maintained and eventually replaced.

Land's uniqueness stems from its distinctive location, fixed supply and immobility. It has no cost of production but is required in the production of all goods and services. It is our most basic resource and the source of all wealth.

Land value comes from ecological and social endowments, not the personal activities of individuals. It varies by location and available amenities. It increases because of people's competitive desire to use the best land sites. Since land is fixed in supply, demand ought to be (and under ideal conditions, is) the sole determinant of land value. As the demand for land increases, its rental value (or sale price) will increase proportionally. Collecting a land value tax will enable the community to attain a sustainable and growing revenue base for funding community services. Land is visible and can't leave the community because it is taxed.

Raising revenue needs from land value taxes would allow lowering taxes on buildings, production and distribution of goods which would foster economic activity. With increased private funds available by reduced taxes on productive activities, new small businesses could begin, with new investment and opportunity to be involved in productive activities. New jobs would be created and wages would increase. Collecting land value taxes would provide the sustainable public revenue for the community's economy.

California and Proposition 13

The opportunity to test the claim that rent provided sufficient revenue to pay for all public expenditure came with a political initiative in my home state of California.

Proposition 13, which became law, had been presented to the state's voters by two real estate dealers, who wanted to curb the property tax. Proposition 13 proposed limitations on assessment increases. Assessed values would be increased by not more than 2% a year unless a property is sold, when it would go on the assessment role at its sale price. For property tax purposes, the assessment for all existing dwellings and improvements would be rolled back to valuations in the base year of 1975-1976.

Mason Gaffney warned that this would be regressive, but he realized that it was what home-owners wanted. He wrote:

> People have objected that exempting buildings would reduce the tax base. Again, in today's context, forget it. People are asking that the tax base be reduced. Public bodies may take comfort in the fact that the tax reduction caused by exempting buildings is much less than might at first appear because the exemption of buildings from tax is capitalized into higher land values. And there is no economic limit on how high the land tax rate may go, once the public accepts the system.
>
> (Gaffney 1978)

To compensate for the loss of revenue from the property tax, two responses were possible: raise new revenue to fund community development and infrastructure, or under-fund public services. Both occurred, and this triggered a process which placed California at a disadvantage to other states which tapped abundant property tax revenue and benefitted from lower taxes on sales and income (Box 7:2).

For the 2011 election year, an Initiative was proposed to replace Proposition 13 with a land value tax. The plan was to eliminate taxes on sales, income and buildings and replace the lost revenue with a charge of 75% of land rental values. I was invited to review the Comprehensive Tax Reform Initiative, as it was called. What would be the impact on the state's revenue?

I estimated that the flow of state and local government revenue would *increase* by $43 billion over the current revenue. To arrive at this conclusion, I had to evaluate existing data and make adjustments and assumptions to fill the data void. Three major items had to be analyzed to:

Box 7:2

Property Taxation and the Prosperity League

Mason Gaffney and a New Hampshire newspaper editor, Richard Noyes, compared all the states in the US to establish how Proposition 13 had affected California. Their hypothesis: capping the property tax (which would raise property prices) and substituting sales taxes would drive the Sunny State down the league table.

Within 12 years of the curb being placed on the property tax, California dropped from 7th to 12th place in personal income. In the 1990s, when other states boomed, unemployment rose in California as municipal governments retrenched on investment in infrastructure such as highways.

In contrast, New Hampshire was the only state in the Union where more than half of both state and local revenue was drawn from the property tax. Improved assessment of property values, together with the removal of personal property from the tax base, saw a substantial rise in land values. And despite the state's relative disadvantage in its natural resource endowments, and inclement weather, personal incomes rose faster than those states that chose to suppress the property tax. The rapid rise up the income league tables was explained by the low taxes on incomes and profits and the relatively high rates of taxation on real estate (Gaffney and Noyes 1998: 215-219).

---

1   adjust the aggregate assessed value of real property as reported by the Board of Equalization, to reflect current market values;
2   determine the percentage of total value that was land value; and
3   apply a realistic percentage factor to the capitalized value (selling price) to arrive at land rental values.

Taxable Value   For the 2007-2008 fiscal year, the California Board of Equalization recorded a valuation of $4.448 trillion. However, this aggregate taxable value was far less than aggregate actual market value. The under-assessment was attributable to Proposition 13, which confined increases in assessed values to no more than 2% a year. This limitation had resulted in massive undervaluation of land and improvements. My house in Anaheim illustrates what had happened. It was assessed at approximately $80,000, but its market value was $380,000 (2010). Thus, for tax purposes, my home was assessed at only 21% of its value.

Hundreds of thousands of single family residences, multi-unit residential properties, farms, commercial and retail properties which, like my house, have remained under the same ownership for decades were grossly under-assessed for tax purposes. The ownership of corporations, limited partnerships and limited liability companies can change while the business entity itself stays on title to real property. That property increasingly becomes under-assessed. Even properties which were acquired by their present owners 15 years ago or less were frequently under-assessed in California by a substantial percentage due to the restrictions imposed by Proposition 13.

The Board of Equalization itself recognizes this problem. It noted in its August 2009 overview of property taxation (Publication 29) that, because of Proposition 13, similar properties can have substantially different assessed values due solely to the dates on which the properties were purchased. *Disparities result wherever significant appreciation in property values occurs over time.* This means that Proposition 13 converted the market value-based property tax system to a mechanism for transferring publicly-created value into private hands. As a result of this anomaly, I had to apply a substantial correction factor to the $4.448 trillion of taxable value, to arrive at a realistic estimate of current aggregate market value for land and improvements.

In my opinion, assessments typically lag market values in a range of 33% to 61%. An adjustment in this range will correct predicted values to between $6 trillion and $7 trillion. Considering the variance in acquisition dates and adjusted values in the real estate database, I believe that 47% represents the average corrective increase needed to adjust assessed (taxable) aggregate value to market aggregate value in California.

Separating Land from Buildings   Statistics reported by the Board of Equalization for the 2007-2008 fiscal year (Board of Equalization August 2009) show that land constitutes about 44.6% of total assessed value. This figure, however, is skewed by Proposition 13. The increase in market value which is disregarded under current law is largely land value.

Current assessment practices may also contribute to the under-valuation of land. Based on my review of actual assessments, it appears that California assessors may use current replacement costs to value buildings/improvements without taking depreciation and obsolescence into account. This tends to overstate the value of improvements and, thus, to under-value land.

The following percentage of land value (LV) to total property value (PV) was found for California's major metropolitan areas, updated to the first quarter of 2009:

Los Angeles:	=	65.0%
Sacramento:	=	40.6%
San Diego:	=	61.8%
San Jose:	=	75.4%
Santa Ana:	=	75.4%
San Bernardino:	=	33.1%
San Francisco:	=	73.7%

Source: Davis and Palumbo (2007: 352-384).

While non-residential property is not included in this data, my experience is that these ratios realistically represent real estate in its various uses. In the major cities the ratio of land to building values often exceeds 80%. In rural districts the ratio may be less than 30%.

It my opinion, the proper percentage of aggregate land value in California falls in an overall range of 47% to 53% of the total value of real property. I believe that 50% is an appropriate state-wide average.

The Rent of Land   Rental value can be calculated either by using an average ratio or multiplier between rent and selling price, or by using a percentage rate of return on the capitalized value (selling price).

The real estate market provides excellent evidence of rental values. Gross annual rent multipliers typically fall within a range of from 12 to 24 times the annual gross rent for single family homes. The multipliers would vary greatly due to amenities, services and locations. In terms of a percent of market value, a range of 4.5% to 8.5% would be typical for single family dwellings. In my opinion, a 6.5% rental rate of return on the capitalized value of real property is an appropriate state-wide average.

For example:

To calculate market value:
Annual rent $26,000 × 15.4 multiplier = $400,000 market value
Annual rent $26,000 ÷ 6.5% rental rate = $400,000 market value

To calculate annual rent
Market value $400,000 ÷ 15.4 multiplier = annual rent $26,000
Market value $400,000 × 6.5% rental rate = annual rent $26,000

Table 7:1

California Revenue under Varying Assumptions
($ billions)

Assumptions	Low		Likely		High
California Board of Equalization Real estate taxable value	$4,448	$4,448	$4,448	$4,448	$4,448
Correction factor Real estate taxable value x Correction factor	133% $5,916	140% $6,227	**147%** $6,539	154% $6,850	161% $7,161
Per cent land value Land taxable value x Per cent land value	47% $2,780	48.5% $3,020	**50%** $3,269	51.5% $3,528	53% $3,795
Per cent rental value **Land rental value** x Per cent rental value	4.5% $125	5.5% $166	**6.5%** $213	7.5% $265	8.5% $323
Taxable portion **Land rent taxes** x Taxable portion	75% $94	75% $125	75% **$159**	75% $198	75% $242

Commercial multipliers and rental rates, while different, may be similar overall to residential rates. Because they are usually investments they may obtain higher overall rates of return. Apartments may have lower rates and industrial may have higher rates of return.

I have prepared the above chart to show the range of revenue that may be raised from the total taxable value of $4.4 billion, under different assumptions. My table shows five different assumptions for the three variables: updating taxable values, estimating land taxable value and estimating the total land rental value.

If we assume a taxable portion of 75%: when the 'LOW case' assumption is applied, the outcome is $94 billion in annual revenue, while under the 'HIGH case' assumption the outcome is $242 billion. In my view, the assumptions in the middle range are the most reasonable for all three variables, yielding an outcome of $159 billion in annual revenue.

This means that, if the Comprehensive Tax Reform Initiative had become law the State of California could have replaced all of the existing revenue sources and raised additional revenue of $43 billion over current revenue.

The initiative was submitted to the California Attorney General and California Secretary of State. The Legislative Analyst's Office approved a fiscal analysis. Unfortunately, an initiative also required signatures on petitions from 8% of the registered voters before an amendment to the state constitution could be proposed and placed upon the ballot. The cost of securing these signatures was prohibitive, and the initiative did not go to the ballot.

Auditing the Rent of Land

That it is practical for existing fiscal jurisdictions to transform their revenue practices to the one that delivers the best outcomes for all citizens is illustrated by my experience in the Canadian province of British Columbia.

In 1973 I had completed a re-assessment of real estate in the City of Hartford, Connecticut. The results of correcting assessments were beneficial for the poorer north-side residents, but they meant large tax increases for the land affluent south-side residents. Although the work was excellent, the results hurt the affluent and influential residents. The politicians were unhappy. I decided to look for a job where my work would be appreciated.

Mason Gaffney had been appointed by a newly elected parliament to head their Research Institute in Canada. He told me the government wanted to improve the property tax and raise a greater proportion of revenue from land and the value of natural resources. I met the Provincial Premier and was hired as a consultant to review and make recommendations for improving the assessment systems in the Province of British Columbia. I began by reviewing their assessment history (Box 7:3).

Early in 1974 an all-party committee of the Legislature conducted a comprehensive study on assessments and reported its conclusions in these terms:

1   The Committee accepts as a basic premise that equalization of assessment of all lands and improvements in British Columbia is essential to the achievement of equity in real property taxation in this Province.

2   The Committee deems it worthwhile to note that the assessment procedures in British Columbia are carried out by assessors employed by the Municipalities and by assessors employed by the Provincial Government.

Box 7:3

Towards Fair Dealing in Property Taxation

Real estate assessment equity and fairness has long been a goal in British Columbia. Assessments have been made since the 1800s. In the 1920s many cities had adopted a land value tax. Edward Denison 'Single Tax' Taylor served eight terms as Mayor of the City of Vancouver.

In 1953 the Assessment Equalization Act was enacted to equalize assessments for school purposes throughout the Province. Beginning in the late 1960's, restrictions were placed upon the amount by which individual assessments could be increased. This caused distortions and inequities in relationships within and between the classes of properties.

Prior to the introduction of the Assessment Act in 1974, real property assessment legislation was contained in the Assessment Equalization Act, Municipal Act, Taxation Act, Public Schools Act and the Vancouver Charter. These statutes prescribed the basis for raising revenue for municipal, regional, school and hospital purposes.

---

3   The briefs submitted to the Committee clearly suggest that this division of assessment responsibility results in two major problems, an inefficient distribution of assessment personnel and the apparent control of assessors by the taxing authority.

4   Therefore the Committee recommends that legislation be introduced at the current session to create a Province-wide Assessment Authority. This Authority must be independent of the taxing function (either municipal or provincial) and its control must be such as will result unmistakably in complete independence.

5   The purpose of the Authority is to establish and maintain assessments that are uniform in the whole of the Province in accordance with the Assessment Act.

The BC Assessment Authority   I recommended a province-wide Assessment Authority that was independent of the taxing function (both municipal and provincial). Annual reassessment of land and improvements at market value was essential to achieve equity in real property taxation. The Authority was created in July 1974 and I was appointed as the Assessment Commissioner and Chief Executive Officer at the end of the year.

The purpose of the Authority was to establish and maintain assessments that were uniform across the province. New laws enabled school taxes to be collected province-wide and redistributed as needed. Municipalities could adopt a land value tax but they all chose to use the new full value assessment base for property taxes.

The Assessment Authority combined and improved the records of all of the former assessment units. The assessing units were consolidated into 27 area offices. In 1974 they produced the first province-wide assessment list totaling $42,200,000,000. The total number of properties was 879,126.

Area assessors were appointed, each to serve several municipalities and the surrounding unorganized provincial lands. Approximately 95% of the former municipal and provincial staff came to work for the new Authority. The staff at year end was 764. An initial Year 1 goal was to value all land at actual value, at which assessors were experienced.

The head office developed systems for data processing, mapping, microfilm, roll production, statutory reports, appraisal and office systems. It was necessary to develop the best systems and methods and then standardize differing field and office records. Success would be achieved by simplifying the handling of property transfers and new construction, expanding training programs, revising the appraisal manuals, expanding technical support and developing a mass land and property valuation system.

Two assessment rolls were produced for the calendar years 1975 and 1976, one showing actual market value and the other reflecting the existing 1974 assessed value levels. The actual value assessment list was used by the provincial study committee to develop information for legislative action, which included changes to market values for calculating taxes and school tax reform. To avoid unexpected and dramatic change on under-assessed properties, a phase-in formula was provided.

British Columbia Today   In 2015, the British Columbia Assessment Authority has been in business for 41 years. It set the standard for updating assessed values annually. It is considered the most efficient assessment organization in the world. The province has grown dramatically.

- ✔ Total population is 4,600,000, with *per capita* income of $51,135.
- ✔ In a land mass of 364,764 square miles, the total number of properties is 1,974,000.

✔ The total assessed value is $1,206 trillion, of which 50% ($603 billion) is land value.

✔ Revenue from the property tax is $6,800,000,000 (approximately $3.4 billion from land).

From 1974 to 2015 the property tax base has grown by 29 times and the land portion of the property tax base has grown from 39% to over 50%. The dynamic impact is measured in economic growth rates. British Columbia has outpaced other Canadian provinces and many countries in the world. The growth rate of land value has exceeded growth in the value of buildings and other improvements on the land. Raising more of its revenue from land rent made it possible to moderate the tax burden on buildings and on production. With increased funds left in private hands, new small businesses have flourished. Jobs have been created and wages have increased. Collecting land value taxes has provided the sustainable public revenue for the community's economy.

The West Coast as a New Frontier

My studies of property markets in California and British Columbia confirm the arguments advanced by Henry George in *Progress and Poverty*. Rent is a buoyant fiscal base that is capable of funding the services of modern states – and this is the case, even if we ignore the fact that the expenditure side of governance would decline (fewer welfare demands would be made on the public purse).

George likened the land market, which was beset by imperfections like speculation, to an unconscious universal cartel which withheld much good land from full use and drove labor and investors out to lower productivity land. Since his day, the West Coast has been burdened by heavy taxes on labor and capital. But it is possible to eliminate such taxes and allow after-tax wage rates to rise.

The rise of wages in the geo-classical fiscal system implies a rise of Gross Domestic Product (GDP). The rise would result from removing the burdens of current taxes, which would increase the marginal productivity of labor. The original western frontier closed in the 1890s, when all the land of the New World had been appropriated by the earliest settlers, leaving late-comers at a disadvantage. But fiscal reform would be like re-opening the frontier, an 'internal frontier,' because it would end the artificial scarcity of land. The poverty endured today would come to an end, as Henry George predicted, by the expedient of enlightened fiscal governance.

References

Board of Equalization California. (2009). http://www.boe.ca.gov/annual/pdf/2009/3-revenues 09.pdf.

Davis, Morris A. and Michael G. Palumbo (2007). 'The Price of Residential Land in Large US Cities', *Journal of Urban Economics*, 63(1); data Located at Land and Property Values in the US, Lincoln Institute of Land Policy.

Gaffney, Mason (1978), 'Proposition 13: an Alternative Reform', *The Center Magazine*, Santa Barbara, (Nov./Dec.). Originally presented as 'Tax Limitation and its Alternatives' at a meeting of the Center for the Study of Democratic Institutions, Santa Barbara, (August 1978).

Gaffney, Mason and Richard Noyes (1998), 'The Income-Stimulating Incentives of the Property Tax', in Fred Harrison, ed., *The Losses of Nations: Deadweight Politics versus Public Rent Dividends*, London, Othila.

Hayek, F.A. (1960), *The Constitution of Liberty*, London, Routledge & Kegan Paul.

Kay, J.A., and M.A. King (1990), *The British Tax System*, 5th edn., Oxford, Oxford University Press.

Stiglitz, Joseph (1986), *Economics of the Public Sector*, New York, W.W. Norton.

8

Corporate Land Bankers as Rent Seekers

DIRK LÖHR

NEOCLASSICAL economics has left its mark on business economics, as a result of merging land with capital (Gaffney 1994: 39-40). This has had serious consequences for the theory of the firm. According to the textbooks, firms are institutions which combine the factors of production labour, capital and land. Since the outlawing of slavery, humans can no longer be shown as assets in financial statements (Johnston 2013). As for land in corporate hands, it is treated as of minor significance. Firms are thus generally considered as representing 'capital'.

Extraordinary profits in so-called 'competitive markets', according to the theory taught in universities today, are supposed to be pushed down to a 'normal' level sooner or later. This is supposed to result from competition from new market entrants or from an increase of capital investment. How, then, do we explain the ability of some corporations to sustain high profits in such markets? I argue that equity basically does not finance 'capital' and that the core of the profit of successful companies is fundamentally not capital earnings (apart from premiums for risk, for inflation and imputed employer's salaries). Instead, in line with Gaffney (1994), I argue that the extra profits received by 'high performers' are economic rents, of which land rent is the archetype. Moreover, I follow Gaffney in viewing successful corporations as large collections of land.

I extend this perspective to other 'key assets' (Gaffney 1988/1997: 7): these go beyond physical land but they share similar features. Hence *I consider investments in a firm's equity as indirect investments in land and similar rent-generating assets, which I will call key assets.*

Key Assets as Real Options

Key assets might take the form of exclusive real options (call options; see Myers, 1977; http://www.realoptions.org). A (real) option gives the right, but not the obligation, to carry out a follow-up investment (Box 8:1). The follow-up investment might be postponed until current insecurity disappears or good business opportunities appear. Hence such an investment strategy has some flexibility, which has an intrinsic value in an insecure world. Land, for example, can be considered as such a real option. Follow-up investments in buildings can be postponed until the opportunity is right. But other key assets may serve as exclusive initial investments within such a sequential investment strategy. Just like land, they have a low elasticity of production and substitution; the chance for future profits can be secured exclusively. Some examples are provided in Table 8:1.

Table 8:1

Key assets as exclusive real options: some examples

Initial investment	Follow-up investment
(Reserve) land, location	Setting up a building/business on a unique location. Yields: Land rents
Patent rights	Exclusive commercial exploitation (knowledge as source) Yields: Patent rents.
Oil concessions, water rights	Exclusive commercial exploitation of the source. Yields: Resource rents.
Liquidity	Universal possibilities, provided by cash. Exchange option for economic rents.

Source: Loehr 2013b, Table 1.

Thus, equity reflects the value of a portfolio of exclusive real options as key assets. Like a financial option, it is also better to buy a real option using equity instead of debts. This becomes clearer if we consider the traces which key assets leave on the asset side of financial statements.

➤ Land as a real option is the most important key asset (cf. Gaffney 1988/1997: 1). Businesses that want to expand need suitable new locations. This includes the reservation of sites for a later development as well as land as collateral for additional loans that are needed for the business expansion (cf. Gaffney 1970: 167). However, if land is not used and the real option provided by land is not exercised (no building is constructed), cash flows cannot be generated. Hence no interest can be paid. Moreover, land has infinite termination; this is why there is no regular depreciation on land. Hence a loan cannot be amortized. Because the value of land may change, the amortization may also not be guaranteed out of possible sale proceeds. The same holds true for interest rates, since land rents are a residual, and may be very volatile. Interpreting the balance sheet to assess the impact of holding land out of use, for instance, is problematic, because of the influence of neoclassical theory (the merging of land and buildings into a single asset). Basically, land's share in real estate and in total assets has to be estimated, not least because the value of land in the firm's financial statements tends to be undervalued – not only in the USA (Gaffney 1970: 167-182).

➤ Certain intangible assets can also be considered as exclusive real options. Knowledge, for example, is attributed to the factor labour, but the law on intellectual property rights may attribute to knowledge characteristics similar to property rights of land. Patent rights, in particular, are a real option (see Table 1). They are necessary for the expansion of business activities. However, because the outcome of research activities is uncertain (Kaserer and Lenz 2009), no amortization and interest can be guaranteed. Moreover, parts of the patent portfolio might not be used for commercial exploitation, but (for instance) to block competitors. Thus it is difficult to say whether and when a patent rent may be earned. In these and other cases, financing of these intangible assets by equity is a more solid way than by loans.

➤ Interests in other companies are exclusive real options (Loehr and Rams 2000). Such interests may be a means of getting access to their key assets. However, interests in other companies also should not be financed by loans for similar reasons as for land: there is no depreciation out of which the amortization of loans could be paid. Moreover, the returns are residuals – similar to land rents. They are insecure and thus do not provide a sound basis for a guaranteed interest payment.

➤ Gaffney (1994: 49) is correct to emphasise that money is not the same as capital. Money, or liquidity, is a universal exchange option. The 'liquidity premium' of Keynes might also be interpreted as a special sort of option premium. Gaffney (1977: 377) recognizes the similar features between cash and land. However, cash or cash equivalents do not earn high yields, and neither is there any amortization. Hence liquidity should not be covered by loans either.

Without access to such key assets, founding or expanding a company and reaping economic rents is hardly feasible. This access is provided by equity. However, endowment of equity depends on the distribution of wealth and income. That is why wealthy stakeholders have better access to key assets than the poor.

The Mirror Hypothesis

For the reasons mentioned above, equity is expected to reflect the value of key assets. This is the mirror hypothesis (Loehr 2013a, 2013b). It reflects reality if the financial base of a company is sound. The mirror hypothesis may be confirmed in an average consideration by using data from Germany. Deutsche Bundesbank extrapolates the whole economy by using a data pool of 130,000 sets of financial statements for 2013 (Deutsche Bundesbank 2015). These statements meet the requirements of the German Commercial Code (Handelsgesetzbuch, HGB). However, the share of land in real property is estimated 'freehand'. It is treated as representing 25% of the book value of property, which in the past has been a typical rate for Germany. Equity and interests on the one hand and receivables and liabilities on the other are not consolidated. Subject to that proviso, the sum of the shares of intangible assets, land, (unconsolidated) interests in companies and cash approximately equals the unconsolidated share of equity in total assets. Table 2 shows the share of key assets and the share of equity in total assets.

The share of key assets in total assets corresponds to the share of equity over time. Both the proportional market value and the proportional book value of the equity increased over time. Despite the decreasing interest rates of recent years, the share of gross wages ('Arbeitnehmerentgelte') in national income also decreased from 67.9% (2004) to 66.6% in 2013 (German Federal Statistical Office 2014). Although German official

Table 8:2

The Mirror Hypothesis: German companies in total

	1998-2001	2002-2005	2006-2009	2010-2013
Share of key assets	21.9%	25.9%	25.9%	26.3%
Share of equity	20.4%	23.7%	25.2%	27.7%
For information:				
Average capital market interest rate	4.3%	3.8%	3.9%	2.0%
Profits as % of national income	8.8%	9.0%	11.2%	11.3%
Profits as % of non-labour income	30.1%	29.1%	32.3%	34.6%

Sources: Deutsche Bundesbank 2015; the present author's calculations.

statistics do not provide sound information in this regard, the decline of the capital market interest rates did not benefit labour that much, but – as in other countries – primarily worked in favour of the location rents and other economic rents (Rognlie 2015; Loehr 2013a, 2013b). Thus the rising share of profits in the national income and the non-labour income *cannot be explained by considering profits essentially as income from capital, but as economic rents.*

An Unknown Economic Law

The correspondence between equity and key assets also provides an answer to the old question of whether or not there is an optimum structure of corporate finance (see for instance Modigliani and Miller 1958). However, this correspondence is not enforced by any regulation, and it is not even taught as a management rule. What we have identified, then, is compliance with an unknown economic law. The argument that this is not possible does not hold true. Sotelo (1995) explains that economic laws may operate even if nobody knows about them. Thus, as in the 'law of large numbers', a gearing to the 'mirror hypothesis' has to be expected for the economy as a whole. Deviations between individual companies, however, may be significant. Also different industries and different legal forms have different ratios of key assets to equity. An important reason for such variations is the different growth rates of companies, industries and legal forms;

the more growth, the higher the under-funding with equity. Table 8:3 shows that the average relationship between key assets and equity for all companies was 0.9 between 1997 and 2013. The key assets were slightly leveraged, probably due to the decreasing level of interest rates. Total assets grew by a factor of 1.7 during that period. Both the average ratio of key assets to equity and average growth of total assets of the average are standardized at 100%. The four most important industries (measured by capitalization) and legal forms are assessed.

Table 8:3

Mirror hypothesis and company growth

No.	Industry	Ratio key assets to equity	Standardized (as %)	Growth (of total assets; 1997-2013)	Standardized (as %)
0	Total	0.9	**100%**	1.7	**100%**
Industries:					
1	Production	0.9	**99%**	1.7	**102%**
2	Manufacturing	0.9	**103%**	1.9	**113%**
3	Information, communication	1.3	**146%**	2.1	**126%**
4	Corporate services	1.0	**115%**	1.8	**108%**
Legal forms and size:					
1	Small and medium-sized corporations	0.5	**60%**	1.5	**88%**
2	Small and medium-sized non-corporations	0.7	**78%**	1.3	**77%**
3	Big corporations	1.0	**111%**	1.9	**113%**
4	Big non-corporations	1.0	**109%**	1.7	**98%**

Sources: Deutsche Bundesbank 2015; the present author's calculations.

Table 8:3 confirms the importance of equity endowment for growth. In particular, initial public offerings (IPOs) open up new possibilities for business expansion.

The German Commercial Code refers to book values; thus hidden reserves and goodwill are not considered (cf. Gaffney 1970: 160). Since most of the companies are not listed, these components are difficult to assess and distinguish from each other. However, this is not necessary in order to support the mirror hypothesis. If hidden reserves (in land) and goodwill were added to the book value of the key assets, equity would also have to be increased by the same amount. This means the share of key assets and equity in total assets increases, but the key assets still correspond to equity. Thus the result does not change.

Elsewhere (Loehr 2013b: 113, Table IV), I have demonstrated that the mirror hypothesis also holds true if parts of the hidden reserves are disclosed using the International Financial Reporting Standards (IFRS), which are adopted by companies that are publicly listed on stock exchanges. Moreover, within IFRS the relative share of equity also reflects the relative level of land prices of different countries. For instance, using data from 1995 to 2011, the average price/income ratio for German real estate was about 75% of the British ratio. Also the unweighted equity ratio of German companies was about 75% of the British ratio, and the ratio of the value of German and British key assets was some 79%. Since unweighted data prevent the dominance of big companies in the dataset, they are probably a better indicator of the general ratio than weighted data. This also emphasises that without equity, access to key assets is difficult, and without key assets, there is no access to economic rents. Corporations are the most effective legal form for gaining access to large amounts of equity, and thus open the way for access to a large amount of economic rents (Loehr 2014; see also Table 8:3).

Profits and Rents

Company profits do not only comprise imputed employer's salaries and risk premiums; they also include economic rents. The rent on land and other key assets is a (exclusive) residual income. The owner of an improved site or an agricultural site only receives what is left after using the income to pay out the other production factors. The equity capital investor receives a residual income as well: the profit. This is not an analogy, but a homology. Rents are the very 'core' of company profits (Loehr 2013a, 2013b), and at least some economists concur with the interpretation of profits as an economic rent (Daepp and Schaltegger 2004). Hence, first and foremost, company profit reflects the rent-earning capacity of its portfolio of key assets, as Table 8:4 illustrates.

Table 8:4

Key assets, rents and profits
(modified from Loehr 2013b, Table 2)

Assets	Liabilities	Economic base
Exclusive initial investments/ key assets (e.g. land): rent as residual income	Equity: profit as residual income (includes: rent, imputed employer's salaries and risk premium)	Factor land in a broad sense, other key assets
Follow-up investments (e.g. improvements of sites)	Loans: Interest as contract income	Factor capital

Textbooks do not even discuss the common features of rents and profits due to the inconsistencies of the mainstream approach. Important sticking points are, for instance, the famous microeconomic crossover of demand and supply and the concepts of consumer rents and producer rents. Here, I refrain from criticizing the common interpretation of the demand curve, although the neoclassical concept is problematic (cf. Keen 2004). Instead, I focus on the upward-sloping supply curve. The standard theory derives this curve by aggregating the rising marginal cost curves of the individual firms. Sraffa (1926) was one of the first economists who argued against this concept. His criticism was picked up by Keen (2004: 54). Gutenberg (1983) advanced considerable theoretical arguments against the generalization of rising marginal costs. Indeed, there is no empirical evidence for the dominance of rising marginal costs considered at the level of individual firms, as neoclassical theory asserts (Gutenberg 1983: 390-394; Monopolkommission, 1986). Empirically, the marginal cost curve seems to run parallel to the X-axis in most cases (Gutenberg, 1983: 390).

However, adding up flat individual marginal cost curves would result in a flat market supply curve. But the total market supply curve in so-called competitive markets cannot be generally flat. In this case, no producer rent would exist at company level. Since the producer rent measures the contribution margin of a company, the sum of contribution margins (as the difference between market prices and marginal costs) would tend toward zero. This conclusion is obviously completely absurd. It seems that we are running into a dilemma (Loehr 2013b):

➤ On the one hand, from an individual company's view, the arguments against a rising marginal cost curve are of convincing theoretical coherence and overwhelming empirical evidence.

➤ On the other hand, from the viewpoint of the economy as a whole, there must obviously be something like a producer rent.

The contradiction might be resolved by referring to elementary findings of classical theory.

Classical economists knew that the best locations were occupied first. With rising production, more and more producers have to switch to second- and third-best locations. At each of these locations, production is carried out with more-or-less constant marginal costs (and falling average costs). However, the production costs of the second-best location are higher than at the best location, and the production costs of the third-best location will exceed those of the second-best location (Gaffney 1994: 50-51). Similar patterns can also be observed for other key assets. If, for example, licenses for process patents are no longer available, there is no access to the best technology. Hence second- or third-best technology has to be used. As a consequence, the production costs will be higher compared with using the best technology.

Thus the producer rent in so-called competitive markets is basically nothing other than the differential rent which is connected with the key assets – in particular land (Loehr 2013a, 2013b). Alfred Marshall (1893) noted: 'Producer's surplus is a convenient name for the genus of which the rent of land is the leading species.'

As mentioned above, land and other key assets are exclusive. So also are (land) rents, as they can hardly be challenged by competition. In contrast, according to neoclassical theory profits can basically be contested in a competitive economy, at least in the long run. If this were true, the correlation between the value of land and the value of company shares should not be too high – at least in the long run. However, if the core of the profits is an economic rent, the power of competition would be limited and a high correlation is to be expected. Elsewhere (Loehr 2013b), I referred to indications taken from the studies of Stone and Ziemba (1993), who assessed the relationship between land prices and stock prices in Japan. Commercial land, in particular, had a close connection to stock prices. According to Ziemba (1991), the correlation was about 0.99 from 1955 until 1988. During that time, land was the most important key asset. Patents became important in a later period, after the TRIPS agreement was put in place (1995). Thereafter, apparently a 'diffusion' of the land rent to other key assets took place. As a consequence, the correlation between land and company values decreased. However, more research is necessary in this regard.

Also in other countries, any significant deviation between the development of land and stock prices must be caused by differences in the development of land rents and profits – at least in the long run. This conclusion is obvious if we assume that other relevant factors such as general inflation or the development of interest rates have similar effects on the prices of land and stocks. In Germany, the correlation between the stock index (DAX) and the real estate index was some 0.72 between 2000 and 2014 (significance level: 0.01). In the UK (from 1966 until 2011), the correlation between the FTSE 100 Index and the House Price Index was about 0.83 (significance level: 0.01; Loehr 2013b).

Hence, on average, equity seems to reflect the accessibility to and the value of the key assets, which are exclusive real options. When they are exercised, they earn exclusive (land) rents, which are the core of the company profits. Since corporations have particularly good access to equity, their chance of getting a large piece of the 'cake' of economic rents is correspondingly high.

The Costs

'There is no such thing as a free lunch.' Whereas rents are reaped privately, costs are externalized. On the one hand, this refers to costs of valorization of key assets. For example, any location would not be valuable without positive externalities of agglomeration (with congestion costs in parallel), the appropriation of the forces of nature (e.g. with externalized costs of degradation) or the efforts of the public (costs of infrastructure; Gaffney 1970: 195; Gaffney 1994: 50). Considering the latter, the state can even be considered as a 'rent-creating institution' (Harrison, 2006). Substantially all patents are based on a recombination of some parts of knowledge, which is a common good, created by efforts of the community. Generally, key assets in private hands privatize the benefits of public efforts.

In addition, corporations, in particular, cause further costs, as Gaffney stresses (Gaffney 1970; Gaffney 1994). For instance, limited liability transfers risk costs of operations onto third parties. The special ability to collect equity drives concentration and hampers competition at the expense of suppliers or consumers (Loehr 2014).

Debunking Land Rents:
Case Studies

I will illustrate the arguments provided above with three case studies; the fourth case, on the energy sector, appears as an appendix. These are taken from Germany.

If social insurance contributions are included, Germany might be considered a high-tax country. In particular, the tax wedge between total labour costs to the employer and the corresponding net take-home pay for average single workers without children was the third-highest of all OECD countries in 2015 (OECD 2015). As Mason Gaffney (1994: 370-381) stressed with his 'ATCOR' and 'EBCOR' principles, higher taxation means lower land rents and land values. Such low land values are an important reason why the land question is not under particular observation in Germany. This makes it all the more interesting to assess whether land plays an important role as a key company asset in Germany.

McDonald-land: *I'm lovin' it*

As an experiment, ask people: 'What is the business of McDonald's?' Probably 99% of them will answer: 'Of course, McDonald's is a burger joint.' *Wrong!* McDonald's is one of the world's biggest real estate companies (Love 1987). McDonald's first chief executive, Harry Sonneborn, reportedly told investors: 'The only reason we sell 15¢ hamburgers is because they are the greatest provider of revenue from which our tenants can pay us rent' (Jargon 2015). The company owns more than one-third of the sites on which the 30,000 branches are located worldwide. Although the other sites have been leased, the company also benefits from location advantages in a similar way as discounters on leased sites are doing (on which, see more below). Hence property and strategically important locations are at the core of McDonald's corporate policy – regardless of whether McDonald's itself or a franchisee carries out the operations. In 2015, a proposal by a large shareholder to spin off the real estate activities into a real estate investment trust ('McDonald-land') was rejected by the company. Depending on the location, the land rents differ. However, it is estimated that McDonald's gets more cash from the land rents than from other franchise fees.

In simplified terms, McDonald's makes money on real estate via two methods:

➤ It buys and sells properties. Often these are restaurant lots, but this is not necessarily always the case. McDonald's will buy properties that it feels are, or will be, sought-after locations. Of course it sells properties that are under-performing.

➤ On top of the franchise fee that McDonald's charges its franchisees to use the 'McDonald's' name (in Germany, this is usually a service fee of 5% of net sales: McDonald's 2015), it charges rent to the franchisees to use the corporately owned properties (Dadlani 2008). This is because normally McDonald's buys the restaurant lots and pays the costs for setting up the restaurant building. The franchise rights are granted within a leasehold contract for a period of normally 20 years. Thus the land rent from the restaurants is the core of the profits of McDonald's (Loehr 2013a). Rental income from franchisees accounted for more than one-fifth of the group's $27.4 billion in total revenue in 2014 – it represents a growing part of its business. Rent payments from franchisees have risen 26% to $6.1 billion over the five years to 2014. In 2014, the McDonald's group received $0.08 billion from initial fees from the lessees (compensation for initial investments in the restaurant lot made by McDonald's), $3.09 billion from royalties and $6.11 billion from renting out property (Jargon 2015).

No wonder that McDonald's outperforms the competitors (N.N./ Aktiencheck 2013). In terms of the mirror hypothesis, in 2014 McDonald's' key assets amounted to 36% of total assets, with equity at 37% (McDonald's 2014).

One may admire the corporate strategy of McDonald's. However, McDonald's makes use of location advantages that have been created by the public, which include agglomeration, infrastructure etc. It makes use of these advantages without appropriate compensation. Moreover, many other costs are externalized. This happens in the value chain by backwards integration, which means by controlling the resource base. Many of the products cause high external costs in environmental and social terms. If all these damages were compensated, the price of a burger would have to be multiplied.

Supermarkets and discounters

Public discussion in Germany about the shortcomings of the economic system is focused on money and banks. These aspects are important.

However, the richest Germans are not bankers but the owners of production and distribution companies. They made their fortune not in monopolistic but in highly competitive markets. The wealth of the heirs of the Albrecht brothers ('Aldi' discounters) has been estimated at about €35 bn. (N.N./Huffington Post 2013), while the assets of Dieter Schwarz ('Lidl' discounters and others) are valued at some €11 bn. They are among the richest families in the world.

How are mere discounters able to triumph commercially? The standard answer in textbooks refers to their high efficiency. Typically, such discounters focus on a narrow product range of daily necessities with a high turnover. The merchandise is presented in a simple way. Successful discounters have a high share of retail brands instead of producer brands – a consequence of the advancing backwards-integration of the value chain. In the value chain, logistics is highly efficient (low transportation costs). Within this concept, discounters achieve a high floor-space turnover in combination with low personnel costs.

There is also another reason why discounters seem to be a striking counter-example to our thesis that land rents are the core of economic profits. In Germany, discounters generally operate on leased land. The land rents go into the pockets of other private stakeholders; it is not the owners of the discounter chains who seem to be the beneficiaries from land rents. Is Mason Gaffney wrong (at least for Germany) when he states that retail chains are mainly land based (Gaffney 1970: 167)? I do not think so. For German discounters, the key to success is the occupation of many sites at the right location, as is the case for distribution companies. The secret of the success of the discounters is the difference between the subjective value of the suitable sites for the discounter chains and the market value.

The strategy of discounter chains is the multiplication of a certain business concept. This is why they occupy new locations. And with every new location, *their* purchasing power is increased. For the 'battle' of the discounters is not won on the consumer side of their business, but by putting pressure on their suppliers.

More branches need more locations, which in the past have been granted generously to the established discounter chains by the land use planners. In Germany, just four companies (Edeka, Rewe, Aldi and the Schwarz group with Lidl and Kaufland) control about 85% of the suitable locations – and thereby the food retail market (German Federal Cartel Office 2014; Bialdiga 2014). It is possible to reach a discounter from any

place in Germany within a ten-minute drive by car. The occupation of
enough suitable locations is an important as well as underestimated
success factor. No success without favourable locations – as the failure of
Walmart in Germany impressively demonstrated (Knorr and Arndt 2003).

Most of the discounters are located at the periphery of the agglomerations, where the location rents are comparatively low. Such large-scale
retailers replace capital and labour with land, which is also a consequence
of the high relative prices of the mobile factors of production due to
conventional taxation (Gaffney 1970: 193-194). Nonetheless, the chosen
locations normally have good access to highways and transport networks,
and they provide convenient parking facilities. Car owners find it much
more convenient to travel to a discounter than to shop in the city centre
where they have to carry the heavy bags long distances to the few available
parking places. Thus discounters save transportation costs and, due to
their agglomeration at certain locations, costs of searching, to the benefit
of the customers. This means they attract a huge share of the purchasing
power of the central locations, despite being located in the periphery.

The discounters pay comparatively low land rents in such peripheral
locations. Sucking the demand from the centre and paying the costs
of land of the periphery – that is the reason why the subjective values of
the leased locations for the discounters by far exceed the market values
for the owners. In case of a merger or acquisition, the financial statements
do not show this difference in 'property' but in 'intangible assets' ('goodwill'). The difference between the low market value and the high subjective value on the one hand along with the flexibility of leasehold in case
of market changes on the other hand are important reasons why German
discounters prefer leasing instead of buying.

Paying the land rents of the periphery and taking the purchasing power
of the centre – this mismatch of benefits and costs has consequences.
In order to be profitable, a full-range provider with revenues of €5,000
per sq m and ca. 1,500 sq m of space needs revenues of at least €7.5m in
Germany (NABU, n.d.). This is the purchasing power for food of about
5,000 habitants. Almost the same holds true for a discounter with
800 sq m of space, which has 1.5 to 2 times as much space productivity
as a full-range provider. Two or three such discounters in the suburbs of
a sub-central city with maybe 20,000 habitants may erase the smaller
owner-run food shops in the centre. This is one important reason
why the cores of many smaller cities in Germany are slowly dying.
In particular, more and more elderly people without cars are missing

shopping opportunities for their daily needs. Meanwhile, many municipalities recognize the mistakes they have made in the past with their generous land use planning in favour of non-integrated locations for discounters and full-range providers. However, due to German planning law it is almost impossible to correct these mistakes. Once developed as a commercial area and privatized, the land use is fixed – a one-way street.

Time slots at coordinated airports

Land rents are of high importance for the least grounded industry of all – the aviation industry. I do not propose to discuss airports themselves, which not only benefit from airport and infrastructure fees but also from renting out parking spaces and shops. For Fraport AG, which runs Frankfurt Airport, shops are by far the highest contributor to EBIT (earnings before interests and taxes) and more important than the airport and infrastructure fees (Fraport 2015a, Table 16 and 1: 60, graph 9). I also do not delve into the fact that the parking and landing fees include, for instance, an add-on for noise, which can also be interpreted as a species of land rent (the residents who suffer from that noise, however, do not see any of that money: Fraport 2015b).

Instead, I shall consider the time dimension of 'land' for aviation (Gaffney 1994: 43). At so called 'coordinated airports', the time slots for starting and landing are scarce; thus the take-off and landing rights have to be allocated to the competing airlines in some way. So far, in the US only three airports (LaGuardia and John F. Kennedy in New York and Reagan Washington National in Washington D.C.) are coordinated airports. In the European Union, all hub airports and a lot of hub-supporting airports are coordinated (Olbrich et al. 2009: 208). Those airlines which are allowed to start and land at favourable times do better business than their competitors. Hence the value of favourable time slots, which are normally valid for one scheduling period (N.N./Airliners.de 2009), might be quite high – in some cases it might be the major share of the value of an airline company and exceed the value of the aircraft fleet. In 2007, for example, one time slot was reported to be valued at €41m (Olbrich et al. 2009: 208, n.7). However, according to IATA rules, time slots are allocated basically by means of 'grandfathering'. An airline company to which the same right was allocated twice in succession is granted the same right in each subsequent period. In most cases, the airlines only pay an administration fee, which is a fraction of the value of the time slot. The beneficiaries are the big and established airline companies. The only restriction on the 'grandfather' rule is the 'use or lose rule', according to which a company may lose its rights if it uses them for less than 80% of the current period (Zirm 2011:12). However, this rule might be circumvented by selling the right. Hence the time slots are basically tradable assets which are allocated to the biggest airline companies for free, according to the IATA rules (Zirm 2011: 11, 16). The lost revenues are covered by taxpayers. Under the rules for allocating time slots, newcomers do not have a real chance of entering the market. This, in turn, reduces the competition faced by the established airline companies. Not surprisingly, established airlines prefer the grand-fathering system for allocating time slots (Zirm 2011: 18-20, 71).

Conclusions

Successful companies are rent-taking institutions. What makes firms valuable is the discounting of future income without costs (and risks). This is nothing other than rents, as illuminated by the case studies. If the business concept of any successful company is assessed carefully enough, economic rents will emerge as the core of the profit. The foundation of these rents is what I call 'key assets' – this is land or at least assets with features that are similar to land.

A look at the Forbes list of global high performers substantiates the thesis that the success of companies is based to a high degree on the rents of key assets (Forbes 2015). Considering oil, gas, patents (software) etc., the dependency on key assets is obvious (ExxonMobil, Royal Dutch Shell, Chevron, BHP Billilton, Apple, Microsoft; see also Gaffney 1970: 162-163). JP Morgan as an investment bank also deals with company interests and derivatives on other key assets. Telecom services (Vodafone) are based to a large degree on telephone networks, locations and intellectual property rights. The so-called 'out-performers' are the most successful rent-seekers.

Meanwhile, business economics is also starting to understand com-panies as a portfolio of real options. Some real options are exclusive keys to economic rents and of strategic importance. If such options are not exercised, other stakeholders might be blocked from access. If they are exercised, economic rents can be collected. Against this background, location-bound industries have an obvious relationship to the original and most important 'key asset', which is land and natural resources. Considering 'footloose industries', this connection is more concealed. Their success is often based on other key assets (particularly patents) or another bias between performance and consideration (as in the discounter example). I showed that the 'sound way' to acquire key assets is basically through equity. Interestingly, a higher debt ratio than expected according to the mirror hypothesis may reflect a leveraged growth strategy, but can also be a sign of a deep crisis. For instance, the high performer Bayer financed some acquisitions in 2014 with debt, whereas the low performing major energy provider RWE financed its record loss in 2013 (€2.8 bn.) with debt (RWE 2014).

If we consider companies as portfolios of real options, we have to take into account that key assets as real options need an underwriter (in contrast to other types of real options). Real options such as land are only valuable for private investors to the extent that the land rents are privatized and the public renounces the yields – although the public valorized the land and created the economic opportunities on it. Privatizing the benefits while pushing the costs onto the public is nothing other than externalization. And externalization is one important reason for market failure. For instance, in principle the bigger the company, the lower the relative effective tax burden. Moreover, the exclusivity of real options means that the concentration of the economy increases and the competitive regime is eroded.

Rent-seeking can also contribute to the decline of large companies. Looking for instance at the energy companies, the 'drug' of economic rents extracted out of the base load power plants caused a deep crisis. In particular RWE (Essen, Germany), did not recognize the sign of the times. The appendix of this chapter tells the story of the rent generating capacity of base load power plants in the past. RWE remained stuck in these rent extracting technologies and thus was left behind in the energy turnaround.

To achieve optimum outcomes, the performance of companies ought to rest on their products and their efficiency, and not on rent-seeking. This could be achieved by skimming off the economic rents by applying the Henry George principle. This means that 'key assets' such as land would be 'decapitalized'; their value would be transferred to the public. This would make access to key assets possible without first commanding a huge amount of equity. The outcome would be an increase in new market entrants, and heightened competition. Furthermore, the public could be compensated for providing the infrastructure on which commercial entities relied for their activities. Rent-seeking would be replaced by improvements in the quality of services provided to customers.

Appendix

Electricity Production: the Greenhouse for Rents

In Germany, the market for electricity is a greenhouse for economic rents. To illustrate why the profits of the large energy producers have been mainly land rents, we shall focus on the example of brown coal-fired plants. Even in the present transition period to renewable energy, brown coal plants remain the backbone of German electricity supply.

On the supply side of the electricity market, the 'merit order' (an operational ranking of the different types of power plants, see Figure 1) is of crucial importance for electricity pricing. In the schematic Figure 1, P* is the equilibrium price for electricity. X* is the equilibrium output.

The merit order starts with the power plants with the lowest marginal costs. Additional power plants with higher marginal costs are switched

Figure 8:1

Merit order and market clearing price

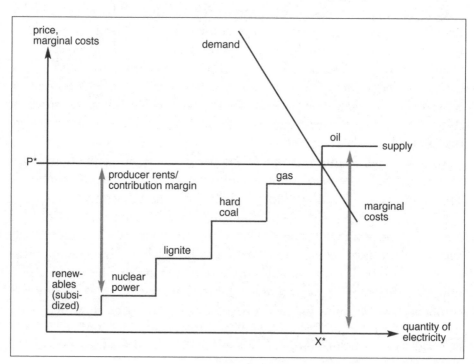

on until the demand is covered. The electricity price is determined by the last offer accepted (market clearing price P*). Base load plants (nuclear power plants, brown coal fired plants) are characterized by huge investments per unit area and high fixed costs, while the marginal costs are quite low. This cost situation is reversed for peak load power plants. In the traditional energy mix, base load power plants (nuclear power, lignite) could earn the highest marginal profits (so called 'contribution margins'), measured by the difference between the electricity market price and low marginal costs. The excess of contribution margins over fixed costs is profit. Hence the contribution margins of those base load power plants that are already amortized are almost pure profit and at the same time almost pure economic rents.

Due to the requirement for high capital investment, firms currently operating base load power plants cannot be easily challenged. Before the phasing out of nuclear energy, about 96% of all base load capacities were owned by the big four electricity suppliers (RWE, E.ON, Vattenfall and EnBW; Vorholz, 2006). Additional competition barriers include the long time span for planning and approval, and the regulatory uncertainties (for example, the past debate about the phasing out of nuclear power and the current debate about phasing out the coal fired plants). Following the decision of the German government to exit nuclear power generation, new nuclear power plants are not being approved. Moreover, the potential for power plants, driven by water power is exhausted in Germany. For these and other reasons, the market for base load power production was basically not contestable for potential competitors. However, the economic rents of base load power plants are nothing other than 'hidden' land rents. For example, due to the high transportation costs of brown coal, such coal-fired plants need an associated brown coal mine (in Germany: traditionally in the Ruhr area, in Central Germany around Halle and Leipzig and in the Lausitz area) or at least an inland port or a railway line nearby. It is no coincidence that the biggest share of the German brown coal resources was owned by RWE, Vattenfall and E.ON. Furthermore, the centres of consumption should not be located more than about 70 km away in order to avoid transmission and distribution losses. Such consumption centres are big agglomerations, as for instance the Ruhr area. Also the connection to the transmission network must be ensured. Tourism and the environment should not be seriously affected. Planning and approval decides if and how much rent may be earned. Not every planned power plant passes the planning and approval process. In brief, a brown coal fired plant can only be set up at very special locations. The availability of such a scarce location is a privilege for the company. It allows it to earn differential rents (which are higher profits, compared to the power plant with the highest marginal costs in use). In essence, these profits are nothing other than privatized land rents. The energy companies are usually able to lease or buy these locations on favourable terms; often, indeed, the locations are sold cheaply by the state.

A significant share of the costs of brown coal fired plants is externalized. (1) The infrastructural services they use are provided by the public. Suitable locations are rare, which means they are valuable. Energy companies secure these locations for only a fraction of their economic value. And so, because the state foregoes income from these scarce locations, the financial deficit is transferred onto other stakeholders (mostly workers). (2) The exploitation fees for the coal are quite low. 3) Environmental and social costs are externalized; the European Emission Trading scheme is only able to internalize a fraction of the external costs caused by air pollution.

Within the proposal to transform German energy policy in favour of green energy, an increasing number of base load power plants are threatened with being replaced by renewable power plants. The 'Big Four' (RWE, E.ON, Vattenfall, EnBW) in the German electricity market have to fear for their economic rents, which have been strongly defended in the past.

Green technologies for energy production also generate economic rents, as illustrated by onshore windmills. An average German farmer may earn a rent of some €300 to €500 per year by leasing out one hectare of farmland. However, if he is allowed to lease out this land to a windmill-operator, he can increase his rent from €30,000 to €50,000 per hectare. This is why, in the past, a huge part of the subsidies of the Renewable Energy Law (Erneuerbare-Energien-Gesetz) have been allocated to landowners. However, this rent-taking is only possible if the land use-plan allows the operation of a windmill on certain sites. This allowance is a privilege, which is granted to the land owners for free. However, these privileges are less concentrated than was the case with the privilege, granted in the past, of operating a base load power plant. Hence they cannot serve as a foundation for concentrated economic power of the kind that arose with the former permissions for operating base load power plants.

References

Bayer (2014), Annual Report 2014 (Geschäftsbericht 2014), Leverkusen, Germany.

Bialdiga, K. (2014), *Kartellamt kritisiert Macht der Lebensmittelketten*, SZ.de, (Sept 24). http://www.sued deutsche.de/wirtschaft/einzelhandel-kartellamt-kritisiert-macht-der-lebensmittelketten-1.2144792

Clark, J.B. (1893), 'The Genesis of Capital', *Yale Review*, 11, pp.302-315.

Dadlani, A. (2008), *McDonald's is a Real Estate Company*, Seeking Alpha, (April 23). http://seeking alpha.com/article/73533-mcdonalds-is-a-real-estate-company

Daepp, M. and Schaltegger, C.A. (2004), *Moderne Steuersysteme – Grundfragen und Systemvorschläge*, Eidgenössische Steuerverwaltung, Bern.

Deutsche Bundesbank (2015), *Hochgerechnete Angaben aus Jahresabschlüssen deutscher Unternehmen*. Statistische Sonderveröffentlichung 5, (May).

Fraport (2015a), Annual Report 2014 (Geschäftsbericht 2014), Frankfurt.

Fraport (2015b), Airport Charges according to Art. 19b Air Traffic Act (LuftVG); Charges for Central Ground Handling Infrastructure, Fraport AG, Frankfurt. http://www.fraport.de/content/fraport/de/misc/binaer/kompetenzen/aviation-services/flug—und-terminalbetrieb/flughafenentgelte-2015/jcr:content.file/entgelte-charges-2015.pdf

Forbes. (2015), *Global Highperformers*. http://www.forbes.com/global2000/list/#tab:overall

Gaffney, M. (1970), 'Adequacy of Land as a Tax Base,' in Holland, D, ed., *The Assessment of Land Value*, Madison: University of Wisconsin Press.

Gaffney, M. (1977), 'Social and Economic Aspects of Foreign Investment in United States Land', *Natural Resources Journal*, 17.

Gaffney, M. (1988/1997), 'Who owns Southern California? Notes by Mason Gaffney on concentration of landholdings', unpublished revised version, (May 3).

Gaffney, M. (1994), 'Land as a Distinctive Factor of Production', in N. Tideman, ed., *Land and Taxation*, London, Shepheard-Walwyn.

Gaffney, M. (2009), 'The Hidden Taxable Capacity of Land: Enough and to Spare', in *International Journal of Social Economics*, 36, pp.328-411.

George, H. (1885), *Fortschritt und Armut*, Otto Hendel, Halle a.d. Saale.

German Federal Statistical Office (Statistisches Bundesamt) (2014), Statistisches Jahrbuch (Statistics Yearbook) 2014, Wiesbaden.

German Federal Cartel Office (2014), Sektoruntersuchung Lebensmitteleinzelhandel – Ergebnisse und Schlussfolgerungen, (Sept 24). http://www.bundeskartellamt.de/SharedDocs/Publikation/DE/Sektoruntersuchungen/Sektoruntersuchung%20LEH-Thesen-PM.pdf?__blob=publication File&v=3

Gutenberg, E. (1983), *Grundlagen der Betriebswirtschaftslehre*, Erster Band: Die Produktion, 24, ed., Berlin/Heidelberg/New York, Springer.

Harrison, F. (2006), *Ricardo's Law: House Prices and the Great Tax Clawback Scam*, Shepheard-Walwyn, London.

Jargon, J. (2015), 'McDonald's Lands in a Real Estate Dilemma', *The Wall Street Journal*, (Aug 25). http://www.wsj.com/articles/mcdonalds-lands-in-a-real-estate-dilemma-1440495181

Johnston, K. (2013), 'The Messy Link between Slave Owners and Modern Management', *Forbes*, (Jan 16). http://www.forbes.com/sites/hbsworkingknowledge/2013/01/16/the-messy-link-between-slave-owners-and-modern-management/#2715e4857a0b6839e01adfa8

Kaserer, C. and Lenz, U. (2009), *Wachstum und Unabhängigkeit durch Eigenkapitalfinanzierung*, Xetra/Deutsche Börse Group, Frankfurt.

Keen, S. (2004), *Debunking Economics – The Naked Emperor of the Social Sciences*, Zed Books, London/New York.

Knight, F.H. (1946/1951), 'Capital and Interest', in W. Feliner, and B. Haley eds., *Readings in the Theory of Income Distribution*, Selected by a Committee of the American Economic Association, The Blakiston Co., Philadelphia.

Knorr, A. and A. Arndt (2003), *Wal-Mart in Deutschland – eine verfehlte Internationalisierungsstrategie*,

Materialien des Wissenschaftsschwerpunktes 'Globalisierung der Weltwirtschaft'. University of Bremen.

Löhr, D. (2013a), *Prinzip Rentenökonomie – wenn Eigentum zu Diebstahl wird*, Metropolis, Marburg.

Löhr, D. (2013b), 'Equity and the hidden factor land: a hypothesis', *Society and Business Review*, 8.

Löhr, D. (2014), 'The hidden rent-seeking capacity of corporations', *International Journal of Social Economics*, 41.

Löhr, D. and Rams, A. (2000), 'Unternehmensbewertung mit Realoptionen: Berücksichtigung strategisch-dynamischer Flexibilität', *Betriebsberater*, 55.

Love, J. (1987), 'Big Macs, Fries, and Real Estate', *Financial Executive* 4.

Marshall, A. (1893), 'On rent', *Economic Journal*, 3.

McDonald's (2014), Annual Report 2014, Oak Brook, Illinois.

McDonald's (2015), Konditionen bei McDonald's.https://www.mcdonalds.de/documents/75202/3597430/Konditionen+bei+McDonald.pdf/d1658131-fc11-4730-b140-d4ddbe32ec40

F. Machlup. (1961/2000), *Die wirtschaftlichen Grundlagen des Patentrechts*, Study written for the Subcommittee on Patents, Trademarks and Copyrights of the US Senate. Reprint in German: *Fragen der Freiheit*, 253.

Modigliani, F. and M.H. Miller (1958), 'The Cost of Capital, Corporate Finance and the Theory of Investment', *American Economic Review*, 48.

Monopolkommission (1986), Hauptgutachten VI (1984/1985), Gesamtwirtschaftliche Chancen und Risiken wachsender Unternehmensgrößen. Nomos, Baden-Baden.

Myers, S.C. (1977), 'Determinants of Corporate Borrowing', *The Journal of Financial Economics*, 5.

NABU (n.d.), Flächenverbrauch durch Einkaufszentren. https://www.nabu.de/umwelt-und-ressourcen/bauen/hintergrund/04787.html

N.N./Airliners.de (2009), Zeitnischen – das Gold für die Luftfahrt. Airliners.de, (Aug 12). http://www.airliners.de/slots---das-gold-fuer-die-luftfahrt/18810

N.N./Aktiencheck (2013), O.V., McDonald's-Aktie: Kampf um 100-Dollar-Marke! in Aktiencheck.de vom (Nov 15). http://www.aktiencheck.de/exklusiv/Artikel-McDonald_s_Aktie_Kampf_um_100_Dollar_Marke-5366537

N.N./The Huffington Post (2013), 'Die 20 reichsten Deutschen', *The Huffington Post*, (Oct 14). http://www.huffingtonpost.de/2013/10/10/reichste-deutsche_n_4075441.html

OECD (2015), *Taxing Wages 2015 – Germany*. http://www.oecd.org/germany/taxing-wages-germany.pdf

Olbrich, M., Dallmayr, D and Zilch, C. (2009), 'Zur IFRS-Bilanzierung immaterieller Vermögenswerte aufgrund von immateriellen Zuwendungen – eine Analyse am Beispiel von Start-und Landerechten', *Betriebswirtschaftliche Forschung und Praxis*, 61.

Rognlie, M. (2015), 'Deciphering the fall and rise in the net capital share', BPEA conference draft, (March 19-20). http://www.brookings.edu/~/media/projects/bpea/spring-2015/2015a_rognlie.pdf

RWE (2014), Annual Report 2014 (Geschäftsbericht 2014), Essen.

Schwartz, E. S. (2003), *Patents and R&D as Real Options*, NBER Working Paper 10114, (November). http://www.nber.org/papers/w10114.

Sotelo, R. (1995), 'Die WertV ist tot, es lebe die WertV', *Grundstücksmarkt und Grundstückswert*, 6.

Sraffa, P. (1926), 'The Law of Returns under Competitive Conditions', *Economic Journal*, 40, pp.538-550.

Stone, D. and Ziemba, W.T. (1993), 'Land and Stock Prices in Japan', *Journal of Economic Perspectives*, 7, pp.149-165.

Vorholz, F. (2006), 'Vom Stromschlag getroffen. Verbraucher, Firmen – das ganze Land leidet unter den hohen Preisen der Energieversorger', *Die Zeit*, 20.07.

Ziemba, W.T. (1991), 'The Chicken or the Egg: Land and Stock Prices in Japan', in W.T. Ziemba, W. Bailey and Y. Hamao, eds., *Japanese Financial Market Research*, North Holland: Amsterdam.

Zirm, M. (2011), *Die Vergabe von Start- und Landerechten auf Flughäfen – Internationale, europäische und nationale Regelwerke*, VDM Verlag Dr. Müller, Saarbrücken.

9

Tax Dodging and the Coming Tax Wars

TERRY DWYER

T HE 21ST century started as a century of wars with 9/11 (9 September 2001). The late 20th century 'war on drugs' has variously expanded into 'war on terrorism', war on 'terrorist financing', war on 'money laundering' and since the Global Financial Crisis of 2007 (GFC) has expanded further into the 'war on tax cheats'.

The 'war on tax cheats' generates almost universal public approval. It is therefore not surprising that international organisations and government talkfests such as the OECD (Organisation for Economic Co-operation and Development) and the G20 (Group of 20) have found it easy to persuade most governments to sign up to a coordinated assault against personal and corporate 'tax dodgers'. The OECD/G20 attacks on 'tax havens' and personal and corporate 'tax dodgers' through 'initiatives' for Automatic Exchange of taxpayer Information (AEOI) and against Base Erosion and Profit Shifting (BEPS) have met with virtually universal and uncritical acceptance and proceeded at a pace which would have been unthinkable 20 years ago. Politicians anticipate an easy increase in revenue from 'enforcement of existing tax laws' while ordinary taxpayers anticipate lower (or at least not increased) tax burdens because somebody else will be paying.

But before one goes to war, any rational person would ask for an account of the benefits and the costs. Rational wars are fought to plunder or enslave other peoples. However, a war may be rational from the point of view of some interest groups in society even though irrational for society as a whole. Groups who are losers from a war may be among the most enthusiastic for its commencement.

I argue here that this 'war on tax cheats' is unfortunate and that the whole project spawned by the OECD (1998) and adopted by the G20 (2010, para 39) for wiping out tax havens and catching personal and corporate tax dodgers is fundamentally misconceived and legally illegitimate. Further, far from being a victimless war against social miscreants, it is a serious 'tax war' between sovereign nations, one which risks escalation from a 'phoney war' of words into real economic wars as damaging to the world as the trade wars of the 1930s. Tax wars, like tariff wars, start out as wars of plunder and end with mutual impoverishment for many and riches for a few. By contrast, I will explain why a fiscal system based on the taxation of rent elegantly avoids all cross-border tax conflicts and conforms to legal norms regarding national and private rights – as well as being far more economically efficient.

The Basic Problem of International Tax

The basic problem (if it is a problem) of international tax is that there is no such thing. Taxation is a sovereign act. It is the act of a sovereign with power to raise debts enforceable against his subjects, or against persons within his territory, as their contributions to his fisc. Under constitutional governments, the sovereign usually requires some form of consent from the governed. Maitland (1920: 67-68, 95) observes that in English law the idea that taxation is a free-will offering to the lord and a gift by consent (originally individual consent) lies deep in English history and is the basis of the later demand that such consent to grants, aids or subsidies for the Crown had to be sought from elected representatives as authorised agents of the common people. It is interesting to note that abbots and bishops sometimes refused to make gifts to the King – he was meant to live 'off his own' (Blackstone [1765-1783: I.8:306], Coffield [1970], Sabine [1980]).

Sovereignty is inherently territorial. A sovereign can be reasonably sure that he can make his commands obeyed within his sovereign territory: he cannot be sure that his commands (even when directed to his subjects) will be obeyed, if obedience depends upon things being done elsewhere. Further, a command directed to a subject carrying out an activity elsewhere may be countered by another sovereign's commands or claims.

Thus the sovereign of country A may say that his subjects shall pay income tax on income they derive from country B, but the sovereign of country B may say they should pay income tax to him first (and, perhaps, to no one else). If the sovereign of country B declines to assist the sovereign of country A, that sovereign may find his extra-territorial tax demands are futile, whether or not the subjects of country A legally or illegally arrange their affairs in country B so that their income from country B is not remitted to or reportable to the sovereign of country A. The sovereign of country A is like King Canute commanding the incoming tide to halt but, unlike Canute, not having the wisdom to understand the limit of his powers.

It is a basic principle of public international law that no sovereign must obey another. While most sovereigns do not go out of their way to obstruct the commands of other sovereigns, they are under no obligation whatsoever to assist them and they are certainly under no obligation to assist any other sovereign collect his taxes upon transactions taking place within their territory. To collect taxes within your country for another country is to be its vassal or subject State, much as its defeated foes rendered tribute to the Roman Empire.

Thus arise unavoidable problems of international taxation – extra-territoriality and double taxation. You may not know where income is earned or generated, or where it is received or earned, or by whom and, even when you do know, you may find another sovereign who thinks he has the prior right to tax it – or to exempt it. Either way, he is under no obligation to you to enforce your income or value added or any other taxes within his territory. In fact, it is most likely in his interest not to do so. When Louis XIV was punishing Huguenots, His Britannic Majesty across the English Channel was happy to welcome them and profit from their skills and industry. Nor did the Swiss Confederation ever have any interest in turning away refugees and their money from European wars or conflicts from the French Revolution through the revolutions of 1848 to past World War II.

In theory, if all countries could agree in every case on what was income, the source of that income, and all agreed only to tax income arising in each one's country, there would be no international income tax conflicts. That is far from the facts of life – and similar problems arise with value added taxes.

Residence and Source

When Pitt the Younger invented income taxation in 1798 to finance Great Britain's resistance to Napoleon, he had to consider what kinds of income to tax. He adopted a schedular system under which incomes were classified as rent, trading profits or emoluments of employment or interest on moneys etc. He did not attempt to tax income arising outside Great Britain but did seek to tax the designated classes of income if received in Great Britain (the origin of the British remittance system of taxation of overseas income).

Notwithstanding recent denunciation of the 'remittance system', Pitt the Younger was not a fool. One assumes he did not want to tax directly income arising overseas in the colonies given that he was acutely aware of the American Revolution and Pitt the Elder's (1775, 1776) spirited support, drawn from ancient precedent, for resistance by colonies to extraterritorial taxation by the mother country, a resistance based on 'the great, fundamental, essential maxim of your liberties, that no subject of England shall be taxed but by his own consent'. Yet Pitt the Younger would have been well aware of the great West Indian sugar barons and East India nabobs then living in London on their overseas profits. Accordingly, while exempting ordinary wage earners, he sought to tax incomes arising from overseas, without infringing upon colonial fiscal autonomy, by taxing such incomes when remitted into Great Britain.

Of course, things change and it is an irony of history that the remittance system is now seen as a form of 'onshore tax haven' for Arab and Russian billionaires and expatriate bankers living in London without paying anything like the tax paid by most of Her Majesty's subjects. Be that as it may, it nicely illustrates the problem which has been with income tax from the very start.

If you want to tax income, you have to define your tax base with legal precision. You have to define 'income'. You have to define the taxing point, you have to define the taxpayer and you have to define when and how it is to be collected. Because income does not exist in a state of nature (contrary to the naive illusions of some economists) and because any tax has to be supported by a law which defines these things, questions immediately emerge. What is 'income'? When is income 'income'? Is income still income after it has been invested somewhere else? Who is the owner of the income? Where does that owner live? What nationality does that owner have? Is that owner one of our subjects or citizens? Where is the income generated?

Thus every income tax system has to contemplate at the very least, the *residence* of the taxpayer and the *source* of his income. There is very little point in trying to tax foreigners living in other countries on income they get and spend outside your borders. They and their governments would laugh at you. Hence most countries seize upon who is within their territorial jurisdiction – that is to say, who is 'resident' within their country. It would be absurd to tax your own citizens but to exempt foreign merchants living within your country and making profits from trading within it.

Residence seems an easy concept. Most of us have only one home. Yet the simple concept of residence quickly became a battleground of litigation and remains so. Is a man who has his house in Ireland but visits London every week for business a UK resident or not? Is a billionaire, who has four houses and spends his time across them most years, a resident of any country or a vagabond with no fixed residence? Thus each country has to create, whether by legislation or by case law, rules as to when an individual is considered resident and how residence is gained or lost for tax purposes. The problem becomes even more severe when we look at companies. Is a company 'tax resident' in the place where it is been incorporated (the US tax law test)? Or is it resident in the place where it has its 'central management and control', usually where the Board of Directors meets to conduct its business (the traditional UK test)? Or is it neither of these places or both? What happens if two countries adopt different tests and both consider the company a tax resident? Who gets to tax the company's income?

The problems of residence are bad enough but the question of the *source* of income is worse. Does a wage or salary earner get his income where he signs his contract of employment, where he is paid or where he performs his work or his duties or in the country whose law governs the contract of employment or where he is appointed to an office? This is a non-trivial question. There are many thousands of individuals working around the world under contracts of employment entered into in country A, who are paid in country B and may be working in country C (two examples are international civil servants and offshore oil workers).

Is the source of interest income where the interest is paid, where the loan contract is made, or where the security (if any) for the loan is given, or where the loan funds are made available to the borrower? Each of these places may be different.

Even better, let us ask ourselves where trading profits arise. Do they arise where the contract of sale is made, where payment is made, where the contract is performed or where the inputs or value-added are injected? This was the problem the Vestey brothers put to the post-World War I Royal Commission into Income Tax and to which they never got a satisfactory answer (Shaxson 2012: 37-38). Unlike most taxpayers unhappy with bureaucratic non-answers, they resorted to self-help and engaged the assistance of lawyers, making sure the Vestey family did not pay UK tax on overseas income for decades (Blue Star Line 2016). The answers to these questions are thus not merely of academic interest to economists (who often lose the questions in their models) but also to taxpayers and tax lawyers (who are acutely aware of them, find the practical answers and put them to good use for their clients).

The reality is that once there is a cross-border dimension to income tax, some form of international agreement or unilateral concession on countries' respective taxing rights is absolutely necessary unless nations wish to see trade and commerce destroyed altogether in many cases.

The original solution to problems of international double taxation was unilateral. The home country, taxing on the basis of residence, would exempt foreign income or give credit to its residents for the foreign tax they had paid on foreign income. For example, within the British Empire, the Australian colonies gave unilateral credit to colonial taxpayers deriving UK income which had been taxed already by the UK. Unilateral tax relief for foreign taxes on foreign income is a political and economic necessity for countries (such as the UK and USA) which have companies with trading interests across the world. Interestingly, the USA has spent much effort over the years trying to tax foreign income, but at the same time has tried to mitigate the adverse effects on American exports. The net result may be that the USA gets no tax revenue from its foreign tax regime because the USA credits foreign taxes and allows active income of subsidiaries to remain untaxed (Grubert and Mutti, 1995). Yet the use by US companies of low rate tax havens may eventually even enhance US tax collections (Hines and Rice, 1994).

Double Tax Treaties

In the 1920s, the League of Nations promoted model income tax treaties which divided up income taxing rights between residence and source countries. The general idea was that tax primacy would remain with the residence countries (where the taxpayer lived and enjoyed public services from the expenditure of that money), while the source countries would be allowed to levy taxes on income arising within their borders up to a point at which residence countries would be obliged to give credit against their own taxes so that there was no double taxation. Essentially it was a colonial model which reflected the 19th century export of capital. It was designed to allow the Mother Country (such as the UK) to raise the taxes it needed on overseas income to build ships to enforce the Pax Britannica. Since World War II, it has sustained the Pax Americana. This model has remained essentially unchanged to the present day notwithstanding many permutations.

It becomes immediately obvious that the historical tax treaty model discriminates against the source countries in favour of the residence countries by limiting the withholding taxes which source countries are allowed to impose.

Areas of particular difficulty arise with dual residents (whether persons or companies) and the source of trading profits. In the case of dual resident companies, primacy may be given in treaty 'tiebreakers' to either the place of 'central management and control' (reflecting the traditional UK approach) or to the 'place of incorporation' (reflecting the US approach).

Trading profits, as Adam Smith (1776: Ch V ii f: 848-849) foresaw, are difficult and elusive to tax. The historical solution to the problem of 'source' in looking at possible double taxation of trading profits has been to draw a distinction between trading 'with' a country and trading 'within' that country. Thus, most treaties exempt trading profits derived by a taxpayer from a treaty partner unless that taxpayer has created a 'permanent establishment' within the country of apparent source. Because tax treaties have usually reflected the interests of the former Great Powers who were the capital exporters of the 19th and 20th centuries, tax treaties tend to ensure that a permanent establishment is not accidentally established and that various preliminary or ancillary business activities do not amount to the creation of a permanent establishment. Activities such as merely maintaining a representative office, a warehouse or a computer server do not amount to the creation of a permanent establishment or the creation of a taxable presence in a jurisdiction.

Because tax treaties are bilateral agreements between sovereigns, it is not surprising that from time to time they differ. European countries often had zero or very low withholding tax rates on interest or royalty income. Given differences between tax treaties, it was hardly surprising that from the 1950s the practice of treaty shopping arose. Just as litigants or merchants may often choose the jurisdiction in which they commence litigation (forum shopping) or whose law governs a contract or a trust, so multinationals or other taxpayers may choose to create companies or trusts in country A in order to invest or hold assets in country B while all the time they are resident in country C. If the company or trust created in the intermediate country can get a better deal on withholding taxes in country B and country A does not tax the income much, then the ultimate investor in country C can be better off than if the investment were made directly from country C.

After some hesitation about whether treaty shopping was a 'use' or 'abuse' of treaties, some countries and lately the OECD itself have, in recent years, tried to limit such advantageous use of treaties by trying to overlay various tests in order for claimants to benefit from tax treaties, such as a requirement for a real presence for a company or trust or, notably in the case of the United States, requirements about beneficial owners of the entities claiming the benefit of reduced treaty withholding rates. Such tests may defeat the whole purpose of double tax treaties by resurrecting disguised double taxation.

Paradoxically, while most countries were anxious to tax the foreign income of their residents, they were equally anxious to promote exports and the trading activities of their own companies or businesses. Accordingly, many countries either unilaterally exempted or deferred taxation on foreign earnings until such time as the earnings were repatriated to the home country (a modern version of Pitt's remittance system). Some countries, notably in Latin America, even adhered historically to a strict territorial concept of taxation where they unilaterally exempted foreign source income on the basis that it was not really theirs to tax, an attitude shared by Hong Kong's colonial Inland Revenue Ordinance (which has been crucial to the rise of Hong Kong as a world financial centre and which Singapore has moved towards, effectively perfecting its remittance system).

In this international tax universe, 'tax havens', such as Switzerland, Hong Kong, Singapore, the Cayman Islands, the Channel Islands and many other places, were happy to profit as conduits through which investments might be made or trade conducted. Later on, countries such as Ireland decided to lower their company tax rates and join 'tax havens' in the competition to become locations for base holding companies and multinational group trading activities. (Many countries dislike the term 'tax haven' but it has no clearly defined meaning. Australia, for example, is a death duty haven. Perhaps the simplest definition is 'a country not as greedy and stupid as you are').

Originally most tax havens did not have any tax treaties with high tax countries and the price of using the tax haven could be to suffer a high withholding tax rate (e.g. 30%) on income coming into that tax haven. Countries such as Ireland, the Netherlands or Luxembourg had many tax treaties and income flowing into them might well enjoy very low withholding rates of zero, 5% or 10% as opposed to 15%, 20% or 30%. Furthermore, these and other countries such as Cyprus or Malta are members of the European Union and enterprises established within those countries have the benefit of free movement of capital and trade within the EU.

Few people (apart from OECD bureaucrats peddling their 1998 'Harmful Tax Competition' agenda) really worried much about this state of affairs until the global financial crisis of 2008 and the collapse of tax revenues, notably in European welfare states. While many countries had been going bankrupt slowly, the global financial crisis reduced substantially the scope for pretending there was no long-term fiscal problem in many European countries. Similarly, the United States, facing the fiscal burden of being the world's policeman in the age of post-Cold War terrorism (just as it was hoping to get a fiscal dividend from the end of the Cold War), showed renewed interest in offshore tax evasion by US taxpayers.

Accordingly, it was time for the 'big countries' to demonise the little countries which happened to be tax havens. All the big countries and their OECD advisers and later the G20 happily subscribed to the idea that wiping out international tax avoidance would help refill their coffers and be a politically costless way of raising revenue and fixing deficits.

Unfortunately, this politico/economic agenda is as simple-minded as it is simple. It is potentially extremely destructive of world trade and prosperity but, worse, of national sovereignty, constitutional government and the most basic privacy rights of citizens across the globe (as recognized in part even by sympathetic commentators [Grinberg, Itai & Pauwelyn, Joost, 2015]).

First, it is a delusion to think that billions of dollars of untaxed income sits in tax havens. Most tax haven transactions are designed to eliminate double taxation or to defer taxation rather than eliminate it permanently. Tax havens are usually merely conduits for transactions between other countries. This becomes obvious once one looks at the example of banking. An international bank may borrow millions from a Eurodollar offering in London. While it may not have to withhold tax on interest paid to investors, they will have to pay tax on the interest. When those Eurodollar proceeds are placed in a Cayman Islands branch, they may be lent to a business in the USA or Europe or anywhere else. Wherever the funds are lent, the chances are that the country of residence of the borrower will demand some kind of withholding tax as a condition of deductibility of the interest. True, that rate of withholding tax may not be at the top marginal tax rate, but in the case of a tax haven, will likely be at 10% to 30%. So *some* tax will be being collected both in the country where the funds are used and in the country where the funds were originally borrowed. It may not be as much tax as would be collected if the money had been lent directly from one country to the other, but it will rarely be zero.

Turning to trading profits, it is true that with the skilful use of tax treaty definitions, some great American corporations such as Apple and Google have been able to avoid much source country tax, both in European jurisdictions and elsewhere. But what is almost invariably forgotten is that the US Treasury is looking over their shoulders with keen interest. Given that the USA is the country of residence of the ultimate owning corporation of many trading subsidiaries, what we are looking at is not tax avoidance or tax evasion but tax deferral.

At the end of the day, every dollar of tax avoided in Europe by Apple or Google adds to the pool of overseas profits of their subsidiaries and stands liable to pay US tax when repatriated back to the US parent to pay dividends. When Apple pays a settlement to Italian tax investigators to satisfy alleged Italian tax debts (Guardian 2015), those tax payments are most likely creditable against US income tax on repatriated earnings – the US Treasury ultimately pays, not Apple.

That is why the US Treasury and, more importantly, the US Senate are starting to feel that the whole OECD 'base erosion and profit shifting' (BEPS) agenda to combat so-called corporate tax dodging is an attempt by European countries to have a free lunch at the expense of the US Treasury (Rubin 2016). The first signs of the emerging tax wars are becoming visible as the US Treasury attacks the EU, and other nations take note (*Shanghai Daily*, 2016).

This brings us brutally back to the starting point – all taxation is fundamentally a sovereign act. What the OECD has marked out since

1998 is a road to war – a war for treasure. Sovereign countries are in conflict. There are no 'Treasure Islands' where they may find hidden loot to share – and, even if there were, one might recall Adam Smith's (1776, I.xi.n; 256) observations on the failure of treasure to make Spain truly rich. The vast bulk of the money flowing through tax havens has gone on to be invested in other G20 or OECD economies.

> *What the OECD has marked out since 1998 is a road to war – a war for treasure. Sovereign countries are in conflict. There are no 'Treasure Islands' where they may find hidden loot to share.*

What is really happening in the aftermath of the global financial crisis is an acceleration of the underlying tension between residence and source countries. The European countries used to see themselves as capital exporters rather than source countries. Now they see themselves a source countries being exploited by American corporations representing a capital exporter.

The United States, on the other hand, sees itself as having provided the Europeans for over 70 years with a nuclear umbrella and low defence expenses under which they have erected their demographically unsustainable welfare states. A United States Senator may legitimately ask why the US should assist European countries tax Google or Apple, thereby reducing US tax revenues, when it is the US which bears the burden (whether sensibly accepted or not) of monitoring worldwide terrorism and sending troops and planes to fight it on the ground or bomb it from above?

What we are seeing in international tax is 'policy schizophrenia'. You cannot have it both ways. You cannot say the country of residence has the ultimate power to tax while demanding that you can collect taxes as you wish at source.

The problems of international income taxation in the early 21st century are just as they were nearly 100 years before. The ever-present but latent tension between the 'source' and the 'residence' principles is generating legal and economic folly in international tax policy whereby countries, at the instigation of the OECD, are tearing up centuries of legal precedent and international law. No sovereign has the right to tell another sovereign the latter must aid the collection of taxes by the former. The OECD is promulgating (its own) newly-invented 'international standards' which run clean contrary to the most basic rules of international law

---

Box 9:1

Income Taxation and Trade Wars

It is worth recalling the effects of the US Smoot-Hawley tariff in the 1930s. That unilateral protectionist tariff devastated world trade and made the Great Depression worse. Income tax, no less than tariffs, is a tax on trade. The power to tax is the power to destroy. There is serious risk that the tax wars now emerging between major economies could end up destroying productive trade and investment, disrupting supply chains, reducing productivity and lowering living standards – as well as tax revenues across nations. Tax wars are a 'negative sum game', where those indulging in a 'game of chicken' may end up wiping each other out as well as inflicting collateral damage on bystanders.

(Panama, 2015). The only surprising thing is that so many countries have foolishly endorsed the OECD agenda, perhaps because most public officials and politicians believe that there is money to be had for nothing.

Serious tax policy questions for policymakers should now be apparent. At an economic policy level,

➤ how does one thwart so-called 'corporate tax dodgers' without shooting oneself in the head? Do you really want to start an international tax war?

➤ Do you really want to suppress the benefits of global specialisation and international trade (Box 9:1)?

➤ Do you really think that raising the cost of mobile capital is a good idea? If so, why do you continue to exempt or impose low tax rates on interest and royalty income flowing to foreigners (as almost all OECD countries do)?

➤ Do you want to drive away foreign investors who do useful things such as building factories, employing your people and raising skill levels and wages?

At a legal policy level, what does enforcement of world-wide residence or citizenship taxation ultimately require? You must find out what income is arising overseas to persons resident in your country. You may go further. You may want to try to tax the incomes of companies and trusts in third countries which you deem to be 'accruing' to your resident taxpayers.

You cannot ultimately enforce such laws unless you turn every other country's financial institutions, tax authorities, courts and police into your spies and enforcement agencies. This is what the OECD and G20 agendas are trying to do with universal 'automatic information exchange' and 'mutual assistance' in tax matters. Of course, there is little that is mutual or involved by way of exchange when it comes to smaller countries.

Worse, from the point of view of citizens of the larger, 'advanced' countries, this necessarily inflicts damage on fundamental human rights. It destroys constitutional traditions built up over centuries which deny the unlimited power of the State to invade people's private affairs without judicial warrant or just cause. Sooner or later, citizens and smaller countries will revolt. Just as American colonists declared 'no taxation without representation', maintaining the ancient idea that all taxes are granted by the consent of the governed, so smaller countries and their peoples will ask why they are expected to become unpaid tax collectors and enforcers for countries for the 'First World' when they and their citizens get no benefits from the bloated social welfare expenditures of European welfare states. If Pacific Islands like Vanuatu have no or low income taxes because clan lands provide a social security net, reducing the needs for welfare expenditures, why should they be collecting taxes for other, richer, countries which refuse to lower income taxes by taxing their land values for social expenditures? If one collects taxes for another country, surely you should demand work visas, medical benefits and pensions from that country as a *quid pro quo*.

> *If Pacific Islands like Vanuatu have no or low income taxes because clan lands provide a social security net, reducing the needs for welfare expenditures, why should they be collecting taxes for other, richer, countries which refuse to lower income taxes by taxing their land values for social expenditures?*

It is time to return to fundamentals. Taxation is a sovereign act. Yes, *in theory*, a sovereign can make orders addressed to anyone in the world. But only his subjects and those in his jurisdiction will be concerned to obey them. Moreover, those of his subjects living elsewhere will be more concerned to obey the laws of the place they are in – when in Rome, do as the Romans do.

If you are a sovereign and you want revenue, it behoves you to look first and last to your own territory. As Adam Smith recognised (1776:

V.ii.f: 848), you will have problems seeking to draw a revenue from your own subjects in relation to their affairs or interests overseas, as contrasted with taxing the value of land within your territory.

Thinking more deeply about the nature of taxation, at the end of the day, all income and all expenditures out of income represent the factor incomes of land, labour or capital, as Adam Smith observed (1776: I.vi: 68-71). Other incomes, such as dividends, interest or pensions are merely distributions out of the incomes of these three great original factor incomes, which Adam Smith described as rent, wages or profits.

This basic tax intuition remains perfectly valid. There are only three things you can tax – land, labour or capital. Only one of those three cannot emigrate, die off, stop reproducing, go on strike, quit, wear or rust out, be hidden in an offshore bank account or become decrepit. The only time land vanishes as a tax base is when there is anarchy and no peace, order or public services (perhaps Somalia is an example). As Adam Smith remarked (1776: V.ii.e; 844), the rents of lands are uniquely due to the good government of the sovereign. It is therefore reasonable that a sovereign not only look to taxing the value of the lands augmented by his activities but look to taxing those lands *exclusively*.

We now see the fundamental fallacy of the OECD agenda foolishly driving the world toward disastrous tax wars. The tax treaty system has been framed on the false basis that all incomes arise only from labour earnings or capital income. Land income is ignored as such and mistakenly treated as a subset of capital income. True, some countries are concerned when they see land and resource profits going to foreigners as low taxed royalties, etc. But there is little they can do about it under the OECD international tax treaty system if the foreigner takes care to use the 'business profits' article skilfully or thinly capitalizes a resource investment, turning land income into exempt or low taxed income. *The emerging tax wars are really about who is going to tax the incomes of mobile labour and capital.*

How to Prevent the Tax Wars

The way to end the tax wars before they start doing lasting damage to countries' economic and legal systems is to return to strict territoriality – to tax land, the immobile factor of production. You can cut or abolish income and other taxes by switching to a simple rate on land values (that is, upon the value of all natural resources in their unimproved state or where improvements are obsolete, for example land where buildings are being demolished).

A land value tax is inherently territorial. It requires no tax treaties to make it effective. It requires no subordination or intimidation of foreign countries.

- ✔ It leaves productive international trade and capital investment free to flourish.
- ✔ It requires no vexatious inquisition into the private affairs of citizens. It is as transparent as a simple land register.
- ✔ Its cost of collection is cheap compared to income taxes or value added taxes (VAT/GST).
- ✔ It is unavoidable, being a clog on the title – if you do not pay, the land can be sold to collect the land value tax. Foreign landholders cannot plan around it.
- ✔ It requires no complex audits, no draconian subversion of the rule of law, reversal of the onus of proof or criminalization of commercial conduct.

Only two questions are required. Who is the registered owner of this land and what is its unimproved value devoid of desired improvements made by the owner or his predecessor in title? Cadastral surveys to answer these two questions are much easier to do by way of mass assessment than to audit millions of taxpayers and their affairs onshore and offshore.

Nor should anyone be allowed to say that land values are not enough to support a reasonable level of government spending. Dwyer (2003), and others (see Holland, 1970) demonstrate that land values are much larger than realized. Oil-rich States have often mainly lived off just one form of land revenues – their oil royalties. Of major economies, Russia in a curious way has renationalized oil revenues as a major part of its public revenues but has not reversed, through land or rent charges, other dirty privatizations of land and other natural resources. What would the land values of all the cities of Europe or the USA be worth as tax bases?

Unfortunately, the OECD dissembles when it comes to land value taxes. They know that taxes on 'immobile property' (of which the only true example are taxes on land values) are superior to other taxes and have zero excess burden (Johansson, Heady, Arnold, Brys and L. Vartia [2008). The OECD candidly admits 'As for tax hikes, they should rely on the least growth-distorting instruments. Taxes on immobile bases,

such as property ... are less distortive than those on factor income (such
as personal and corporate income)'. (OECD, n.d: 9). 'Where revenue hikes
are needed, emphasis should be placed on the least distortive taxes, such
as those on property rather than on labour and income.' (Gurria, 2010).
An OECD researcher once confessed to the writer that though it was
correct in theory to tax land values rather than wages or capital, the problem was basically political. So the OECD and IMF still advocate polices
of higher VAT or GST to tax workers and world-wide residence or pseudo-
residence income taxation as the basis for attacking tax havens and 'tax
dodgers'.

This is intellectual nonsense. If you are upset that Apple or Google
or any other foreigner is not paying income taxes in your country,
why would you increase VAT or GST to cut corporate income taxes? By
definition, VAT or GST exempts foreigners drawing income from your
country and spending that income in their own countries. VAT/GST is a
tax on local consumers. It exempts capital income by refunding tax paid
on business purchases. It taxes human capital formation by taxing money
spent raising children, a consideration which Adam Smith foresaw (1776:
V.ii.k: 872-873) and which Europe should have thought about as it now
sees demographic fiscal disaster emerging.

By contrast, a general land value tax thus *indirectly* (but pervasively)
captures the ultimate benefits of all foreign trade or investment, as labour
and capital compete away any differential returns. What is also overlooked
is that as Henry George remarked (1879, IX.1: 435-436) 'No man can
keep to himself the good he may do, any more than he can keep the
bad... Nature laughs at a miser'. If Apple and Google make profits, they
do so by providing services which raise productivity and real incomes.
They save consumers and producers time and money. Even if they avoid
local income taxes and defer US taxes by carefully using income tax treaty
definitions of permanent establishment, source and low withholding
rates, they cannot appropriate to themselves all of the economic surplus
they generate. Apple or Google or any other multinational company
trading 'with' or 'within' a country helps generate higher land values
directly or indirectly. Its warehouses, representative offices or franchise
stores all help generate land rents, as do the increased profits of those
using its wares.

> If multinationals move in and gradually bid up wages and salaries,
> what happen to residential land values?

➤ If multinationals bid for office or warehouse space what happens to commercial land values?

➤ If local businesses become more efficient and profitable using imported technologies or services, what happens to land values?

Only land values, as Adam Smith (1776), John Stuart Mill (1848-71), Henry George (1879) and others saw, can permanently capture and reflect rising differential productivity of labour or capital.

Conclusion

The secret of thwarting international tax dodgers is – *don't bother.* You do not need to! Tax land values instead.

It is not necessary to create international tax Gestapos with financial institutions becoming State informants spying on their customers. There need be no public outrage over directors of multinational companies doing what they are legally bound to do as fiduciaries in maximizing after-tax profits for shareholders. It is not necessary to vilify people whose only 'crime' is to understand and step past silly tax laws (as Mason Gaffney remarked to the author in 1982: 'If one is condemned to live in a corrupt system, it is preferable to be a beneficiary rather than a victim'). It is totally unnecessary, as well as economically and politically danger-ous, for countries to embark on a round of tax wars which will be as damaging as a global tariff war.

International tax competition is actually an optimizing process (Sinn 1993: 43-44, 70), since the economically optimal rate of tax on both labour and capital is zero, as demonstrated by Judd (1985), Chamley (1986), Zhu (1992) Correia (1996), Jones, Manuelli and Rossi (1997) and Karanountias (2013). Models, of course, are only as good as their assumptions and a contrary model by Gottardi, Kajii and Nakajima (2015) implicitly assumes land values do not exist to be taxed.

Instead of chasing multinationals and individuals around the world, just tax land values so you can cut corporate and personal income tax rates down towards zero. Accept that mobile or manipulable incomes will always flow, like water, to the lowest tax rate. But, in doing so, they fertilize the adjacent lands and enrich most the lands through or to which they flow. By employing land value taxes, which have zero excess burden (Feldstein, 1976), to reduce or abolish other taxes, every country can enhance the benefits of international trade and investment while making sure it is on a level to be a participant drawing from the ultimate reservoir.

In closing, one should pay tribute to the native and original genius of Henry George (1879, 1891). He saw that collection of land rent for public revenue offered the elegant and congruent solution for avoiding domestic tax disincentives, international tax conflicts, the corruption of legal systems (Smith 1776, V.ii.k: 828; George, 1891: 8; Cooper, 1997) and destruction of citizens' natural rights, such as privacy, in the interests of tax collectors (OECD, 2015).

References

Blackstone, Sir William (1765-1783), *Commentaries on the Laws of England*, reprinted with commentary by W.D. Lewis, Geo. T. Bisel, Philadelphia, 1922.

Blue Star Line (2016), *Biography of William Vestey*. http://www.bluestarline.org/william_vestey.htm (accessed 19 March).

Chamley, Christophe (1986), 'Optimal Taxation of Capital Income in General Equilibrium with Infinite Lives', *Econometrica*, vol 54.

Correia, Isabel H. (1996), 'Should capital income be taxed in the steady state?', *Journal of Public Economics*, vol 60.

Coffield, James (1970), *A Popular History of Taxation: From Ancient to Modern Times*, Longman, London.

Cooper, Graeme S, editor. (1997), *Tax Avoidance and the Rule of Law*, International Bureau of Fiscal Documentation, Amsterdam.

Dwyer, Terry (2000), '"Harmful" Tax Competition and the Future of Offshore Financial Centres such as Vanuatu', *Pacific Economic Bulletin*, 15(1).

Dwyer, Terry (2002), '"Harmful" Tax Competition and the Future of Offshore Financial Centres', *Journal of Money Laundering Control*, 5(4).

Dwyer, Terry (2003), 'The Taxable Capacity of Australian Land and Resources', *Australian Tax Forum*, 18(1).

Dwyer, Terry (2013), 'Trash or treasure? Offshore under attack – Review of Shaxson's Treasure Islands', *Offshore Investment*, 235, April.

Feldstein, Martin (1976), 'On the theory of tax reform', *Journal of Public Economics*, 6 July-August.

G20 (2010), *Seoul Summit Document*, (12 November). http://www.g20.utoronto.ca/2010/g20seoul-doc.pdf

Gaffney, Mason (1998), 'International tax competition: harmful or beneficial?', *Offshore Investment*, 90, October.

Gaffney, Mason (1999), 'International Tax Competition: Harmful or Beneficial?', *Journal of International Trust and Corporate Planning*, 7(1).

Gaffney, Mason (1999), 'Taxation and economic growth', *Offshore Investment*, 99, September.

George, Henry (1879), *Progress and Poverty*, reprinted New York, Robert Schalkenbach Foundation, 1971.

George, Henry (1886), *Protection or Free Trade: An Examination of the Tariff Question with Especial Regard to the Interests of Labour*, reprinted Robert Schalkenbach Foundation, New York, 1980.

George, Henry (1891), *The Condition of Labour: An Open Letter to Pope Leo XIII.*, New York, 1891; reprinted, London, Land & Liberty Press, 1947.

Gottardi, Piero; Kajii, Atsushi and Tomoyki Nakajima (2015), 'Optimal Taxation and Debt with Uninsurable Risks to Human Capital Accumulation', *American Economic Review*, 105(11).

Guardian, (2015) 'Apple agrees to pay £234m to settle Italian tax dispute' (30 December), http://www.theguardian.com/business/2015/dec/30/apple-pays-234m-settle-italian-tax-dispute (accessed 19 March 2016).

Grinberg,Itai & Pauwelyn, Joost (2015), 'The Emergence of a New International Tax Regime, The OECD's Package of Base Erosion and Profit Shifting (BEPS), *ASIL Insights*, American Society of International Law. https://www.asil.org/insights/volume/19/issue/24/emergence-new-international-tax-regime-oecd%E2%80%99s-package-base-erosion-and (accessed 19 March 2016).

Grinberg, Itai & Pauwelyn, Joost (2015) 19(24), 'The Emergence of a New International Tax Regime: The OECD's Package on Base Erosion and Profit Shifting (BEPS)', *ASIL Insights*, American Society of International Law. http://www.asil.org/insights/volume/19/issue/24/emergence-new-international-tax-regime-oecd%E2%80%99s-package-base-erosion-and (accessed 19 March 2016).

Grubert, Harry and Mutti, John (1995), 'Taxing Multinationals in a World with Portfolio Flows and R&D: Is Capital Export Neutrality Obsolete?' *International Tax and Public Finance,.. 2.

Guardian (2015), 'Apple agrees to pay £234m to settle Italian tax dispute', (30th December). http://www.theguardian.com/business/2015/dec/30/apple-pays-234m-settle-italian-tax-dispute (accessed 19 March 2016).

Gurría, Angel (2010), *Fiscal consolidation: Remarks by OECD Secretary-General, delivered at the International Forum of Americas*, Montreal, 7 June.

G20 (2010) *Seoul Summit Document*, 12 November. http://www.g20.utoronto.ca/2010/g20seoul-doc.pdf

Grubert, Harry and Mutti, John (1995), 'Taxing Multinationals in a World with Portfolio Flows and R&D: Is Capital Export Neutrality Obsolete?', *International Tax and Public Finance*, 2.

Hines, James R. Jr and Rice, Eric M. (1994), 'Fiscal Paradise: Foreign Tax Havens and American Business', *Quarterly Journal of Economics*, 109, February.

Holland, Daniel M., ed. (1970), *The Assessment of Land Value*, Madison: University of Wisconsin Press.

Johansson, Å., C. Heady, J. Arnold, B. Brys and L. Vartia (2008), 'Taxation and Economic Growth', *OECD Economics Department Working Papers*, No. 620.

Jones, Larry E., Rodolfo Manuelli and Peter E. Rossi (1997), 'On the Optimal Taxation of Capital Income', *Journal of Economic Theory*, 73(1).

Judd, Kenneth L. (1985), 'Redistributive Taxation in a Simple Perfect Foresight Model', *Journal of Public Economics*, 28(1).

Karanountias, Anastasios (2013), *Optimal Fiscal Policy with Recursive Preferences*, Federal Reserve Bank of Atlanta Working Paper, 2013-07.

MacArthur, Brian, (ed.) (1996), *The Penguin Book of Historic Speeches*, London.

Maitland, F.W. (1920), *The Constitutional History of England*, Cambridge University Press, 1920.

Mill, John Stuart (1848-1871), *Principles of Political Economy: With Some of Their Applications to Social Philosophy*, variorum edition by J.M. Robson. Vols. II and III, *Collected Works of John Stuart Mill*, University of Toronto Press, 1965.

Pitt, William, the Elder (1775), 'The kingdom is undone', Speech in House of Lords, 20 January, reprinted in MacArthur (ed).

Pitt, William, the Elder (1766), 'I rejoice that America has resisted', Speech in the House of Commons on the Stamp Act, 14 January, reprinted in MaArthur (ed) (1996).

OECD (1998), *Harmful Tax Competition: An Emerging Global Issue*, Paris.

OECD (n.d., 2010?) *Preparing Fiscal Consolidation*, Economics Department. http://www.oecd.org/tax/public-finance/44829122.pdf (accessed 19 March 2016)

OECD (2015), *Standard for Automatic Exchange of Financial Account Information: Common Reporting Standard*, Paris. http://www.oecd.org/ctp/exchange-of-tax-information/automatic-exchange-financial-account-information-common-reporting-standard.pdf (accessed 20 March 2016).

Panama, Government of (2015), Letter from its lawyers to OECD (17 September). http://www.eduardomorgan.com/blog/wp-content/uploads/2015/12/Letter-A.-Gurria-from-J.-Bacchus.pdf (accessed 19 March 2016).

Rubin, Richard (2016), *Senators Ask White House to Consider Retaliatory Tax Measure on EU* (15 January). http://www.morningstar.com/news/dow-jones/europe/TDJNDN_2016011510485/senators-ask-white-house-to-consider-retaliatory-tax-measure-on-eu.print.html (accessed 19 March 2016).

Sabine, B.E.V. (1980), *A Short History of Taxation*, London, Butterworths.

Shanghai Daily (2016), 'US attacks EU tax probes as unfair', (1 February). http://www.shanghaidaily.com/business/finance/US-attacks-EU-tax-probes-as-unfair/shdaily.shtml (accessed 19 March 2016).

Shaxson, Nicholas (2012), *Treasure Islands: Tax Havens and the Men who Stole the World*, Vintage, London.

Sinn, Stefan (1993), 'Competition for Capital: On the Role of Governments in an Integrated World Economy', *Kiel University Institute of Economics Discussion Papers No 253*, J.C.B. Mohr, Tubingen.

Smith, Adam (1776), *An Inquiry into the Nature and Causes of the Wealth of Nations*, Glasgow Edition, Oxford, 1976.

Zhu, Xiaodong (1992), 'Optimal Fiscal Policy in a Stochastic Growth Model', *Journal of Economic Theory*, 58(2).

10
Enlightenment's
Food for Thought

DUNCAN PICKARD

T HE WORLD needs a new Scottish Enlightenment. That need is
nowhere better illustrated than in Scotland itself. How such
enlightenment might be nurtured in the 21st century is illuminated by the key doctrine that was developed in Scotland in the 18th
century. Members of the Scottish Enlightenment asserted the fundamental importance of *human reason combined with a rejection of any authority that
could not be justified by reason.* The members relevant to the topic of land are
Adam Smith, William Ogilvie and Robert Burns.

Adam Smith is best known for his analysis of the means by which
wealth is created and distributed between the factors involved in its
production.[1] His analysis has not been bettered, and those who seek to
establish a prosperous society where justice prevails and inequality of
health and opportunity are minimised should not just accept other's
interpretations of Smith's work. Modern economics should be accurately
called 'Anti-classical' because it ignores the distinction between 'Land'
and 'Capital' which Smith understood as fundamental to how wealth
is created. His picture of a successful political economy was strongly
influenced by his appreciation of morality. He accepted that the pursuit

---

1 Smith, Adam (1776), *The Wealth of Nations.*

of self-interest was beneficial to wealth production, but he did not claim that greed was good. He was well aware of the need for good governance to ensure that the adverse effects of monopolies were prevented.

William Ogilvie was a contemporary of Adam Smith and although less well known, his *Essay on the Right of Property in Land* (1781) is central to all considerations of economic prosperity and social justice.[2] Ogilvie was the Professor of Humanity at the University of Aberdeen and a close friend of Robert Burns. Burns' words should be studied closely to appreciate what he meant by 'freedom' and 'independence'. The freedom from tyranny that he sought was not the tyranny of a foreign power but that of the landowners in Scotland. He wrote his poem *'Scots! Wha hae wi' Wallace bled'* in 1793 just after Thomas Muir had been convicted for having a copy of Thomas Paine's *The Rights of Man*. Burns only narrowly escaped conviction for a similar offence. The words of Burns' poem were not a call to his compatriots to revive old national feuds, but to confront the tyrants who enslaved working people by their 'Divine Right' to claim ownership of the land. Not many are aware of his desire to improve the condition of poor, oppressed people everywhere. He agreed with Ogilvie, whose *Essay* is a well-reasoned discourse on the fundamental birthright which everyone has to a share in the earth's natural resources.

Ogilvie traced the 'oppression, misery, injustice and poverty of the majority' to the unjust acquisition of the 'Right of Property in Land' by a minority of people who owned land and 'preserved their power to claim the rent resulting from the labour of others'. The introduction to his *Essay* states, 'with respect to property in land, that system which now prevails is derived from an age not deserving to be extolled for its legislative wisdom and is in need of reformation and improvement'. Ogilvie was scathing of the 'Divine Right' which landowners claimed to justify their ownership. *That ownership was according to the Law but it was law devoid of justice.* Today in Scotland land owners object to proposals for land reform by saying that their ownership of land is a 'fundamental human right'. That assertion cannot be true, because it only applies to people who own land. Those who do not own land are excluded from the 'fundamental human right' to own any at all, as we shall see in the case of Scotland.

The reformation and improvement which Ogilvie proposed was that the annual rent of land (which Smith called 'ground rent') should be

---

2 Ogilvie, William (1781), 'Essay on the Right of Property in Land', in *Birthright in Land*, London, Othilla Press (1997).

collected by the government to pay for its functions. His opinion on the appropriate source of government revenue was similar to that of Adam Smith, but he went further; he regarded it as inherently unjust to levy taxes on landless working people whilst leaving those who owned land to keep any of its unearned rental revenue. Burns and Ogilvie agreed that people cannot enjoy freedom and independence merely by gaining political freedom. This has to be combined with economic freedom, which cannot occur when the earnings of their labour are taxed by the state, leaving the unearned rent of land with those who have the legal but unjust right to claim ownership of it.

In Scotland, the conflict between land owners and tenant farmers continues to this day.

> ➤ Tenants seek greater security of tenure and more compensation at the end of a tenancy for their improvements to houses and other buildings.
> ➤ Land owners are reluctant to extend existing tenancies or to grant new long-term agreements.

The fundamental problem is the high market price of farm land, and the distortions that arise from unjust laws that sanctify the maldistribution of income.

The primary function of farming is to use land for the production of food, but farmers must accept their responsibility for preserving, if not enhancing, the fertility of land. The condition of farming in Scotland today gives much cause for concern.

> ➤ Many farmers are dependent on subsidies. They prefer to rely on the government to divert taxpayers' money to maintain their standard of living rather than thinking of ways to farm more efficiently.
> ➤ Others have ambition to own as much land as they can, which reduces the chances for potential newcomers to farm on their own account.
> ➤ The market price of farmland is far higher than can be justified by current produce prices and yields.
> ➤ The plight of many dairy farmers is symptomatic of the lack of self-reliance in general; they maximise their output of milk without considering whether there is a market for it at a price which would cover the production costs.

Land Prices and Rural Unemployment

There is an almost universal belief among farmers that high land prices are beneficial to farming. I contend that high land prices are a curse on farming. I do not deny that some landowning farmers become very rich from high prices, but only when they sell, most of them making more money from selling their farms than they did throughout the time they were farming. There is a clear distinction between what is beneficial to a few farmers and what might be beneficial to farming in general and especially to those who want to farm but have no land.

In Scotland the average price of farmland is more than £4,000 per acre (2016), an increase of 17% over the previous year. The average price of arable land is £8,000 per acre. The market price of land is much higher than can be justified by its productive capacity. Take as an example land for growing wheat which is capable of yielding 3 tonnes per acre: the current price of wheat ex farm is less than £120 per tonne. This gives a gross income of £360 per acre. The current cost of growing wheat is about £115 per tonne or £345 per acre, leaving a surplus of £15 per acre. With arable land at £8,000 per acre and the cost of borrowing at about 4%, the annual interest cost is £320 per acre, clearly unaffordable at current wheat prices. The price of wheat would need consistently to be £250 per tonne to justify a purchase price for arable land of £8,000 per acre.

The traditional method for estimating the price of a farm which would enable the purchaser to fund a mortgage and to make a living puts the price of a farm at 20 times its rent. This was the basis of the price we paid for our farm in 1992. It was also the basis for the price we paid for the first piece of farmland we bought in 1975. The RICS (Royal Institute of Chartered Surveyors) *Land Market Survey* (2015) reports that the average rent of arable land is £85 per acre. This means its purchase price *ought* to be £1,700 per acre. The current acreage price of £8,000 is 4.7 times more expensive than its productive capacity would justify and its rent would be £400 per acre.

Why is the Market Price of Farmland so High?

There are five primary reasons why the price of land that is fit for producing food is above what its productive capacity justifies.

1   The rising price of farmland is attractive to non-farmers who have

money to invest. They are not concerned with the land's productive capacity; they hope for increases in its price.

2   Farmland is favourably treated for taxation. Inheritance tax and Capital Gains Tax are avoidable and 'farmland is an efficient asset for the transfer of wealth'.[3]

3   Farmers buy about half of the land offered for sale. Those who own their farms free of debt can afford more land by averaging the cost of new borrowing over the whole of their enlarged farms.

4   Landowning farmers who receive subsidies which are surplus to requirements invest in more land and thereby increase their subsidy income.

5   Rent-seeking banks persuade owner-occupiers with no mortgage to buy more land.

Most farmers who buy more land claim that larger farms are more efficient, but they do not define efficiency. The only measure of efficiency which consistently increases with increasing farm size is output per person employed. Other measures, such as output per unit area or per unit of invested capital, seldom do. It is also claimed that economies of scale are gained when farms become bigger, but true economies of scale are very difficult to find in farming.

Rural communities are seriously disadvantaged when the State's perverse tax system interferes with the market for land.

1   Young newcomers to farming are prevented from buying land unl less they have access to money from elsewhere.

2   There is an effective monopoly in farmland purchasing when only those who already own land are able to buy, which results in large farms becoming larger, and smaller farms becoming fewer.

3   Landowners are unwilling to offer land for rent except on short leases because land which is subject to a long term tenancy has a market price which is about half that of freehold land.

4   Landowners are unwilling to sell farms to their long-lease tenants because the price differential means that the tenants could make a substantial financial gain by selling at the freehold price.

5   If an 'Absolute Right to Buy' provision is introduced, tenants could not exercise the Right to Buy because the freehold price is too high. In other words, such a legal provision would be cosmetic.

---

3 Savills (2014), Market Survey, Agricultural Land.

The Common Agricultural Policy

Another major problem for Scottish farmers is the Common Agricultural Policy and the fact that subsidies make up a large part of farm incomes. How have farmers become so dependent on subsidies such that, as soon as reductions in their income support are proposed, their leaders issue dire warnings of the total collapse of agriculture?

The lack of willingness to question the validity of pronouncements from politicians, economists and farming 'experts' indicates that many farmers prefer others to do their thinking, and for 'the government' to cushion them from any adverse consequences of their own decisions. The subsidy culture nurtures this attitude. If farmers challenge the imposition of policies which are detrimental to their ability to farm effectively, the threat of withdrawal of subsidy income is sufficient to guarantee submission. The Common Agricultural Policy of the European Union has never been what its name implies. Since its inception it has been a Social Welfare Policy, to provide income support for small farms in continental Europe, especially in France. The main beneficiaries of farm subsidies are those who own land; tenant farmers pay most, if not all of their subsidy money to their landlords as rent.

> *The main beneficiaries of farm subsidies are those who own land; tenant farmers pay most, if not all of their subsidy money to their landlords as rent.*

The claim that 90% of farmers would go out of business without subsidies is an easily discredited claim.[4] It is based on examining farm accounts and deducting the subsidy from the income from farming. Farmers are then seen to be left with insufficient revenue to cover the costs of their labour and capital inputs. The official statistics of farm incomes are a very unreliable guide to the actual incomes. They are constructed as 'an index of incomes to allow comparisons to be made over time and between countries'.[5]

Most farmers are not as poor as they are reported to be. The number of those who are not farming profitably could be decreased if all farmers were as competent and diligent as the top 25%. Farmers do not work harder if they can achieve their ambitions by working less and receiving income support. Too many have risked their businesses by refusing to

---

4 Scottish Local Tax Commission Report (2015), The Scottish Government.
5 AGRA Europe (2015), Britain's EU Exit would devastate nation's farmers, October 24.

diversify their enterprises. They concentrate on one or two activities (and streams of revenue), even where the land has traditionally been used for mixed farming and involved different types of livestock and crops.

The negative effects of farm subsidies are seldom acknowledged. Apart from allowing inefficiency to prevail, they increase the market price of farmland because those of us who have surplus subsidy income find that the best way of investing it is to buy more land. The high price of land makes it impossible for newcomers who are not already rich, to start farming. *More food could be produced in the UK, but is not, because subsidies allow farmers to use their land below its optimal potential.* I define subsidies as non means-tested income support for wealthy landowners.

The Collection of Annual Ground Rent

The Local Tax Reform Commission, appointed by the Scottish Government in 2015, concluded that the collection of ground rent should be seriously considered as a source of funding for local government in Scotland.[6] What would happen if the rental value of land (excluding the sum paid for the use of the land owner's capital on the land) was collected to both fund the necessary functions of government and abolish the taxes that harm the agricultural sector?

The first benefit would stem from reduction in the time and money spent on record keeping and accountancy, which would increase the time available for farming. The next most noticeable effect would be a reduction in the market price of land, because speculative investment in land would no longer be profitable. If the charge on all land was based on its optimal permitted use, the owner of unused land would either use it or sell it to someone who would do so. The cost of gaining access to farmland would fall, bringing it closer to levels affordable to those who want to start farming. Politicians and the farmers' union leaders are always willing to proclaim their support for more opportunities for young people to become farmers, but they persist in defending tax policies which prevent those opportunities from appearing. The current system encourages farmers to maximise the area of land they own. A more enlightened fiscal system would result in them minimising their holdings to optimise profitability and minimise the land rental charge. The land vacated would be available to newcomers.

---

6 Gaffney, Mason (1992), 'Rising inequality and falling property tax rates', in *Land Ownership and Taxation in American Agriculture*, Gene Wunderlich, ed., Westview Press.

Box 10:1

Why a 'Tax' might be Both Good, and Bad

Whenever property taxes are discussed the common reaction is that farms and farmland should be exempted.* There is also a common belief that property tax relief is good for farmers. This is refuted by Mason Gaffney. His research in the USA showed that exemption from property tax for agricultural land increases the likelihood that it will attract those looking primarily for tax shelters and speculative investments. Such non-productive incentives ultimately inflate land prices, making it increasingly difficult for working farmers to access and maintain land for agricultural use. The fiscal jurisdictions with lower property taxes also had larger average farm sizes and more unequal distribution of farm sizes along with more under-used land and lack of land improvement. Gaffney's findings indicated that property taxes on farm buildings as well as land penalised smaller farms and supressed improvements. Taxes on land values promoted the efficient use of agricultural land and supported the overall viability of smaller farm operations.

*Here, I use the word 'Tax' to mean, according to the Oxford Dictionary, 'a contribution to state revenue compulsorily levied on individuals, property or businesses'.

The number of occupiers of farm holdings in Scotland fell by almost 2,000 in the 10 years up to 2015. This is an indication of the number of smaller farms which have been bought by larger farm businesses. Conventional wisdom says that these smaller farms had to be taken over because their size was too small for them to be financially viable. The example of a farm in my neighbourhood, which was sold a few years ago, shows that this conclusion is false. The farm has 185 acres and the previous farmer grew wheat and potatoes and kept cattle and sheep. He had inherited his farm from his father and had no debt. He made a comfortable living and the farm was obviously financially viable as an independent holding. It ceased to be so when it was bought by a large farm business for a price of £1.2m. Its market price based on the 20x annual rent formula would have been £314,500. It is their high market price which makes many farms unviable, not their lack of potential to provide a living for a family.

The average farm size in Scotland is almost five times that of the other 27 countries in the European Union. Within the UK it is more than twice the average size in England and two and a half times that in Wales and Northern Ireland. There is scope for many more farm units and independent farmers in Scotland. The ability for more people to make a living on remote and less fertile land in Scotland would improve if their taxes were abolished. Such land is capable of producing sufficient income to pay wages and interest to sustain labour and maintain capital but not to pay rent. Under such conditions, the annual ground rent charge would not be payable. Unless there is radical tax and land reform in Scotland the traditional 'family farm' will become a thing of the past and the majority of the farmland will be owned and farmed by 'agribusinesses'. That is the conclusion implied by a major piece of research into the impact of the US property tax by Mason Gaffney (Box 10:1).

The number of people employed in farming continues to decline. Between 2004 and 2014 the regular workforce on Scottish farms fell from 63,832 to 59,636, a drop of 4,196. The data from our farm show why this is happening. We employ two full-time staff and we are obliged to send about one-third of each man's pay to the Inland Revenue each month. This means that we employ two staff members and send the take-home pay for another to the government. Contrast this with what happens when we buy another tractor. The investment allowance is an attractive incentive to buy more farm machinery, so it should be no surprise that the size of tractors is increasing and the number of farm workers is falling.

The abolition of income taxes and the introduction of a charge on the rental value of land would allow more people to be gainfully employed. Not only would the cash costs of employment be reduced but also the costs of stress associated with complying with the outdated, complicated and disincentive tax laws. Farmers would have the incentive to become reasonably rich from farming their land, not trying to become unreasonably rich by owning as much land as possible to capture the unearned increase in its market price. Farmers should gain their rewards for *'farming smarter, not bigger'*

Why I Opt for AGR

I am often asked why I, as a land owning farmer, am advocating the abolition of taxes and their replacement with an annual charge on the rental value of land. The current excessively high market price of our farm is no advantage to me and my family because we have no wish to sell. We have not earned the £3m by which its market price has increased since we bought it 23 years ago. Furthermore, that increase in the price of land is a disadvantage to our desire for the next generations of our family to continue to farm it. If our son has to pay an equal share of the market price to his brothers and sister he will have to sell the farm to do so. If the price was close to what its productive capacity would justify, however, there would be no problem. I estimate that the farm would be more profitable if taxes were abolished and replaced by an annual ground rental (AGR).

If all taxes were abolished, how much AGR would we pay?

➤ The rental value of farmland would be higher than the current average rent we pay for the use of land without buildings. Since taxes come out of rent (see Feder, Ch. 2 of this volume), the removal of taxes would enable rental values to rise. But compared with the payment of income taxes on behalf of our employees, the payment of an annual rental charge would be closely linked to our ability to pay.

➤ Under the existing tax regime, when we employ someone we have to pay the going rate related to the person's skills. But the amount of tax we pay is related to the wage *irrespective of whether the farm is profitable enough to afford to pay.* Compare that with rent. When we negotiate a rent with a landowner, the rent we bid is based on the estimated potential profitability of the animals or crops we plan to produce.

So, as of today, it would be difficult to say *how much* I would pay in AGR. But I can say with certainty that the annual payment would correspond to *what I could afford to pay* as an efficient farmer.

The Rental Value of Farmland

There is currently a serious problem with negotiating the rent of farm-land based on the average of prices paid in the open market. Some bids for summer grazing exceed £200 per acre. Why would someone pay £200 for six months' grazing when the average rent for whole farms is much less? Farmers who own their land can afford to pay a very high price for a small amount of additional grazing land because, when this rent is averaged over the total farmed area, it is easily afforded. Rents for whole farms are usually closely related to the productive capacity of the land when taking into account the seasonal variations in yields, costs of production and product prices. There are instances of land owners and their agents who use the average market price of rents to justify increases in rent for their long-term tenants. Most landowners with farms on long leases are wise enough to leave their tenants with all the work and the

---

Box 10:2

How Downsizing turns into Asset Stripping

Prior to the last 25 or 30 years farms were sold as a whole: the farmhouse was included is the price paid for the farm. That is seldom the case today because of the massive increase in the market price of houses. If a good farmhouse in a favourable location is worth £500,000, and if the farm has 150 acres of good arable land its market price will be about £1m. Although such a farm would be capable of providing a reasonable living for a young farming family, they would not be able to afford it. It is, however, within the reach of someone wanting to sell a modest house in the London area to live in the countryside. Such a person could buy the farm, sell most of the land to neighbouring farmers and have plenty of money left over.

---

risks and negotiate the rents accordingly. This position would still pertain after an annual ground rent is introduced because land owners would be entitled to keep the rent for the buildings and other improvements they provide, and they would enjoy the benefits of the abolition of taxes on their incomes. The losers after this change would be those who hold potentially productive land out of use. They will either have to use it or pass it on to someone who can do so.

With the introduction of the AGR to pay for public services, the market price of land would fall. What happens to farmers who have bought at inflated prices? They would see their asset turn into 'negative equity'. This need not be a problem when the ability to farm profitably is increased by the abolition of taxes. The market price of land has become the only criterion used by banks to secure a loan, instead of the borrower's ability to repay. This is a relatively recent development. When land prices are rising lenders need to know little or nothing about the borrower's business or his skill in running it when they can rely on being able to sell the land and recover from their bad lending decision. It seems to be grossly unfair that the borrower is left with all the responsibility for a bad debt whilst the banks as lenders accept none and expect to be repaid in full.

We cannot interrogate the agricultural sector without taking into account the ripple effects from the urban house market. The motive for owning residential property has a huge impact on the inability of people to break into farming. Most young people are attracted to the ownership of a house because rising prices make this asset the most attractive form of investment. The exemption from Capital Gains Tax enables the owner-occupiers of houses to accumulate the unearned rental value which is translated into higher house prices. This, in turn, triggers the ripple effects on communities in the countryside (Box 10:2).

The use of the current stock of houses is very inefficient. The UK Government estimates that, in England alone, about 600,000 dwellings are held vacant, 200,000 of them on a long-term basis.[7] And yet, we are told that there is a severe shortage of houses and that many more need to be built! Furthermore, we are told that there is a lack of suitable land available on which to build. How can this be so? The amount of suitable building land in urban areas is huge, but its owners have no incentive to develop it, because vacant land is free of Council Tax. If the government collected the annual ground rent of this land it would be developed and the average price of land for building would fall. The beneficial knock-on effect on the price of houses on farms would enable more young people to become farmers.

It is often claimed that the UK is an overcrowded country. Compared with Hong Kong, we have plenty of space. The population of Hong Kong is about 7m living on a land area of 426 square miles; the county ('Kingdom') of Fife in Scotland has about 365,000 people and an area of 512 square miles. The average standard of living in Hong Kong is higher than that in Fife, mostly because its land is used to its optimal potential and much of the revenue for government funding is obtained from the collection of ground rent. People are allowed to keep what they earn, for very few pay income tax and there is no VAT.

A new Scottish Enlightenment, based on the legacies of Adam Smith, William Ogilvie and, especially, Robert Burns, is needed to guide Radical Tax and Land Reform and allow all the people of Scotland to have equality of opportunity on the way to prosperity. Burns is known to millions around the world and his popularity is not only because of the beautiful poems he wrote about his love for the lassies. He empathised with the miserable plight of working people everywhere who suffered under the handicap of a landowning minority. He witnessed the early death of his father through excessively hard work on a tenanted farm with a ruthless landowner.

---

7 https://www.gov.uk/government/statistical-data-sets/live-tables-on-dwelling-stock-including-vacants

PART III

Prophetic Voices

Trust in governments and respect for authority has diminished to levels that are dangerous to democracy. The global economic crisis of 2008 and its painful aftermath confirmed people's suspicion that the knowledge base was not as firmly grounded as its guardians claimed. Elections produced hung parliaments across Europe and strange candidates for presidential power in the United States.

The European Union is riven with shocking levels of unemployment and an institutional incapacity to raise growth rates. Migration from a war-torn Middle East threatens the continent's post-World War II settlement. In China, authoritarian power struggles to keep control of a runaway economy. Across the globe, governments continue to search for policies that might help them to rebalance their systems for producing wealth. High finance is at the heart of these crises, but conventional doctrines are failing to equip policy-makers with the tools to steer their societies towards sustainable peace and prosperity.

The rise of the far Left in Greece and Spain and of the far Right in France and Germany casts dark shadows. Spain and the United Kingdom are threatened with demands for a breakup of the state. Similar voices are heard in France (from the Basques) and in Italy (the Northern League). In the United States, the Right demands 'small government,' but policy-makers are ill-equipped to protect citizens who are marooned in poverty.

Mason Gaffney has shown how episodes of Great Awakenings inspired by religious leaders led to progressive reforms in America. Today, intellectual elites invoke secular arguments to exclude religion from political discourse, but their record has not vindicated the 'evidence-based' approach to policy-making. The centres of learning have failed to equip leaders with wisdom in place of obsolete dogmas.

New voices are needed.

The authors of Part III search for the prophetic voices that might inspire people to chart a new course in the 21st century.

211

11

False Hopes in Euroland

FERNANDO SCORNIK GERSTEIN

W HEN SOCIETIES tip into severe crisis, new voices may emerge to point towards a new future. The social role of such voices was loud in biblical times: prophets warned of doom as they sought to persuade people to mend their ways. In the history of America, religious awakening preceded each wave of radical reform (Gaffney 2010). Spiritual strength aroused the social determination to correct what was perceived as wrong in the way communities conducted their affairs.

A century ago, Winston S. Churchill raised his voice to warn of the damage that was being done to society by the private exploitation of the nation's rental income. If the landlords had permitted the Liberal Government's Budget of 1909 to be implemented, would the social benefits that Churchill predicted have materialised? Britain would have benefited from the evolution of a different kind of economy, one that would have avoided (or at least mitigated) the terrible impact of the Depression of the 1930s. In the event, the law was not implemented, so we do not have the empirical evidence to evaluate Churchill's prophesy.

History tells us that false prophets are ever present in our midst. Some may be well-intentioned but ill-informed. Others may be malevolent, as the world discovered when Germany presented Adolf Hitler with a political platform in 1933. The challenge, then, is to determine whether people can trust the emerging leaders. How do we judge whether their messages really do shine a hopeful light on the future? That question is urgent for us today, for our globalised society finds itself in the worst economic crisis since the 1930s. It is now clear to everyone that our existing leaders have lost their way. Their doctrines of governance were false – otherwise, the world would not have been blindly driven into the financial crisis of 2008. And people would not have been forced to endure the 'austerity' policies that followed the banking crisis, which have caused the global economy to sink into the doldrums.

The citizens of Europe today feel betrayed by their political leaders. That is why they no longer respect authority. Throughout the European Union, new leaders have emerged to try and guide their nations away from the policies enforced on them by governments in the post-2008 era. We have seen the rise of a new political party in Italy inspired by a comedian. In France, the rise of the National Front, and in Slovakia, the rise of new far-right parties, evoke fears of the return of neo-fascism onto the European political scene. Such fears were reinforced by the rise of populist German nationalism, the voices rallying around anti-immigrant slogans. The European Central Bank struggled to create social stability across the continent by expending large sums to buoy up the Eurozone economy, but the results were insufficient to restore order in Portugal: here, the election of a socialist political party to power came with promises to overturn the commitments of the previous government. Similar social disturbances occurred in the United Kingdom, with the emergence of radical socialism and right-wing opportunism.

Mainstream political analysts had difficulty making sense of these eruptions. Tony Blair, who was Prime Minister of Britain for 10 years, confessed: 'I really mean it when I say that I'm not sure I fully understand politics right now, which is an odd thing to say when I've spent my life in it' (Luce 2016). Much the same has happened in the United States. Popular discontent with the long-run decline in wages, and with the breakdown in public services, led to the rise of eccentric politicians from both the Left and the Right. Political debates were not informed in a way that produced clarity. One professor (Larry Sabato, from the University of Virginia) explained that 'Sadly, we are in a post-factual era. It is amazing and more than a little frightening' (BBC 2016).

Ours is now a world locked into a terrible state of confusion over political philosophy and the arts of governance. We need to inform ourselves about the errors of past and present public policies, so that we can exercise democratic choice with wisdom. A good starting point is the country that gave the world the idea of democracy.

Greece: The Global Minotaur

The Crisis of 2008 exposed Greece as a nation that was victimised by high levels of corruption and debt. The population became prisoners of their creditors. The rise of Syriza, a new left-wing party, claimed that it would oppose the austerity policies imposed on the people by financial institutions that still upheld the conventional economic policies that had caused the financial crisis in the first place. The guardians of conventional wisdom drove Greece deeper into sovereign debt as it borrowed money from the IMF, the European Central Bank and the European Union (the Troika). Syriza promised to release Greece from the shackles of debt and free its citizens so that they could rebuild their communities from the ground up. The saviour arrived on the back of a motorcycle.

Varoufakis.

Yanis Varoufakis.

The professor of economics was elected in 2015. On behalf of the Syriza government, he was nominated to negotiate salvation from the Troika. He knew all about economics, which he had studied in a British university. He taught the subject as a professor in both the western and the southern hemispheres. So when the call came from his people, he was ready. The beams of light from the flashguns of the paparazzi bounced off his bald head as he raced to and fro from the parliament building in Athens, where he had assumed the role of finance minister. The global media elevated him to the rank of superstar.

Varoufakis knew his Greek mythology, from which he drew his inspiration. Laced with the language of Marxism, he contrasted the fall of communism with the crisis in the peripheral economies of Euroland:

> The crash of 2008 exuded the air of a pre-classical, more mythological and thus cruder sequence of events. It is for this reason that this book adopts a title alluding to a period before tragedy was invented. (Varoufakis 2013:22)

The Minotaur was a tragic Greek figure symbolising greed, divine retribution, revenge and suffering. For Varoufakis, the Minotaur symbolised the American Empire. The problems of Europe and the rest of the world could be laid at the door of Washington, DC. But the suffering of the Greek people could be alleviated: Varoufakis was convinced that the Troika could be persuaded to reschedule Greece's debts. But he was not prepared to pay any price. He adamantly refused to comply with the terms laid down by the Troika for the €86bn (£63bn) bailout of the Greek economy. He blasted his way through Europe's corridors of power, to no avail. In the end, he was fired. Syriza retreated and lamely accepted defeat. The harsh austerity terms continued to be imposed by the Troika.

Varoufakis rode off into the sunset on his trusty motorbike. Lucrative speaking engagements came his way, but there was no relief for the people of Greece. Unemployment remained at over 20% and the pensions of the elderly (which had fallen by 40% in the five years up to 2015), were scheduled for a further cut if the country wanted to receive more money from its creditors.

Varoufakis would continue to play the role of saviour, this time by organising a movement to democratise the European Union. But his message was still embedded in a neo-Marxist framework. Could he have offered a different message to the people of Greece, one that might have mobilised them to undertake the reforms that might have led to renewal of the economy? That model was promoted by Joseph Stiglitz. He calls it the Henry George principle. Varoufakis had disclosed his familiarity with that model, but he declined to propose it as a mechanism for resolving the financial problems between Greece and its creditors in Brussels, Frankfurt and Washington DC.

And so, audiences throughout Europe remained frightened, angry and confused. On whom could they rely for sound judgements? Social activists placed special faith in the powers of the Internet. Digital technology had democratised communication, making it possible to by-pass the main-stream media! But how can technology overcome the dysfunctional ideas embedded in the collective consciousness? The story of one prophetic voice, which emerged out of the ether from a small village in Spain, is a warning for all of us.

He Died a Happy Man

Edward Hugh found fame late in life, just in time to die a happy man. The IMF courted him, hedge funds offered him big bucks to act as a consultant and governments – even the White House in Washington, DC – followed his blogs.

From his hideaway in a village outside Barcelona he fired off his blogs to anyone who would listen. And he gathered a large audience, for Edward Hugh had discovered the reason why the European economy would implode. *The New York Times* called him 'the blog Prophet of Euro-zone doom'.

Old age was at the heart of Europe's crisis! The population in Germany was ageing faster than in Spain and Greece, and this would cause the breakup of the European Union (EU). The Germans would save more and spend less on housing. The Spanish and Greeks were younger and would borrow more at low rates of interest to invest in houses. The Euroland experiment would end in tears.

> 'Why haven't these countries converged' with the rest of Europe? he asks. 'It's demographics. As populations age, there are fewer people in their 20s to 40s to buy new houses, so they save more. The younger a country is, the more dependent it is on credit to get growth.'   (Thomas 2010)

Hugh had a solution. Germany would have to withdraw from the single currency, so that the euro would devalue and the peripheral economies could recover their competitiveness.

He was serious. His blogs attracted the attention of professors in California and hedge fund analysts in London. They even offered him money to act as an adviser. And he relished the fact that he was paid to address conferences.

Hugh died on December 29, 2015, at the age of 67. His fame rested on an analysis of demography, the subject on which he had embarked for a doctoral thesis which he failed to complete. But who needs a doctorate when, according to his obituary, his record as 'an economic forecaster was more reliable than many a Nobel Prize winner' (*Daily Telegraph* 2016)? The obituary added:

> Hugh attracted a cult following among financial analysts and the accuracy of his predictions about the Eurozone led to invitations to advise the IMF, international banks, the White House, and the Spanish government. By 2011 he had moved on to Facebook, attracting thousands of new followers.

It was all smoke and mirrors. As Graph 11:1 indicates, countries with the highest GDP *per capita* (such as Germany and Denmark) also had lower levels of home ownership than Spain or Italy. But this had nothing to do with the age profile of the population. German families were less likely to fund a property boom because they were content to rent their homes and to invest their money in the small- and medium-sized businesses (SMEs) that make their economy dynamic. The property boom in Spain and Greece, on the other hand, was all to do with land speculation and the pursuit of capital gains; it was not driven by young families needing new homes.

Graph 11:1
Level of GDP pc vs Homeownership

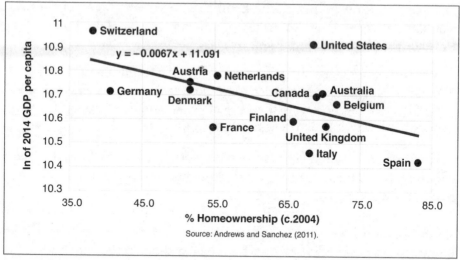

Source: Andrews and Sanchez (2011).

Edward Hugh may have been factually incorrect, but he served a purpose for the people in power. He was a prophet whose predictions – circulated widely via the Internet – did not challenge the economics of the statesmen who created Europe's single currency. Hugh attributed blame to something over which governments have no control – the age of the people who put them in power. And so the politicians were not embarrassed with awkward challenges to their policies.

But Edward Hugh was not the only false prophet to emerge in Euroland.

Spain: The Constitutional Promise

Spain would not have suffered the indignities of the global depression of the 21st century if the politicians of an earlier generation had adopted policies that reflected their commitments in the Agreements of Moncloa (October 1977). They signed those Agreements following the death of the dictator, Gen. Francisco Franco. It was a moment of sincerity in Spanish politics. The agreements declared:

The policy on land and urbanism that we propose is based on three principles: first, that public policies must reflect the social desire for occupation and use of urban land; second, that the plusvalue of urban land belongs in a fundamental way to the Community and, finally, that the public sector must assume the principal role in guaranteeing access to the use of urban land.

The Agreement proposed measures for the public appropriation of land value by increasing the land tax to avoid speculative retention.

Unfortunately, the Spanish Constitution (December 1978) was less emphatic than the Moncloa Agreements. Nevertheless, Article 47 in the chapter called 'Guiding principles of social and economic policies' states: 'All Spaniards have the right to dignity and an adequate home. The public powers will promote the necessary conditions and establish the corresponding rules to make this right effective, by regulating the use of land according to general interest to deter speculation. The community will participate in the land values that originate in the urban action of public entities'.

This was a 'guiding principle'. Nothing serious was done by successive governments. Some measures were introduced: a very mild municipal land value tax law and a capital gains tax with so many exemptions and drafted in such a way that those receiving the largest capital gains paid low amounts. In reality, all type of regulations were enacted which enhanced speculation. Not surprisingly, Spain became the victim of an orgy of speculation and corruption in the real estate sector. The outcome astonished other European nations. The popular reaction began with the rise of the movement called '15M'.

On 15 May 2011 hundreds of thousands of Spaniards took to the streets to protest against the dreadful economic situation. Unemployment reached almost 5m, which was 25% of the work force. People protested against shortages and cuts in spending on the public health system and on public schools. The austerity programme was one of the severest in Europe.

People also protested against the corrupt and inefficient politicians who had ruled the country for the previous 30 years. Their targets were the two main parties: the conservative Partido Popular (PP) and the socialist Partido Socialista Obrero Español (PSOE). Both parties were not only unable to implement remedies for the devastating economic crisis, but, on the contrary, they had profited from land speculation and an incredible level of corruption. The Conservatives were undoubtedly more immersed in corruption (as became evident from the investigations that were launched in 2015), but the Socialists also faced charges of corruption, especially in Andalusia. But politics was overshadowed by the ghosts of the Spanish Civil War. When the country went to the polls, many people still supported Partido Popular due to the fear that the 'reds' – as they call leftist organizations – would come to power. Many people – especially the older generation – recall that civil war, which caused the death of 1m people, and they do not want another one.

And so, in 2016, in what was supposed to be a period of economic recovery, Spain continued to be haunted by the crisis of 2008.

- ❖ *Unemployment* remained at over 4m, with many people out of work for more than two years. Reduced levels of unemployment were in part due to the fact that thousands of people lost all hope and ceased to register as unemployed. Furthermore, thousands of young people emigrated.
- ❖ *New jobs* provided precarious employment, with many people earning low salaries of €300-400 per month. Employees earning €600 per month were privileged.
- ❖ *No income* at all was received by over 1m families: their unemployment benefits had been extinguished.
- ❖ *Poverty* and mal-nutrition among children rose sharply. The queues of people waiting to get food from NGOs were a spectacle never seen before in Spain.

This was the economic situation which the Conservative Government of the Popular Party proclaimed as 'improving'. The state of the nation's finances suggested otherwise. GDP in 2014 was €1,041.160 million. The sovereign debt (2015, Q3) was €1,062.315 million. Sovereign debt equalled the annual GDP. Each Spaniard owed €22.875.

Governments of both the socialist and the conservative parties were unable to prevent the escalation of debt. The recession caused a drop in tax revenue, apart from the revenue from the property tax.

The total public income in 2014 (revenue received by Central Government, the Autonomous Communities, City Halls and the Social Insurance mandatory payments) was €399,733 million. This was about 38% of GDP, one of the lowest levels of taxation in the European Union. That did not imply that the income of the citizens was higher. It meant that the private appropriation of land rent was one of the highest in Europe.

Privately appropriated rent circulating in the Spanish economy amounted to 12% of GDP. This revenue fostered an incredible level of land speculation, thanks to the fact that property taxes were one of the lowest of Europe (a median rate of 0.664% on property values – house and buildings – which were assessed to be just 40% of the market value). This situation not only fostered an extraordinary level of corruption in many City Halls and Autonomous Communities (obtaining a building licence increased the value of land by 10 to 20 times!); it also contributed to the housing crisis.

Spain is an empty country: 93 inhabitants per square kilometre (occupying the 114th place in the world league). In this empty country the new generations of Spaniards have no possibility to access – buying or renting – a decent home. The main obstacle? *The price of land!* Its cost makes the price of residential property completely inaccessible. So now, thanks to the ignorance and corrupt behaviour of some politicians, Spain faces an incredible situation. There are about 1m empty houses, many of them in the hands of banks, while millions of Spaniards cannot have access to them.

We are driven to the only conclusion: the conservative and socialist politicians, in failing to address the problem of land speculation, created the crisis. Instead of promoting policies to curb land speculation, all the measures taken – due to ignorance or bad faith (I do not know which is worst!) – were directed to increase it. The only policy that could end speculation and reduce the price of land to affordable levels is through the fiscal policy of taxing rent. That was the one policy which they had completely ignored.

The pressure on the economy arising from the policy deficit is illustrated by the following numbers:

❖ The cadastral value of urban property (representing just 40% of market value) increased by 308% from 2000 to 2015. Rural property increased by approximately 145%. This compared with the 43% increase in the minimum salary between 2000 and 2015.

❖ As measured by Spain's National Accounts, the nation's rents at current prices increased from €551.333 million in the year 2000 to €839.294 million in 2014, an increase of 52%.

❖ The price per square meter of houses increased from €856.20 in 2000 to €2.101 in 2008, an increase of 145%. In 2015, with the ßgovernment cheerfully announcing the 'end of the crisis', the price per square meter was €1.457, an increase of 70% from the year 2000.[1]

---

1 National Institute of Statistics.

Movements of prices in the land market can be contrasted with what happened in the labour market. The minimum salary increased between 2000 and 2015 by 43%, while the price of housing per square meter increased by approximately 250% by 2008, declining to 170% in 2015. Real estate speculation – correctly called *land* speculation – destroyed the prospects for workers to acquire homes with their normal salaries. They could only do so with banks credits, which were the route to final disaster when workers lost their jobs and could not keep up their mortgage payments.

The Spanish production model was based on land speculation!

This was the context that fostered the movement known as 15M. It started in Madrid in May 2011 and spread rapidly to cities throughout Spain. The movement spawned new political parties: Podemos, and alliances like Unidad Popular, Izquiera Unida (hosting the Communist Party as the main force in it). Other organisations sprang in Valencia, in Galicia and in Catalonia.

The greatest hope for change rested with Podemos. Its charismatic leader, Pablo Iglesias, claimed that the central part of Europe's homeland – the core economy – was privileged because bankers were prejudiced against the peripheral economies. In *Politics in a Time of Crisis: Podemos and the Future of a Democratic Europe* (2015), he wrote:

> Our province of Spain has been selected, along with Greece, Portugal, Italy and Ireland, to act as the slum of the Europe invented by the Party of Wall Street.
>
> (2015:128)

Iglesias provided a robust description of exactly what caused the banking crisis of 2008 (Box 11:1). That problem originated in the real estate sector. Would a Podemos government provide the financial inoculation to prevent another feverish round of property speculation in the future? I had high hopes that Podemos would be willing to transform the tax regime to ensure that Spain would never again be savaged by a real estate sector that put profits before people.

In 2012 I was invited to join the Economic Group of 15M. I found very little understanding of the origin of land speculation and resistance to the proposal to introduce a tax on land values in their program. Nevertheless I was invited to present the case for tax reform on public platforms, and my recommendation to include land taxation in a document issued by different 15M groups in the Spanish capital, Madrid, was approved. Most of the economists who were members of the Economic

Box 11:1

According to Podemos leader Pablo Iglesias, the crisis began in 2006 with the rise of foreclosures in the more impoverished neighbourhoods of some American cities. He wrote in *Politics in a Time of Crisis*:

> The people thrown into the street were African Americans, Latin migrants, single mothers; who cared about them? But in the summer of 2007, the wave of foreclosures began to lap at middle-class white households, and by the end of the year more than two million Americans had lost their homes and another four million were about to do so.
>
> (2015: 110)

These events set off a chain reaction. American banks stopped lending to households and businesses, with the crisis spilling over across Europe, mainly affecting the peripheral countries of Portugal, Ireland, Italy, Greece and Spain. Millions lost their jobs and homes. Public services were then dismantled by means of austerity programmes 'that did away with what used to be called the welfare state'. Iglesias concluded:

> [What] began as a problem in the property market in the American south and southwest spread to the mortgage markets of Ireland and Spain, ravaged the banking systems of Iceland and Latvia, triggered a budget emergency in California and caused an appalling debt crisis in Greece and Spain due to the bailout of the banking sector.

From this chronology, we see the chain of causation. It was the failure of financial policies within the property market that caused the financial crisis of 2008. Those policies were sanctioned by the law-makers whose fiscal policies formulated the way economic incentives were created and how national incomes were distributed.

Group opposed the policy, but many others appreciated its significance.

In 2015 I joined the Economic Group of Podemos and participated in its Taxation Committee. I filed – jointly with Fred Harrison – a comprehensive report called 'The Cultural and Economic Renewal of Spain,' to outline the elements for an economic strategy for the new party. Lay members of the Taxation Committee were supportive. I faced fierce opposition from some economists, but we managed to introduce a paragraph in the final report to recommend land taxation. The response from the political leaders – most came from the Left and the 15M movement – was complete silence. Some of them informed me that it was a fantastic idea, but that 'it is not the time to propose it'. The outcome was reflected in the manifesto produced by Podemos for the local election in Madrid in 2015. Not a word was said about land taxation. In relation to the housing problem, a kind of Stalinist policy was proposed. The intention was to investigate and sanction those who owned more than 10 empty apartments (those who owned eight or nine empty apartments were not to be touched!). This was an absurd attempt to address a problem that could easily be solved by simply shifting the property tax off the value of buildings and onto the current value of land.

Not surprisingly, the proposal was removed from the program that was presented to the public in the general elections of 2015. Instead, the party announced that it would 'create an institutional agreement to establish the directives for programs on housing,' along with 'regulating the integration of a Table of Agreements' (Mesa de concentración) with representation from the state, Autonomous Communities, City Halls, public housing associations, the third sector, tenants, etc. The privatisation of rented public housing would be prohibited. Last but not least, it was proposed to introduce a tax on the owners of empty properties. I explained that this would require a police system to enforce, and that the appropriate policy was to tax all properties equally, which would deter owners from keeping their dwellings unoccupied. My advice was of no avail. The leaders of this 'new' movement were either ignorant or afraid of confronting the rent problem.

The programs offered by Podemos and the Socialist Party did not contain a single measure to tackle land speculation. To compound the error, Podemos proposed to increase taxes. Some of these would aggravate the damage inflicted on the economy. Others had a semblance of fairness to them, like an increase in the Inheritance Tax (which does fall on land) and ecological taxes.

Competing for power in the 2015 election was an array of other new parties, and old parties dressed up in new clothes (like Izquierda Unida, a political formation promoted by the Communist Party). None of them uttered a word about land taxation. The central idea of left-of-centre politicians was to deepen taxes, mainly the direct taxes, to try and soften the impact of VAT, and to tax large fortunes. A tax on financial transactions found favour. All the parties – the Socialists, Podemos, Izquierda Unida and its coalition partner Unidad Popular – made an issue of attacking tax evasion and fiscal fraud, without any realistic proposals for achieving this goal.

Towards the Promised Land?

In the event, the general election of December 2015 failed to produce a decisive outcome (a similar stalemate occurred in the election in Ireland in February 2016). Mariano Rajoy's Popular Party lost its overall majority and its leader declined the offer of the King to try to form a Government. The initiative was shifted in favour of the Socialist party (it had endured the worst election result in its history, but was still the second largest group in Parliament with 90 seats). It sought to do a deal with one of the new parties, Ciudadanos, a right-wing party that was free of the corruption that tainted the Popular Party. It advocated lower taxes, promised to attack fiscal fraud and evasion, but offered not one word in favour of taxing land.

The Agreement proposed to Parliament by the PSOE and Ciudadanos was called 'Agreement for a Government of Reforms and Progress'. Although real estate speculation was the driving force behind Spain's terrible recession, there was scarcely any mention of this fact in the Agreement. In a short paragraph it declared: '*A new more fair taxation system will be implemented*, in which each citizen's contribution would be according to their ability to pay, in the way it is established by the Constitution. At the same time *fiscal reforms will promote the transition to a new economic model*, giving incentives to productive investment, under-takings and innovation, against other types of activities that should be dis-incentivised such as *speculation, contamination or those that contribute to climatic change*' (emphasis added). There was only one reference to speculation in the Program and it was not related to land. Nevertheless it also states that 'the new government shall propose reforms of the taxation system that would increase the revenue without increasing taxes, shifting part of the taxation weight to the wealth and the use of natural finite resources'. We may understand that land is a natural finite resource, but when the Program analysed individual taxes, the only taxes that should be harmonised (not increased), and which were in a way related directly to real estate property (and hence to land), were the Inheritance Tax and the Patrimony Tax. They should be harmonised to end with the competition between both taxes that makes them 'empty' and stating finally that the middle class will be exempted from both taxes.

There was not a word about the direct taxation of the rental income of land.

Regarding the housing problem – a direct consequence of land speculation – with 1m empty houses in the country that people cannot afford to buy or rent, the program included some phrases against evictions, stating that victims should receive a house with a 'social rent according to the economic and family circumstances'. It also urgently proposed 'a Program of Social Renting by an agreement with the banks and the owners of empty properties'.

These were the only forms of action proposed to solve the existing problems and to avoid a new round of land speculation.

The proposal was rejected by the Spanish Parliament on 4th March 2016. The Socialist candidate, Pedro Sánchez, with the support of Ciudadanos, received 131 votes (90 from PSOE, 30 from Ciudadanos and 1 from Coalición Canaria, a party from the Canary Islands). Against him were 219 MPs, which meant all the other parties: PP, Podemos, Izquierda Unida–Unidad Popular and all the independent supporters from the Basque country and Catalonia. The future remained uncertain. An alliance of Socialists-Ciudadanos with Podemos and Izquierda Unida–Unidad Popular appeared extremely difficult. A coalition between PP, the Socialists and Ciudadanos, although promoted by Ciudadanos, was unacceptable to the Socialists. Rajoy was tainted by allegations of corruption and reactionary policies, but a manoeuvre between the parties should not be discounted. The only other option was for the King to call for a new election.

Nothing indicates that the problem of rent appropriation will be tackled in the near future, as none of the political parties is even considering it.

And so, Spain illustrates how the prophets of Euroland from both the Left and the Right who offered to lead their people to the Promised Land have created a political impasse. They aspire to fairness and justice, but their programs reveal that they have chosen the wrong road. Ignoring the way rent works in the economy, and not collecting that stream of revenue to fund the common good, will eventually lead Europe into another nightmare created by land speculation.

Instead of focusing on the financial strategies that would create hope and prosperity for everyone, the politicians remain committed to the tax regime that contributed to the crisis. The EU has standardised the Value Added Tax across the continent. This tax inflicts damaging consequences on everyone, according to the analysis by Mason Gaffney (Gaffney (2013).

New prophetic voices are urgently needed to help with the redirection

of our societies. Will they emerge from among the ranks of existing statesmen? In his analysis of how this happened in the past, Gaffney lamented
the absence of such voices in the United States today.

> Free market panaceas and banker deregulation have collapsed in shame
> and calamity, but nothing has arisen to replace them. Something must
> and will; but what, and how long must we wait? God moves in a mysterious
> way, his wonders to perform. My guess is that Mexican Americans, our
> new despised and feared minority, will take the lead: nothing pulls people
> together like contempt and persecution. They will ally with a variety of
> smaller ethnic groups. Where is the new political genius to pull all these
> disparates together? This leader will appear; many are grasping for the
> brass ring.
>
> (Gaffney 2010: 8)

Gaffney's guess of a Latino response was written six years before the
rise of the real estate magnate Donald Trump as a nominee for the US
presidential election of 2016. Trump's political language included vicious
attacks on people of Mexican heritage. It remains to be seen whether,
out of this community, there does emerge a prophetic voice that is capable
of shining a bright light on the future. Such a beacon is desperately
needed. In Euroland the prophetic voices, so far, have offered nothing
but false hopes.

References

Andrews, D., and A.C. Sanchez (2011), 'The Evolution of Home Ownership Rates in some OECD
Countries: Demographic and Public Policy Influences', *OECD Journal: Economic Studies.*

BBC (2016), Newsnight interview with Prof. Larry Sabato, Director of the Centre for Politics,
University of Virginia, February 24.

Gaffney, Mason (2010), 'Great Awakenings', *CounterPunch*, Vol. 17(22), Dec. 16-31.

— (2013), 'Europe's Fatal Affair with VAT', *GroundSwell*, March-April. http://commonground-
usa.net/gaffney-mason_europes-fatal-affair-with-vat-2013.htm

Harrison, Fred (1983), *The Power in the Land*, London, Shepheard-Walwyn

Hugh, Edward (2015), *Is the Euro Crisis Really Over?*

Iglesias, Pablo (2015), *Politics in a Time of Crisis*, London, Verso.

Luce, Edward (2016), 'Blair warns on electability of Sanders', *Financial Times*, February 24.

Telegraph, Daily (2016), 'Obituary: Edward Hugh: Blogger whose advice was sought by policy makers
after he correctly predicted the Eurozone crisis', January 5.

Thomas, Jr., Landon (2010), 'The Blog Prophet of Doom' *New York Times*. June 9, http://query.
nytimes.com/gst/fullpage.html?res=9500E5DC1E39F93AA35755C0A9669D8B63&
pagewanted=all

Varoufakis, Yanis (2013), *The Global Minotaur*, London, Zed Books.

12

Cries of the Wild

PETER SMITH

I F A GROUP of people was shipwrecked on a desert island, what would be the first set of rules they would have to agree upon? To ensure social cohesion and effective cooperation, the first task would be to agree how to share the natural resources on which they would depend for biological survival. They would expect to be treated as equals. And, conforming to the principle of prudence, they would agree to nurture the riches of nature, since they would not know how long they would be marooned on the island.

The shipwreck story is a metaphor for the evolution of culture. It evokes a vital insight: if there is something fundamentally wrong with the way people use their natural habitat, there is probably something wrong with property rights. A dysfunctional relationship with nature implies a serious defect in the rules, or with the way the rules are enforced. For as individuals, people would not wilfully wreck their natural environments, or malevolently extinguish other species that did not pose an existential threat to them. If they manifest such behaviour, we must search for the possibility that there is something fundamentally wrong with the laws of the land.

Listen carefully to the cries of nature. They tell us that the rules which regulate our behaviour are fundamentally flawed. We have killed countless species. Many more are being extinguished. The anguish this causes echoes from the farthest points of our planet, a message of despair with

229

Box 12:1

Starved to Death by Our Garbage

We treat the oceans as a waste dump. Whales, those intelligent creatures of the oceans, are telling us about the scale of the crime known as acidification. Within a few months at the beginning of 2016, more than 36 whales perished as they were washed up on North Sea beaches. Thirteen of them on a single beach in Germany were examined and were found to have stomachs full of plastic waste. The waste included a 43-foot fisherman's net, a 3-foot cover from a car's engine, and parts of a broken bucket. The environment minister for the north German state of Schleswig-Holstein concluded that the plastic waste "causes them to suffer and at worst, causes them to starve with full stomachs" (Fernandez 2016).

Plastic packaging generates significant negative externalities, which are conservatively valued by the UN Environment Programme at $40 billion. Each year, at least 8 million tonnes of plastics leak into the ocean. This is equivalent to dumping the contents of one garbage truck into the ocean every minute. If the current trend continues, the volume is expected to increase to two per minute by 2030 and four per minute by 2050. There are an estimated 150 million tonnes of plastics in the ocean today. The ocean is expected to contain 1 tonne of plastic for every 3 tonnes of fish by 2025. By 2050, the forecast is for more plastics than fish by weight (World Economic Forum (2016: 7).

the way we live our lives. At stake is not just the plight of other creatures. Humanity itself is at risk.

The global destruction of species is analogous to the mass extinctions that occur when super volcanoes erupt or when asteroids struck the planet hundreds of millions of years ago. Scientists apply the term 'Holocene extinction' to this, the sixth such mass extinction event our planet has faced in its four billion year history. Upwards of 875 extinctions have been documented for the period between 1500 and 2009 by the International Union for Conservation of Nature and Natural Resources, but the rate of extinction may be up to 140,000 species per year (Pimm *et al.*, 1995). The term 'Anthropocene' has been coined to describe how our geology and environment have been so transformed that we have created a new geological age (Waters *et al.* 2016). Efforts to protect wonderful creatures such as tigers, orangutans, elephants and rhinos attract massive support, but population science is telling us that we are losing the battle for conservation. Our children's children may never have the chance to see tigers or orangutans in their natural habitats. The cries of the wild must alert us that the laws that regulate our relationship with nature are not fit for purpose (Box 12:1).

As the director of a conservation charity in Britain, I listen to nature every day. Through my office window I can hear the howl of a wolf and the bellow of a European Bison. But the metaphoric cries from species that we subject to the grotesque abuse of their land are much louder and clearer to my perception. We fail to heed those mortal messages at our peril. This time, we really must adopt the remedies that can secure the future of our species and peaceful co-existence with nature. Earth is a complex web of life. The composition of our atmosphere and minerals are a direct result of biological action. Science is unpicking the com plexities of ecology just as we are destroying these relationships. We only just understand how wolves and beavers change rivers and land, how whales bring to the surface minerals that whole ocean ecosystems depend on, yet every day we are destroying nature. Humanity's future is entwined in the same fate.

The Tragedy of Property Rights

Property rights are at the heart of most conflicts within human societies, and in our relationship with nature. This is insufficiently considered by environmentalists who campaign on behalf of nature. This has worked to the advantage of ideologists who champion private property rights.

The most notorious example of the skewing of the debate on property rights is ecologist Garrett Hardin's article in *Science* (1968). In this, he claimed that the commons were abused by people who, lacking private property rights, allowed their cattle to over-graze the fields. This was *the tragedy of the commons.* But when he was challenged, he conceded that the problem was not with unmanaged commons. The problem was with the inappropriate management of

In many ways, nature conservation has become just another method of rent extraction by landowners who are trying to hide the fact that modern farmers' fields are essentially deserts, devoid of wildlife, and the taxpayer must pay 'rent' if we want wild animals to occupy 'their land'.

Box 12:2

The False Trade-offs

The central dilemma that ecologists and environmentalists face is one in which they are told that efforts to protect nature are treated by most policy-makers as trade-offs between jobs, prosperity and human progress. Environmental campaigners have internalised this argument, so they are captured by the doctrine of dismal choices: they concede that we must forego jobs and economic prosperity for the sake of protecting nature. But this need not be the case. As Mason Gaffney has written (1998:1): 'Understanding [Henry] George's programme, one can see that those allegedly hard choices are false, calculated to unman us and make resolute action seem futile.' Understanding the role of economic rent in the economy enables us to see that its collection would free us to protect nature and our environment and at the same time enjoy the benefits of technological advancement that can be shared by everyone.

the commons (Hardin 1991). Too late: his original thesis continued to multiply like malignant parasites in the economic literature, reinforcing the ideological prejudices of those who wished to turn Mother Earth into money and material for owners who recognised no social or ecological responsibilities.

Mason Gaffney's theses in *The Corruption of Economics* were a seminal moment for me. I realised that the study of economics is central to nature conservation. I have seen the destruction of nature time and time again and come to realise just how our economy rewards those who damage nature and punishes those who try to protect it. The perverse incentives surround us yet seem to go unnoticed.

My work as an ecologist over the last 20 years has had many successes, but I came to understand that I was wrestling with dismal choices and futile trade-offs. And yet, as explained by Gaffney (1998), it took the genius of Henry George to see how the dismal trade-offs could be resolved in happy solutions (Box 12:2).

I now grasped a fuller understanding of why the efforts of nature conservationists were failing, and the futility of our efforts to reverse the loss of biodiversity. I have raised tens of millions of pounds to protect nature, but this was actually funding the destruction of nature elsewhere. I came to understand why the efforts of most charities and government agencies to protect nature were counter-productive. Many of the public policies that I campaigned to enact were undermining my initiatives and were destroying nature.

The Sheep-wrecked Hillsides

Marginal land where it is hard to farm ought to be places where wildlife can still cling on. But these places are as devoid of wildlife as our urban environments. The story of the desolation of these habitats illustrates how nature conservation has become just another method of rent extraction by landowners who are trying to hide the fact that farmers' fields are essentially deserts, devoid of wildlife, and the taxpayer must pay them rent if we want wild animals to occupy 'their land'.

The conservation organisation English Nature published a report showing there was more birdlife in people's back gardens than in rural areas. Landowners turned viciously on this report and ensured that it was expunged from websites so that their myths would continue to flourish.

Wildlife that is clinging on in the more remote hard-to-farm areas is under assault. It is not an easy task to expunge wildlife, but to do so we now train an army of 'land managers' on how to graze the land bare, and how to pour fertilisers and pesticides on the ground to produce a tiny amount of food. By subsidising the use of these marginal areas, we make it expensive. This, in turn, drives people on to even more barren land, thereby pushing the margin of production out to the most unforgiving landscapes. Those who wish to farm battle among themselves to find inexpensive land to rent. Nature's most wild and inaccessible places suffer the collateral damage.

Modern farmers' fields are 'agri-desert', and for that we can blame the system of subsidy payments. Subsidies push farming to destroy wildlife with no regard to the land. They penalise efforts to use land efficiently for food production and wildlife protection. We even subsidise land used by the social elites for hunting, where they burn and graze bare their land to overstock it with grouse and deer, often so that lazy hunters do not have to walk too far to shoot their animal of choice.

Nature conservation organisations do not realise the extent to which their support for such policies have dire unintended consequences for the wildlife they are dedicated to conserving. They lobby to bolster agri-environment schemes that subsidise land that is used less intensively. The perverse consequence is that land that would have been below the margin, and ought to have been left alone, is brought into production. So we have become gardeners of nature. Many conservationists and farmers think they are doing good for nature, but if they left the land alone we would have greater biodiversity.

Rewilding

The rewilding movement has realised that the diversity of life depends not only on allowing vegetation to grow naturally. Nature also needs the complex action of the herbivores that browse the vegetation and the carnivores that keep the herbivores in balance. That process is all but gone in the UK, with just a few places left for the browsing of wild horses or beavers. But we also need wolves and lynx to keep wild populations in check.

Nature conservation organisations have to spend millions of pounds in buying land and then using the labour of thousands of skilled conservationists to try and recreate the lost unique ecological processes that were once provided free by nature. Money is solicited to fund this work. But because of the way our economy works, donations and grants have perverse outcomes. They help to push up the price of land. Ultimately this makes conservation projects harder to get off the ground. In the time I have spent purchasing land for wildlife charities, the price of land has risen over twentyfold.

Furthermore, when conservation charities receive subsidies, similar sums are often granted to other land users. This adds a further upward twist to the price of land that would otherwise have been designated as below the economic margin. So land that is 'farmed for wildlife' actually has less wildlife on it than would be the case if we had left it alone. All of this is at the expense of taxpayers, from whom the subsidies are extracted in return for less biodiversity.

This perverse state of affairs can only be reversed if we introduce a rental charge on land to soak up the subsidies and donations and provide an incentive to allow land of poor quality to revert to the wild.

Tenant farmers support the system of farm subsidies without realising that they are not the beneficiaries. That outcome is well understood.

Agricultural subsidies tend to be capitalised into the purchase and the rental price of agricultural land. Because of higher incomes farmers are prepared to bid more to rent in or purchase extra land. But given that the overall supply of land is fixed, farmers will bid against each other up to the point where the entire increase in profitability is dissipated by the higher cost of land. Thus, it is landowners who are the main beneficiaries of farm support policies.

(Matthews, 2007)

Land that is close to, or below, the margin of worthwhile cultivation, ought to command zero rent. Where rent is payable, it is in the form of the subsidies transferred from taxpayers. A marginal hill farmer's rental payment to his landlord may be made up almost entirely of subsidy, especially if they receive the UK government's enhanced Higher Level Stewardship grants. If those subsidies were withdrawn, sub-marginal farms would give way to wildlife. Biodiversity would be nurtured. The 'ecosystem services' would be performed at no cost to taxpayers.

Subsidies are non-means tested state benefits to landowners who receive them without having to work (see Chapter 10). A small minority of landowners endeavour to protect wildlife out of moral duty, but our system does not support them to the extent it should. The cost to taxpayers of government agri-environment schemes are essentially compensation to landowners for the profits forgone.

If we had a land value tax on land, which replaced income tax and VAT, farmers could get on with the business of farming unencumbered by this economic minefield. Agri-environment subsidies would then really help the environment rather than idle landlords.

Carbon and Climate Change

Carbon is the very substance of life, born in the nuclear furnaces of stars, coalesced into the hearts of planets and then, through the miracle of life, carbon forms the substructure of every organic molecule. Life can be described as the process of turning simple carbon molecules into complex molecules. The evolution of life is about how that process has become more efficient.

Our technological achievements have reversed this process. We release the energy stored in complex carbon molecules as it breaks down into carbon dioxide and other pollutants. We exploit the stored complexity of life, which is formed in coal and oil, to provide the power we need. While this process is natural, our use of fossil fuels has set in motion a chain of effects that could cause calamity to humanity. Atmospheric carbon dioxide is at dangerously high levels. The science is convincing – this will severely affect our climate in coming generations.

This 'wrong' form of carbon could threaten our existence. Scientists and politicians ferociously argue about whether this is the case, when they should be exploring not just *how* carbon is being used but *why* our economic system has wasted this precious natural resource. We need to understand why the policies our politicians have enacted are ineffective at reducing the use of carbon.

This deplorable state of affairs has arisen not only because we use trains, planes, automobiles, and heat for our homes, but because coal and oil are incredibly profitable for those who own the rights to take it from the ground. Those profits are inflated because of the failure to internalise the costs of using them. As a result, we are robbing future generations by depleting those finite natural resources.

The bias in efforts to control the emission of carbon dioxide is illustrated by the 'cap and trade' policy, which also illuminates how property rights have captured the conservation agenda. Cap and trade is designed to enrich the rich and impoverish the poor without reducing the emission of carbon. It gives private companies ownership of the right to pollute and, in turn, the right to rent their privilege to others. Shareholders of polluting companies at a stroke become hereditary barons, milking humanity of their productive labour for the rest of time.

Yet the effort needed to create new technologies that use less natural resources is punished by taxes levied on labour and on the capital that is needed to create these innovations. Many economists like Joseph Stiglitz promote the concept of a simple carbon tax, which is a charge on the rent of a natural resource. This carbon tax would eat into the monopoly profits and reduce the incentives to extract the fossil fuels from the ground. By shifting taxes from wages and trade and on to carbon, we would use less and work more efficiently at manufacturing goods and investing in renewable forms of energy. Our smart phones, televisions, cars and houses would be made in ways that kept carbon safely in the ground and not in the atmosphere. Furthermore, the greater efficiency of land use, and the return of land to a wild state, would help to suck billions of tonnes of carbon back into the ground.

Food or Wildlife

Critics of rewilding and nature conservation claim that it is impossible to have more wildlife because we need the land to grow food. In Britain, the National Farmers Union flies the flag ot 'food security' whenever we canvass the need to nurture nature or cut subsidies. So conservationists should consider how policies on land ownership and taxation affect society, and therefore colour people's views on our relationship with nature.

Feeding the Fat and Starving the Poor   Globally, we produce more food than we consume. Those involved in feeding the starving state that famine is more a question of logistics and physical security than food availability. What is less understood is how economics determines people's ability to feed themselves, for even if we produce more food there is no guarantee that it will reach the hungry.

- ➤ The UK produces probably three times as much food than actually ends up on tables. Food is wasted throughout the chain from farm to dining table.
- ➤ We subsidise foodstuffs such as maize and wheat which is then fed to animals, a vastly inefficient way to use farm crops in the production of meat.
- ➤ Rainforests are being destroyed to produce soya, corn and palm oil that is fed to animals in intensive animal rearing pens. The horrors of these mega factories of half a million pigs or 3,000 cows in tiny 'feedlots' pumped full of antibiotics is an environmental and animal welfare disaster.

Obesity has reached social crisis levels in countries like the USA and UK. This is just one indicator of the fact that the simple production of more food will not in itself solve the problem of hunger. Ultimately, the solution is to share the rent of land to ensure that the poorest receive a square financial deal. That, in turn, through the fiscal/financial chain, would empower them to eat food without abusing nature (Box 12:3).

Water Water Everywhere   The perverse use of water in California, a state suffering from historic water shortages, has long engaged the attention of Mason Gaffney (1969; 2016). Inherited water rights and subsidies have turned the supply of water into a crisis. People who hold the right to use water over-use it on crops such as rice fields. This creates the insane spectacle of field after field of flooded rice paddies in an arid region where there is not enough water to supply homes. In the Palm Springs desert, golf courses bloom while the rivers run dry and there is no water downstream for people or nature. This system of water rights is similar to the one in the UK, where landowners and businesses

Box 12:3

The Rainforest Syndrome

Worldwide, palm oil plantations and soya fields are wiping out tropical rain-forests at a frightening pace. The economic driver is not the growth in human population but the quest for cheap meat for western consumption. This is a lifestyle choice at the expense of the environment. If the rent/revenue policy was applied in all countries, those seeking to use tropical rainforests for soya and palm oil production would have to pay for the privilege: the farmland they create would attract a yearly rental charge. That would change the financial incentives and people's attitudes. Meat would become more expensive, to reflect its true cost. Human health would improve. One paradoxical result: more food would become available for consumption, thereby increasing food security and saving low-income people from starvation. Pristine wildlife habitats would be free of the rental charge.

have inheritable rights. The true value of this water is not reflected in the costs of 'abstraction licenses' and there has been slow progress in reforming the system, consequently, water is still used inefficiently.

If we charged the full cost for the use of water, perverse incentives would be converted into positive incentives. Farmers and businesses would internalise the cost of water into their products and encourage them to minimise its use and maximise its economic potential. Everyone can be allocated a minimum amount of water for health and hygiene, and more efficient ways would be found to water the garden, wash cars or fill swimming pools. The charge for water can be regulated so that rivers and aquifers never run dry and waterways and wetlands can be preserved for wildlife.

We can extend this system of publically shared 'water rents' to third world countries and water starved areas such as Karachi in Pakistan, which endures thousands of deaths a year related to water shortages. In 2015 the lack of water contributed to a calamity where cemeteries had no room to bury the dead. In a system based on water rents there would be enough water for all and funds to invest in public water infrastructure to prevent the recurrence of such calamities.

Some areas suffer from too much water. This is popularly attributed to climate change. In reality, changes in upland agriculture and lowland urban development have altered the way water moves through catchments areas. One cause of the flooding of towns is intensive farming of uplands and floodplains. Wetlands and upland bogs have been drained, so these giant sponges cannot perform their traditional role of absorbing the downfall from heavy rains. Water now flashes over compacted soils, down through subsidised drainage channels into the rivers, where it sluices downstream into the front rooms of people's dwellings.

Restoring the capacity of land to absorb water would be most efficiently achieved through rewilding of upland catchment areas, and protecting the flood plains from urban development. We need to replace existing taxes on property with a site-value only charge – an annual rental charge. Both social and ecological habitats would benefit, in their own ways. One result would be a rise in the location value of economically important areas. In time, higher rental revenue could be used to fund mitigation work and reduce the taxes that damage private enterprise. One beneficiary would be the owner of poor quality land, for whom the fiscal burden would be reduced to zero.

Rewilding and Rodent Power   The rewilding project has an ally in the humble beaver. This amazing rodent will do all the land management work we need to create the giant wetland sponges that will not only hold back the floodwaters; they will allow the water to seep back into our rivers in dry times, providing year-round water flow. Beavers create peaty soils that suck carbon back into the soil and establish a wildlife paradise. Rewilding the catchments areas would cost the tax payer very little, if we allowed the beaver to do the work for us. And yet, nature's creatures are victimised as villains by the culture that accords priority to people who privately own our natural habitats.

Mad Cows: an Epidemiological Nightmare

Intensive meat rearing systems have created an epidemiological nightmare. The UK, for example, is being swept by a bovine TB epidemic, known as mad cow disease. In 2015 the UK Government began to shoot badgers in a futile effort to control TB. The reality is a story full of intrigue and vested interests competing for economic advantage. A whole generation of farmers and 'country people' have forgotten the basic epidemiological science of bovine tuberculosis (bTB). The farming lobby finds it much easier to blame badgers than address the fundamental problems of poor cattle farming.

The introduction of pasteurisation effectively stopped the disease being transferred to humans through drinking milk. Strict controls on cattle movements and herd quarantine ensured a reduction in bTB across the UK, effectively wiping out the disease. The restrictions were relaxed in the 1970s, and bTB began to reappear.

Changes in farming practices have contributed to the epidemic. Cattle live in larger and denser groups and spend more time in large sheds and stockades, thereby exposing herds to bTB. But rather than attribute the spread of the disease to their own practices, the farming lobby is trying to blame badgers, despite the absence of credible scientific evidence. The solution is economic: stop the perverse incentives that reward farming for poor husbandry techniques.

1 Private insurance   The farming industry should pay for bad and illegal practices. The best way to achieve this is by withdrawing government subsidy and compensation payments. Farmers could privately insure themselves against TB. This free market solution would reward good farming practices (lower premiums). High-risk farms would be charged high premiums, and farmers who commit fraud by changing ear tags and other illegal practices would invalidate their insurance.

2 Stricter quarantine   Detailed statistical analysis has shown that it is the movement of cattle from one farm to another that is by far the most important factor in the spread of TB (Gilbert *et al* 2005). The reintroduction of the quarantine measures that were abandoned in the past is key to the control of bTB in the UK.

3 Credible science   Spending large sums of taxpayers' money on trials of shooting and gassing badgers should stop. Devote the funds used to kill badgers to microbiological research of the disease and its control by vaccination in cattle and badgers.

4 Fiscal policy   Taxation should be shaped to promote less intensive agriculture. Current tax policies favour tax-dodgers, land speculators, large landowners and investment in huge capital infrastructure. Fuel, fertilisers and agricultural chemicals enjoy huge subsidies that do not reflect their true cost to society or the environment. Landowners benefit by expanding their buildings and gaining planning permission for huge new cattle sheds. Capital gains from land are tax-free. The cumulative effect is ever more intensive agricultural systems, increased disease and the suffering of animals.

We would rebalance the economy and encourage less intensive farming by removing taxes on wages and trade, and removing the tax perks on large machinery. Government should raise its revenue with an annual charge on ground rent and charges on the rents of natural resources such as oil and minerals. Small farmers would be able to compete on equal terms with industrial farming methods. One outcome would be the reduction in the use of poor quality animal husbandry and the spread of disease.

War, Conflict Resolution & the Refugee Crisis

The war in Syria had its roots in a combination of dysfunctional land practises and the intervention of nature. A drought, high temperatures and the poor allocation of water and grazing rights led to desertification, crop failure and the displacement of 1.5m Syrians. People were transformed from being relatively wealthy farmers to poor urban dwellers. This contributed to the fomentation of discontent that eventually erupted in civil war. To try and stem the tide of refugees flowing into Europe, Western governments tried to restore peace by bombing Syria.

The intervention of those seeking to profit from the crisis, by getting their hands on the spoils of war – in particular, the oil – served as the murderous back-cloth to this and many other conflicts. The anti-war movement lacked a concrete objective, a remedy that would remove the causes of warfare such as environmental destruction and loss of livelihood, and eliminate the incentive of those who seek to profit from war. Only by redistributing resource rents on a democratic basis can we achieve these complex objectives. Rent-sharing removes the perverse incentive to fight over natural resources because these would not be monopolised by one group, corporation or country. Fiscal policy would transform us all into stewards of nature, stewards of peace and reduce the pressure of mass migration, ridding us of the horrors that are being suffered by refugees across the world.

Pirates and Fish in the Oceans

The depletion of fish stocks has reached a critical point. Vested interests are engaged in legal battles surrounding fishing subsidies and quota allocations, but these cannot be resolved until we answer one fundamental question: who owns nature? The answer enables us to develop an

economic formula that recognises the difference between the free gifts of
nature and the value that we create by our labour. Otherwise, the rent-
seeking culture will continue to abuse the natural environment. This is
illustrated by the over-exploitation of fish stocks which may be analysed
with the aid of an ocean-going version of the 'tragedy of the commons'.

Garrett Hardin argued that natural resources were over-exploited –
that there was 'rent dissipation' – because of the absence of private
property rights. His contention was that, by allocating private rights, the
over-grazing of land would cease; self-interest would ensure conservation.
This notion has been extended from the land to the oceans, in the claim
that fishermen were not able to make a profit because of an excessive
number of fishing vessels. This led to the thesis that the grant of fishing
quotas would reduce the number of boats, making it possible for the
remaining fishing firms to make a profit.

How the privatisation of natural resources was spread deep into the
academic economic establishment is traced in Gaffney (2011). The flaw
in the reasoning, in relation to fisheries, was exposed by Seth Macinko,
an associate professor at the department of marine affairs at the University of Rhode Island, and his co-author David Bromley. They explained
how the problem was not with rent dissipation, but with the failure to
protect public ownership rights. That protection included 'rent capture
on behalf of [the] owning public' (Macinko and Bromley 2002: 33).

The European Union failed to learn that lesson. It issued free fishing
quotas which were then converted into financial instruments by the major
fishing corporations. Iceland became one of the victims of this financial-
isation of fishing quotas. The fishing corporations borrowed heavily on
the strength of their valuable quotas, which contributed to the boom that
collapsed the Icelandic economy in 2008.

The solution was not to privatise the fish stocks by handing out free
quotas; it was to charge rents for the privilege of fishing, by leasing the
right to fish. Fishermen would keep what they earned by their labour
and the capital invested in their vessels; rent – the net income, which is
the value above the normal profit to be gained from fishing – would go
into the public purse. This model, as Macinko and Bromley stressed,
would transform the management of fish stocks to everyone's advantage.
The losers would be those who wished to use their quotas to operate as
financial speculators.

If fishing quotas were auctioned every year to the highest bidders,
society could control the amount caught and promote efficiency in the

fishing industry. In effect, the industry would become self-policing. The economic value of fish would be internalised in the cost of the fish to the consumer, which becomes the self-regulating way to protect each species. This negative feedback system can be extended to all of nature's gifts, while at the same time reducing poverty and inequality.

The Value of Nature

Placing a monetary value on nature is controversial among conservationists and environmental campaigners. But the problem is not with valuing nature: it lies with *not* valuing nature properly. Valuation exercises, such as the UK Government's National Ecosystem Assessment, are inadequate. But of greater importance is the issue of how to internalise value in the economy, to help us all to preserve nature.

The sophisticated solution is to transfer taxes off earned incomes and trade and raise revenue from rents. One immediate consequence is the removal of the financial incentives that contribute directly to the destruction of nature. A nuanced system of public finance encourages behaviour that includes: leaving fossil fuels in the ground, reducing farming on marginal habitats, conserving fresh water and allowing nature to bury carbon in the ground.

If we are to enjoy nature at little or no cost to the taxpayer we must abandon land that has little commercial value for growing food, homes and industry. Rewilded locations would not be devoid of people: there would be jobs aplenty for those who are able to help tourists as they flock to these wonderful places to enjoy nature in its raw beauty. But we can only achieve this vision of a natural wonder if we create the incentives for current landowners to embrace change. This can be best achieved by removing agricultural subsidies and converting land rent as a gift bestowed on all of us equally. Farmland would become cheaper and therefore accessible to young farmers. In the UK, I estimate that between 40% and 50% of the land surface could be shared with wildlife.

In caring about nature, we would also help to elevate the quality of people's lives. Eating habits would be improved in tandem with a reduction in the reliance on fossil fuel-based chemicals and the degradation of soils. That would enable conservationists to proceed with the business of nature conservation. We need to learn much more about how animals move from place to place, how populations establish relationships between organisms such as the fungi in the ground, the plants, the flowers, the trees, wild horses and cattle roaming in a natural habitat, and how the wolf and lynx would operate to keep these populations in check – nature's own process of habitat conservation.

References

Andelson, R.V. (1991), *Commons without Tragedy*, London, Shepheard-Walwyn.

Fernandez, Colin (2016), 'Washed up whales had bellies full of plastic', *Daily Mail*, March 26.

Gaffney, Mason (1969), 'Economic Aspects of Water Resource Policy', *American Journal of Economics and Sociology*, 28(2).

_ (1994), 'Neoclassical Economics as a Stratagem against Henry George', in Mason Gaffney and Fred Harrison, *The Corruption of Economics*, London, Shepheard-Walwyn.

_ (1998), 'George's Economics of Abundance: Replacing dismal choices with practical resolutions and synergies', May 17, Speech at Grosvenor Hotel, London. http://www.usbig.net/papers/195-Gaffney—George's%20Economics%20of%20Abundance—Apr09.pdf

_ (2011), 'Sleeping with the Enemy: Economists who Side with Polluters', *Groundswell*, Jan-Feb. and May-June.

_ 'and Merrill Goodall (2016), 'New Life for the Octopus: How Voting Rules Sustain the Power of California's Big Landowners', *American Journal of Economics and Sociology*, Vol 75(3).

Gilbert, M., *et al* (2005), 'Cattle movements and bovine tuberculosis in Great Britain', *Nature*, 435.

Hardin, Garrett (1991), 'The Tragedy of the *Unmanaged* Commons: population and the disguises of Providence', in Robert V. Andelson, ed., *Commons Without Tragedy*, London, Shepheard-Walwyn.

Matthews, Alan (2007), CapReform.EU, More on who benefits from farm subsidies, October 14 2007: http://capreform.eu/more-on-who-benefits-from-farm-subsidies/

Macinko, Seth, and Daniel W. Bromley (2002), *Who Owns America's Fisheries?* http://sethmacinko.com/publications

Pimm, S.L. *et al* (1995), 'The Future of Biodiversity', *Science* (269). http://www.montana.edu/screel/Webpages/conservation%20biology/pimm%20et%20al%20-%20biodiversity.pdf

Waters *et al* (2016), 'The Anthropocene is functionally and stratigraphically distinct from the Holocene', *Science*, January 8, Vol. 351.

World Economic Forum (2016), *The New Plastics Economy*, Geneva. http://www3.weforum.org/docs/WEF_The_New_Plastics_Economy.pdf

13

The Culture of Prosperity

ROGER SANDILANDS

S OMETIMES IT PAYS to 'listen' to what people are doing rather than what they are saying. As Henry George noted in *A Perplexed Philosopher* (1892: 217):

> That thought on social questions is so confused and perplexed, that the aspirations of great bodies of men, deeply though vaguely conscious of injustice, are in all civilized countries being diverted to futile and dangerous remedies, is largely due to the fact that those who assume and are credited with superior knowledge of social and economic laws have devoted their powers, not to showing where the injustice lies but to hiding it; not to clearing common thought but to confusing it.

The United Kingdom has been one victim of this process of power being deployed to cause confusion. A century ago, however, a window of opportunity appeared, and it was opened in 1884 by Henry George. He had arrived from America to address a packed audience in Glasgow's City Halls. He decried the shameful poverty and squalor that existed side by side with so much evidence of growing wealth in the Second City of the Empire. Why was this? George proffered the answer, which resonated with the people of Scotland. They, in turn, gave a mandate to the Liberal Party, which secured a landslide victory in the general election of 1906.

The Liberal MP for Stirling, Henry Campbell Bannerman, was confirmed as Prime Minister, followed in 1908 by Herbert Asquith, the MP for East Fife. Glasgow Corporation was also dominated by Liberals who campaigned strongly for land value taxation. A petition in 1906 was signed by 518 local authorities calling for reform that led to a land valuation bill in 1908 and to Lloyd George's 'People's Budget' of 1909. Both bills were blocked by the landlord-dominated House of Lords. This led in 1911 to the removal of the Lords' power to block finance bills. The process was begun to value the land of the United Kingdom, which had to be halted by outbreak of war in 1914 (Mulvey (2002).

We shall never know how the UK economy might have evolved over the 20th century, if the 1909 Budget had been enacted and further developed in line with the logic of the new fiscal philosophy. But we can derive an idea of what might have happened to transform people's personal lives and the fabric of their communities if we undertake an exercise in counterfactual history.

What would have happened if the rent-revenue policy had been adopted back in the 1970s? How much richer would the people of the UK have been, if the growth rate had been higher by (say) 2% per annum? This is a reasonable but cautious assumption to take as the starting point for analysis. But is it a realistic hypothesis? To avoid indulging in fantasy speculation, we need to be sure of the realism of our speculations. Take, for example, the case of Singapore. Following the departure of the British and the achievement of sovereignty for the island in 1965, Singapore adopted a growth model which delivered an annual average growth rate of 7.6% between 1970-2012 Set against that achievement, it is not unreasonable to suggest that the UK might have grown by an additional 2% per annum if she had adopted measures similar to those that were deployed in Singapore. What was the secret of the former British colony's prosperity?

According to Phang Sock Yong, PhD Harvard and a professor of economics at Singapore Management University (previously my colleague at the National University of Singapore), the city state flourished because the economic model contained 'elements of [Henry] George's land value tax capture'. She explained:

> Soon after independence, the Land Acquisition Act was passed in 1966, which gave the state broad powers to acquire land. In 1973, the concept of a statutory date was introduced, which fixed compensation values for

land acquired at the statutory date, November 30, 1973. State land as a proportion of total land grew from 44% to 76% by 1985 and is now around 90%.

(Phang 2015)

Rents that accrued from growth were ploughed back into funding yet more and improved infrastructure. Taxes that damaged the economy were held down. Thus, we are entitled to take Singapore's performance as a comparator, to gain some sense of what the UK could have achieved – and might still achieve – if she had enjoyed similar fiscal and land-use policies (Sandilands 1992, 2015).

Singapore's annual growth eclipsed the UK's because a far greater proportion of government revenue was derived from the rent of land or from the leasehold sale of public land. This laid the foundation for the nation's stellar annual average growth at a rate triple that of countries like Britain that employed disincentive taxation.

> ➤ In real terms, Singapore's per capita income in constant US$ (base year 2011) rose from US$6,708 in 1970 to $48,630 in 2011, a real increase of 625%. See http://www.indexmundi.com/facts/singapore/gdp-per-capita together with World Bank 2011 data: http://data.worldbank.org/country.
>
> ➤ The comparable figures for the UK were US$19,198 in 1970 and $41,680 in 2011, a far more modest increase of 116%. This meant that the UK, initially nearly three times richer than Singapore in 1970, ended up 17% poorer by 2011.

In Singapore in FY2013, more than a third of all current government revenue of about £28bn (about 16% of GDP)[1] came from levies on the use of space and fixed property. A further £5bn (18% of current revenues) came from sales of government land. In addition, there was undoubtedly much rental income in the corporate income taxes that accounted for 22% of all revenues. The Port of Singapore Authority's revenues, for example, amounted to nearly £2.4bn in 2013, mostly from docking charges. Its 'profits' amounted to about £836m or 36% of revenues, and it paid around £150m in taxes.

Singapore residents pay for the use of land in various other explicit and implicit ways. For example, one cannot buy a new car without first bidding, in a monthly auction, for a 'certificate of entitlement' (COE).

---

1 This is less than half the proportion of total tax revenues in the UK's GDP.

The certificates are issued strictly according to the estimated increase in the carrying capacity of the road system – about 1% a year. A COE for a 1600cc car may cost £33,000 on top of the world price of the car plus 31% import duty. So, a car whose world price is £15,000 would cost around £53,000 in Singapore. Also, there are steep parking charges and charges for entering the Central Business District. These are all effectively charges, or rents, for the use of road space. For those who do not wish to pay such prices, Singapore provides a world-class public ransit system that is funded out of the rents of land.

So Singapore obtains a substantial fraction of all government revenue from property taxes, with correspondingly low taxes on earned incomes and expenditures. As a result of this greater dependence on land-based revenues, Singapore's taxes on personal incomes account for only 13.4% of all government revenue. In the UK, the proportion obtained from personal income taxes in FY 2012-13 was 26.9% plus another 16% in national insurance contributions. The resulting dynamism of the Singapore economy has naturally engendered a self-sustaining virtuous circle of buoyant land values and associated state revenues alongside the personal prosperity of its citizens.

Singapore did have its ups and downs, because her fiscal revolution was incomplete. But with her 7.6% average annual growth (6% per capita) since 1970, *Singapore was able, from a base income only one-third that of the UK, to catch up and overtake the UK within less than 40 years.* So what might the fate of the UK have been, if she had switched her fiscal policies to something resembling Singapore's?

A Vision for the UK

The 1970 real UK GDP (in 2008 prices) was £575.7bn. With the UK population at 55.6m, this represented an average income per head of £10,555 in 2008 pounds. Over the period 1970-2012, the UK's annual average growth rate was 2.52% (2.2% in *per capita* terms). By 2012, UK GDP stood at £1,414.8bn. With a population that had grown by 14.6% to 63.7m, average income per head had slightly more than doubled to £22,211 (again in 2008 pounds). If the overall growth rate average had been just two percentage points higher over the period, at 4.52%, the real UK GDP in 2012 would have been more than 6 times greater, at £3,768.4bn. *Income per head, instead of doubling, would have risen nearly six-fold, to £59,158.* The difference is £36,947 per head. Such is the dramatic effect when people are freed to realise their full economic potential.

Graph 13:1

Scotland/UK Growth Comparison since 1970

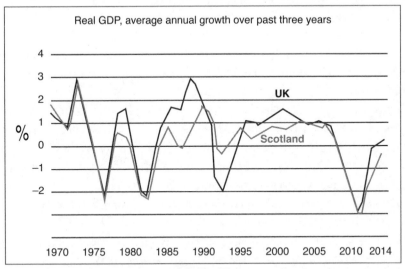

Real GDP, average annual growth over past three years

Source: *Financial Times.*

The gap between Singapore's achievement, and the performance of regional economies within the UK, was even wider. We may illuminate this outcome with the case of Scotland, for two reasons.

1 Historically, Scotland has been one of the most innovative regions within the UK: yet her growth rate has consistently fallen behind that of the UK, as indicated by the trends since 1970 (Figure 13:1).

2 When power was devolved to a Parliament in Edinburgh, Scotland acquired the option to abolish the Income Tax and raise additional revenue from an annual ground rent (AGR) in place of existing property taxes. If those fiscal powers are exercised, might this change the prospects for the people of Scotland?

Holyrood, the Scottish parliament, now has the tools to double Scotland's secular growth rate, re-lay the foundations of the labour market on principles of equity and natural justice and attract entrepreneurs who wish to establish businesses in a labour-friendly environment. To understand why this is a politically feasible strategy, we need to review the relevant historical events that culminated in the Holyrood elections of May 2016.

Embedded Inequality

Scotland is tied to an economic model that has exacerbated inequalities. Of the 34 OECD countries, the UK ranked 29th in terms of income inequality. *The disparity in the distribution of income is the logical outcome of the way in which government fiscal policies favour the activity which economists call rent-seeking.*

The original rent-seekers were the lords and lairds who enclosed the common and clan lands so that they could capture the rents produced by people whose status was converted to that of tenants while their overlords often migrated to the big cities like Edinburgh and London to live off those clan rents, with a diminishing sense of *noblesse oblige*. Since then, rent-seeking has been extended to include those with power in the banking sector, and those who are able to influence public policies in a way that privilege them against their fellow citizens.

This outcome does not square with the vision of a society that was grounded in fair treatment of everyone as equals. In a fair society, the incomes of the producers of new value would remain in the hands of those who worked for their living. But the net income – the economic rent that exists after wages and profits have been paid – would be treated as unique. Economic rent is a composite value that reflects the services of both nature and society. Therefore, as the Scottish moral philosopher Adam Smith pointed out, this was the proper source from which to fund public services (Smith 1776: Bk V, Ch. II, Pt. II, Art.I).

Historically, under the feudal and pre-feudal forms of social organisation, the State was funded out of that net income produced by the working population. In England, for example, we have the data which demonstrates that the state created by William the Conqueror in the 11th century was wholly funded out of the rents generated by the agriculture-based economy (Figure 13:2). It all started to go wrong as the feudal aristocracy decided they had a special entitlement to that rental revenue. They embarked on a historic transformation of the English Constitution so they could take control of the public finances away from monarchs. Their intent was to reduce the revenue collected by the land tax, so that they could pocket the rents themselves. The reciprocal was the invention of new taxes which were directed at the peasants.

The outcome was not just the theft of state revenue. It was also a strategy that suppressed the productive potential of the people. Taxes on wages and consumption, and on the capital that was created by working people, distorted people's incentives to work, invest, and innovate.

Graph 13:2

Land Rent as a % of Public Revenue (1066-1842)

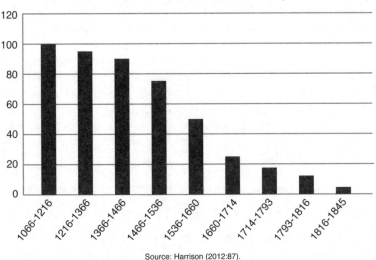

Source: Harrison (2012:87).

❖ Taxes such as those on salt and beer, and on the windows of people's homes, had a corrosive effect on both personal psychology and the fabric of communities.

❖ The privileged accumulation of rents enabled the aristocracy and gentry to evolve a culture that separated them from the rest of the people (Thompson 1991: Ch.2).

Today, the Scottish government asserts that 'everyone has a right to participate fully in society'. It notes the growing concentration of income at the top end of the distribution scale, with what it calls the 'highest *earners*' receiving a greater share of the income in recent years. The problem with this analysis is with the way it analyses the top incomes. In common with all governments and academic analyses of income distribution, such as the widely acclaimed investigation by Thomas Picketty (2014), no attempt is made to differentiate between earned and unearned income.

➢ High incomes that are *earned* imply that the beneficiaries added value to the sum total of wealth. Why penalise them with taxes?

➢ Those who get rich on *unearned* income, wittingly or otherwise, damage the welfare of others. Why should they keep what they do not earn?

> # Box 13:1
>
> ## Adam Smith's 'Peculiar Tax'
>
> 'Both ground-rents and the ordinary rent of land are a species of revenue
> which the owner, in many cases, enjoys without any care or attention of his
> own. Though a part of this revenue should be taken from him in order to
> defray the expenses of the state, no discouragement will thereby be given to
> any sort of industry. *The annual produce of the land and labour of the society,*
> *the real wealth and revenue of the great body of the people, might be the*
> *same after such a tax as before.* Ground-rents, and the ordinary rent of land,
> are, therefore, perhaps, the species of revenue which can best bear to have
> a peculiar tax imposed upon them.'
> (Smith 1776:Bk.V: 370; emphasis added)

The inequality between the rich and the poor which Scotland's
government says it opposes was, and remains, the logical outcome of
conventional modes of governance. The outcome of the privatisation
of socially-created rent is the economics of apartheid. This was not what
Adam Smith envisaged for his native Scotland (see Box 13:1).

The Democratic Deficit

During the UK general election campaign of 2015, the Scottish National
Party focused attention on its determination to abolish inequality by
administering a 'tax system that is fit for the 21st century' (Scottish
Government, 2015:14). The puzzle, however, is that it proposed to retain
the existing way of raising revenue, along with some amendment to the
locally-administered property tax and piecemeal 'land reform' in the guise
of community buy-outs (largely at the general taxpayers' expense). On
the basis of this strategy, the SNP could not realistically expect to
change the course of Scotland's social and economic development. This
conclusion holds, even if the SNP government achieved 'full fiscal
responsibility'.

The SNP called the devolution of fiscal power 'a fairer approach to
taxation'. The implications were examined by the Institute for Fiscal
Studies (IFS). It concluded that Scotland would endure a fiscal deficit
every year up to 2020. The shortfall of revenue in 2020 would be nearly
£10bn. That projection is shown in the top row of forecasts in Table 13:1.

Table 13:1

Scotland's Finances Under Competing Scenarios: £ billions

2013–14	2014-15	2015-16	2016–17	2017–18	2018-19	2019-20
Net Fiscal Balance, 2013–14 (outturn), 2014-15 to 2019-20 (IFS Projections)[1]						
–3.8	–5.9	–7.6	–8.2	–8.5	–8.9	–9.7
Net Gain from Zero-rating Scotland's Income Tax						
11.5	11.5	11.5	11.7	11.9	12.2	12.4

1 David Phillips, 'Full fiscal autonomy delayed? The SNP's plans for further devolution to Scotland', London: IFS, 21 April 2015. http://www.ifs.org.uk/publications/7722

The IFS projections are seriously misleading. They do not include the offsetting gains that could be achieved from fiscal reform. To properly evaluate the SNP claims, the people of Scotland needed a full audit of the fiscal implications. They were entitled to an idea of the full costs associated with current funding policies. Those costs are technically called the 'excess burden' of taxes. The more meaningful term used is 'dead-weight losses'. Economists can measure the wealth and welfare which people *forego* as a direct result of the way government chooses to raise revenue. The IFS failed to provide estimates of those losses for Scotland (Box 13:2).

The scale of the damage caused by taxes remains controversial. HM Treasury claims that the deadweight loss is equal to 30p for every £1 raised (Harrison 2006:155, 156). The 0.3:1 ratio suggests that the Treasury is only taking into account their costs of administering the tax regime, and the costs of administrative compliance by taxpayers. This makes no allowance for the distortions to behaviour that arise from the disincentives created by taxes. Some US economists claim that the total damage is as high as 1.5:1 – that is, a loss in wealth and welfare of $1.50 for every $1 collected by such taxes. The ratio that is recommended by Mason Gaffney is 1:1 (see Ch. 6 in this volume).

If the losses inflicted by 'bad' taxes were eliminated, society would enjoy a net gain if it raised the revenue to fund public services out of socially-created economic rent. Productivity would be improved in a million and one ways.

Box 13:2

Measuring Deadweight Losses

In the general election of 2015, all four major political parties declared they would have to increase taxes if given the power by the electorate. The IFS compared those increases, and concluded: 'None of these parties has provided anything like full details of their fiscal plans for each year of the coming parliament, leaving the electorate somewhat in the dark.' Furthermore, IFS researchers said they had to make many assumptions about the parties' real intentions in order to crunch the numbers (Crawford 2015).

However, the IFS, though hailed as Britain's authoritative independent assessor of tax policies, failed to provide estimates of the deadweight losses of those proposed tax increases. It declines to calculate the deadweight losses because it would have to estimate the damage inflicted by all the marginal tax rates (Adam 2014).

Offering deadweight estimates, no matter how proximate (after all, the IFS was willing to indulge in guesswork in order to pronounce verdicts on the work of others), would at least draw attention to the fact that elected representatives use revenue tools that cause losses, compared to those financial instruments which do not inflict losses on the working population. This, of course, would then highlight in people's minds the possibility of collecting revenue without damaging the economy.

➤ When people are not taxed on earned incomes they may choose to earn more because the additional income does not attract the attention of the taxman. Alternatively, they may choose to receive the benefit in the form of more leisure time.

➤ Investment in capital goods would increase and be employed more efficiently. Under current taxes, capital is diverted to 'tax efficient' projects which may not maximise the satisfaction of consumers, but which minimise the taxes paid by corporations.

Under the rent-revenue formula for public finance, labour and capital resources are devoted to optimising the satisfaction of people who want the goods or services that are made available in the economy. Consumer satisfaction is synchronised with the objectives of the producers. Here, we identify two of the virtues of the rent-revenue strategy.

❖ The abolition of harmful taxes is a self-funding strategy.

As taxes that damage the nation's health and wealth are reduced or terminated, *the rentable value of 'land' in all its forms rises by corresponding sums.* This is explained by the ATCOR thesis – All Taxes Come Out of Rent. The political implications of this are of major significance: in abolishing harmful taxes, *current public services do not have to be sacrificed.* This contrasts with the austerity programme pursued by governments post-2008 in which, to cut budget deficits, taxes were raised or services reduced.

❖ The rent-revenue policy democratises the public's finances.

People exercise the power over when, why and how they fund the services they want to use. This is the case today, for example, in the housing market. When someone chooses the location where she wishes to live, she selects a home on the basis of two criteria.

1 The merits of the building are evaluated: whether it has the required number of bedrooms, for example, and the condition of the amenities.
2 Proximity to the desired public services, such as transport, schools and parks. These are stressed by estate agents as essential information, because their quality and accessibility affect the price of the property.

The anomaly in this arrangement is that the part of the 'house' value which is paid to access the public services is not paid to the public agencies that provide the amenities. Instead, that value (the rent of location) is paid to the vendor of the dwelling. *That payment exposes the pathological character of the tax regime.*

Now consider what would happen if a Scottish government chose to exercise its devolved power over taxation?

❖ As a first step, Scotland could zero-rate the Income Tax.

The net gains are shown in the bottom row in Table 13:1. Replacing the Income Tax with rental charges would deliver an annual net gain to Scotland of *circa* £11bn. Over the five years from 2016 to the Scottish elections of 2021, the people of Scotland would be enriched by nearly £60bn! This contrasts with the outcome under the existing funding arrangements, in which the people of Scotland would continue to accumulate a debt burden that has to be serviced. By eliminating the deadweight losses caused by current taxes, *the projected net gains from re-socialising rent revenues would be able to convert large annual deficits to large annual surpluses.*

If Scotland achieved 'full fiscal autonomy', her government could also decide to get rid of regressive taxes such as VAT, National Insurance Contributions, Customs Duties – all the exactions that distort people's decisions on spending and investing. This would *transform black holes into pots of gold.*

In 2014, the revenue from those taxes levied in Scotland which caused serious damage to the economy added up to about £33bn (in an economy of around £115bn). This calculation excludes those charges that fall directly on rent (such as oil rents). Also excluded are the 'sin taxes' that people may choose to retain, if they wish to deter private activities that impose social costs on others (such as taxes on tobacco and alcohol). If Scotland abolished the damaging taxes and replaced the revenue with rents, the *net gain* in wealth and welfare from this transitional switch would be *circa* £33bn. Thereafter, the economy would operate at a more dynamic growth rate that could conservatively be expected to be double the cramped historic rate.

But would there be sufficient rent to replace the bad taxes so as to retain the current level of public services? This is not a valid way of putting the question. The ATCOR thesis explains that *all taxes come out of rent.* This means that *existing taxes are already derived from the nation's rents*, but they are collected *indirectly* and misleadingly labelled 'income' tax or 'value added tax'. By scrapping this indirect way of raising revenue, the 'savings' would resurface as rents. The graduated introduction of a public charge on those rents, in a revenue neutral transition to the new fiscal system, would progressively reduce the damage hitherto inflicted on the economy. By swapping the indirect for the direct way of collecting the rent, Scotland would rationalise the fiscal system and emancipate her people to achieve ever higher levels of productivity. Through the private and public sectors, the population would share the bonus of the ensuing *increase* in total income.

The first practical step in the direction of this reform was taken in December 2015 when the commission appointed by the Scottish Government identified land value taxation as a potential replacement for the residential property tax. The SNP decided to seek re-election in May 2016 without adopting the option to restructure the tax regime. But that option now remains with the people, if they choose to exercise their democratic right to assert control over their public finances.

The switch to funding policies that draw revenue directly from rent would frame the national budget within the principles of integrity, transparency, accountability and, indeed, natural law (Sandilands 1986). Revenue from North Sea oil rents may diminish to zero over the next 40 years. But Scotland is rich in its educated labour force, which means that she will produce social rents *at an increasing rate* as the productivity of the economy rises under the influence of liberating tax reform.

The people of Scotland have a unique opportunity to scope out the strategies that will actually work for their personal and common good, if they empower their elected representatives to initiate the appropriate fiscal reforms.

If Scotland did once again take the lead, the other nations of the UK would follow suit, as they did in the lead-up to the People's Budget of 1909 (*Geo*philos 2012). This time, assuming the absence of the intervention of a world war, the outcome would be a material prosperity and quality of life greater than the sum of the divided parts.

References

Adam, Stuart (2014), Personal email to Fred Harrison, October 14.

Crawford, Rowena, *et al.*, (2015), 'Post-election Austerity: Parties' Plans Compared', London, Institute of Fiscal Studies (IFS), Briefing Note 117.

Geophilos video (2012), 'Glasgow – Progress and Poverty in the Second City of Empire", https://www.youtube.com/watch?v=XtZ-uOaLZdA

George, Henry (1892), *A Perplexed Philosopher*. https://www.schalkenbach.org/library/henry-george/perplexed-philosopher/pdf/George/pe-Perplexed_philosopher.pdf

Harrison, Fred (2006), *Wheels of Fortune*, London, Institute of Economic Affairs. http://www.iea.org.uk/publications/research/wheels-of-fortune

— (2012), *The Traumatised Society*, London, Shepheard-Walwyn.

Mulvey, Paul (2002), 'The Single Taxers and the Future of Liberalism, 1906-14', *Journal of Liberal Democrat History*, 34/34. Spring/Summer:, 11-15. http://www.liberalhistory.org.uk/wp-content/uploads/2015/05/34-35-Mulvey-Single-Taxers.pdf

Phang Sock Yong (2015), 'Home prices and inequality: Singapore versus other "global superstar cities"', *The Straits Times*, April 3. http://www.straitstimes.com/news/opinion/more-opinion-stories/story/home-prices-and-inequality-singapore-versus-other-global-sup

Picketty, Thomas (2014), *Capital in the Twenty-first Century*, Cambridge, Mass, Belknap Press.

Sandilands, Roger J. (1986), 'Natural Law and the Political Economy of Henry George', *Journal of Economic Studies*, 13:5, pp.4-15. Reprinted in Mark Blaug, ed., *Henry George (1839-1897)*, Cheltenham, Edward Elgar (1992).

— (1992), 'Savings, Investment and Housing in Singapore's Growth, 1965-90', *Savings and Development*, XVI:2.

— ((2015), 'Rewards from Eliminating Deadweight Taxes: The hidden potential of Scotland's land and natural resource rents'. http://www.slrg.scot/

Smith, Adam (1776), *The Wealth of Nations*, Cannan edn (1976).
Scottish Government, The (2015), *Scotland's Economic Strategy*, Edinburgh.
Thompson, E.P. (1991), *Customs in Common*, London, Penguin.

14

The Needed Moral Revolution

NICOLAUS TIDEMAN[1]

HUMANITY NEEDS another moral revolution, a change in consciousness. We need to understand that all people have equal rights to the earth, and we need to bring that understanding to bear on our lives.

We have had other moral revolutions. Between about 1740 and 1880, humanity came to understand that slavery is wrong. (How could it have taken so long?) Between about 1950 and 1990, most people came to understand that women and minorities must be accorded the same political and civil rights as majority males. Most recently we have come to understand that our obligation to respect the dignity of all persons requires that the word 'marriage' be understood to apply to committed relationships between two persons of the same gender.

In moral revolutions our ideas about what is right change in ways that seem impossible before the revolution occurs. These seemingly impossible changes in consciousness are coming ever faster. One might think that they are becoming easier to achieve. But the next moral revolution will be more difficult, perhaps even more difficult than ending slavery.

The next moral revolution will be more difficult because, like ending slavery, it requires people to relinquish what they see as their property. The Latin origin of 'property' is 'proprius,' an adjective whose central

1 I am indebted to Florenz Plassmann for helpful comments.

meaning is 'one's own.' This connection in meaning is reflected in the tendency for people to regard their property as extensions of themselves. Thus a challenge to a person's property can feel like a challenge to one's very self, so it can be expected to be especially difficult for people to undergo a change in consciousness that entails giving up what they understand to be their property, just as it was with ending slavery.

We need this change in consciousness despite its difficulty because, as with ending slavery, justice requires it, and because it offers the only reasonable prospect for a peaceful world. It also offers the prospect of a world that functions more efficiently, but justice would require this moral revolution even if it led to inefficiency. The sections that follow discuss the basis for acknowledging that all people have equal rights to the earth, the consequences for secession, the consequences for the internal structure of a nation, the consequences beyond a single nation, the consequences for environmental care and economic efficiency, the consequences for global peace, and the actions that individuals can take.

Why We Must Acknowledge that All People Have Equal Rights to the Earth

Justice requires us to acknowledge that all people have equal rights to the earth because other people are our moral equals. If anyone asks us, 'Why should this piece of earth belong to you and not to me?' we owe that fellow human being an answer, and the only adequate answer is, 'Because I have left as much for you as I have taken for myself.'

There are other possible answers, but they are inadequate. If we answer, 'Because I bought it,' or 'Because I inherited it,' then the next question will be, 'What was the basis of the claim of ownership of the person from whom you obtained it? Did you 'buy' it from someone who had stolen it?' When titles to pieces of the earth are traced backward in time, they almost always originate in the dispossession of an earlier claimant whose claim was at least as good as that of the dispossessor.

There have been people who have argued that the ability to kill or drive off a previous possessor is a valid basis for ownership. For example, the economist Frank Knight wrote that those who undertake investments in seizing land obtain, on average, only ordinary returns on their investments because

[I]n real life, the original 'appropriation' of such opportunities by private owners involves investment in exploration, in detailed investigation and appraisal by trial and error of the findings, in development work of many kinds necessary to secure and market a product – besides the cost of buying off or killing or driving off previous claimants.[2]

If this were a valid argument, one might argue similarly that thieves obtain only ordinary returns on the resources that they invest in thievery. But obtaining only ordinary returns does not justify either the seizing of land or common theft. The suggestion that paying the cost of 'killing or driving off previous claimants' provides a valid foundation for ownership should be rejected on four different grounds, two of them ethical and two of them efficiency.

First and most fundamentally killing or driving off previous claimants is ethically wrong because it endorses a failure to accord other people – those who are killed or driven off – the respect that they ought to be accorded. Second, it is ethically wrong because it promotes unending conflict, leading to a world where peace can never be expected. It is tempting to think that we might allow past land grabs to stand while stopping future ones, but any future land grabber who manages to hold on for a while will have as good a claim as those who now claim ownership. We will lack a moral basis for stopping future land grabs if we allow existing ones to stand.

From the perspective of efficiency, we ought to reject claims to land that originate in killing or driving off previous claimants because such a practice, in facilitating future land grabs, motivates the socially wasteful use of resources in killing or driving off existing claimants. Finally, tolerance of such aggression produces incentives for socially wasteful use of resources in defending existing claims. For all these reasons we should reject claims of exclusive access whose only justification is that they can be traced back to forcible dispossessions.

Not every claim to exclusive use of a piece of the earth can be traced back to a forcible dispossession. There is another rationale for rejecting claims to exclusive use of disproportionate slices of the earth, a rationale that applies not only to claims that can be traced back to forcible dis possessions but also to claims that can be traced back to ancient first possessions.

Consider an instance of ancient first possession. When asked, 'Why should this piece of earth belong to you and not to me?' the respondent

---

2 Frank H. Knight, 'Some fallacies in the interpretation of social cost', *The Quarterly Journal of Economics* (1924): p.591.

answers, 'Because it came into my hands by a sequence of lawful transfers that can be traced back to the ancient first possessor.' The next step in this dialog will be for the questioner to ask, 'Why should possession traceable to the ancient first possessor give you a claim to more of what nature offers than I can have? Do I not have as much right as you to the things that no person produced?' The possessor may answer, 'The reason that I should have this opportunity and not you is that my antecedent in possession discovered this opportunity. If it had not been for his efforts of discovery, this opportunity might never have been known. No one would have gotten any value from it.'

Now the argument gets a bit complicated. Investments in discovery can be valuable, but things that are found are likely to have been found by others if they had not been found by those who did find them. Those who discover new opportunities have reasonable claims on some special consideration, reflecting the productivity of their efforts, but that does not imply granting full perpetual ownership of newly discovered opportunities to those who discover them. To the extent that new opportunities can be discovered for less than the cost of discovery, a practice of granting full ownership to the discoverer will motivate a 'land rush,' an allocation of an inefficient amount of effort and resources to discovery, dissipating the possible gain from discovering new opportunities. Motivating efficient discovery requires a system of special compensatory consideration, somewhat like patents, but not full ownership in perpetuity. Designing and implementing a system for rewarding discovery that is as efficient as possible is an important public function. Thus we should respond to the possessor, 'Yes, some special consideration is appropriate, in view of the value of your antecedent's efforts, but not full ownership forever. After some amount of time (to be determined by a public process) his effort should not count to give you exclusive possession of the thing he discovered. Since the first possession you rely on was ancient, the amount of time of exclusive possession that would have been suitable compensation for the efforts of your antecedent first possessor has certainly passed by now. It is time for all to have equal rights to this natural opportunity.'

Thus both for possessions that originated in coercive appropriation and for ancient instances of first possession, we should recognize that justice requires that natural opportunities be shared equally. For relatively recent first possessions we should have a publicly agreed rule about the extent of the special consideration that seems likely to motivate the most efficient efforts in discovering new opportunities.

The proposition that people have equal rights to the earth should be distinguished from egalitarianism. Egalitarianism entails sharing all things equally. The rationale for sharing land equally – the obligation to justify exclusive appropriation of opportunities provided by nature – does not apply to human talent or to the product of human effort. We do not appropriate our human talents and thereby exclude others from them. Rather, they are utterly non-transferable components of our beings. No one's possession of talent reduces the talent available to others.

The right of every person to his or her being entails the right to cooperate with whom one chooses in whatever ways are mutually agreed. Thus people have rights to the earnings from their efforts and to the returns from their savings. Still, this does not mean that there can be no taxation of productive efforts. People are free to use their rights to themselves to form societies that tax whatever the society decides democratically to tax. Anyone who objects to the tax is free to live somewhere else.

Equal Rights to the Earth: Consequences for Secession

Suppose that a nation recognizes that all people have equal rights to the earth. What will be implied for the response of that nation's government to a region that seeks to secede? The government of that nation will need to recognize that it cannot claim to have accorded equal rights to the earth to its citizens unless people are free to exercise their equal rights to the earth in collaboration with whom they choose. While there might be some minimum size for seceding regions (perhaps 30,000, the size of the smallest nations today), and it might be appropriate to require agreement by a supermajority to implement a secession (perhaps 60%), in view of the disruption in the lives of those who did not wish to secede, still the nation that recognized that all people have equal rights to the earth would need to acknowledge that, in principle, a region that wished to secede had a right to do so, as long as 1) the seceding region agreed not to prevent anyone who wished to leave to do so, and 2) the seceding region would not be claiming more than their share of the nation's natural opportunities.

Equal Rights to the Earth:
Consequences within a Nation

Next, consider what would be implied for the social organization of a nation that recognized the equal rights of all persons to natural opportunities. In an earlier, pre-market era, recognition of equal rights to natural opportunities would have implied dividing land up, so that everyone had a share of equal value. In a market era people recognize that not everyone has the ability to organize production effectively, so some people make best use of their land rights by allowing others to use the land that they could claim. Thus equal rights to land can be achieved efficiently, by collecting from everyone who has title to land, the rental value the land would have if it were unimproved, and sharing the proceeds equally. A person who wants to use only his share could pay the charge for the land that he was using out of the payment for his share of the proceeds, thereby obtaining 'free' use of his share of land.

For the purpose of sharing the unimproved value of land equally, 'unimproved' means 'in the condition provided by nature,' that is, without any surrounding infrastructure as well as without man-made improvements on the site in question. Thus the unimproved value of land in an urban area would be the value that the land would have as a place to put a city if there were no city there. The additional value that the land has because of the surrounding infrastructure and private development is not value that everyone in the nation can claim. Rather, it belongs to the residents of the city. The city would reasonably collect this part of land rent and use it to finance public services. Thus while justice requires only that the part of land value due to nature be shared equally, it would be reasonable to collect all the rent that parcels of land would have if they were individually unimproved, allocate the part that is not due to nature to the local community, and put the rest in a pot for equal sharing. To the extent that activities of state governments and the federal government raise the value of land, that amount of land rent would be sent to those governments to support those activities. This would permit a substantial reduction in other taxes.

The contents of the pot for equal sharing would include not only land, but a variety of other natural opportunities as well. There would be:

- Water rights
- Mineral rights

- Fishing rights
- Hunting rights
- Spectrum rights

There might be others as well. The rule of sharing the value would apply to all scarce opportunities that are provided by nature. It would *not* apply to human talent or to value produced by human effort.

To determine the value of natural opportunities, the nation that sought to share natural opportunities equally would need assessors. These assessors would operate rather like assessors now operate under property taxes, but with a couple of differences. First, they would assess only land rather than both land and improvements as at present. Second, they would assess rental value rather than selling price.

There are two reasons for assessing rental value rather than selling price. First, rental value is what a nation that sought to share natural opportunities equally would seek to identify and share. Second, if the rental value of an unimproved natural opportunity was fully collected publicly, then the selling price of that unimproved natural opportunity would be zero.

Because selling prices would go to zero, assessors would need to devise new methods of assessment. They could not rely on selling prices as they do now. One possibility would be for the assessors to hold rental auctions of examples of the things they were assessing, with bidders understanding that their bids were offers of rent for some specified number (perhaps three) years. The results from the auctions would be used to set rental values on similar items that had not been subject to rental auctions.

Some natural opportunities, such as mineral deposits, can only be used by being used up. For these natural opportunities, the annual price to be paid would be a combination of the diminution in value from extraction and a possible fee for inadequate use of the opportunity if the rate of extraction was inefficiently slow.

The transition to a society that collected the rent of land publicly, with a consequent fall in land prices toward zero would have stark consequences for homeowners and financial institutions that held mortgages. Homeowners would need to pay their mortgages as well as their land taxes. And financial institutions that had lent on the value of land would find that the collateral for the loans that they held no longer covered the loans. Special measures would be needed to deal with these consequences.

The situation of homeowners would not be as difficult as it seems at first, because the use of the rent of land and other natural opportunities as a source of public revenue would permit reductions in other taxes. Still, if the purpose of public collection of the rent of land is to transfer to the public what has previously been pocketed privately, it is sensible to collect it from those who have been doing the pocketing. In the case of mortgaged land, those who have been pocketing the rent are not the homeowners but rather the recipients of mortgage interest. Thus it is sensible to devise a mechanism for collecting the tax on land from them. The way to do this is to specify that those who have mortgages on land are able to pay the interest on the land component of their mortgages with their tax receipts. In other words, while the person who had title to land would be legally responsible for paying the tax on that land, if there was a mortgage on the land, the title holder could pass on to the mortgage holder as much of the tax as corresponded to the interest on the mortgage on the land.

Mortgages are generally held by financial institutions that have obligations to creditors. The financial institutions would be allowed to pass the land taxes on to their creditors, and so on to the final recipients of the mortgage interest that represented the rent of land. The rationale in justice for designing a land tax to fall primarily on the recipients of mortgage interest is that today the rent of land goes substantially to pay mortgage interest, so it is appropriate that a tax on land fall correspondingly on the recipients of mortgage interest. The public would in effect be saying to citizens, 'If you were counting on pocketing the rent of land directly or indirectly, you are out of luck. We are collecting it to provide public services and to share equally the value of natural opportunities.'

There is the further issue of bank loans that would no longer be supported by collateral. Managers of financial institutions would be unhappy. For the United States, this situation must be considered separately in 'no recourse' states and in other states. In the 12 'no recourse' states, a mortgagee has the right to turn mortgaged property over to the lender and walk away from the loan. Financial institutions in these states might need to be restructured. That is, because it would be likely that many borrowers would be walking away from loans that now exceeded the value of the mortgaged property, the creditors of these financial institutions would need to accept that the institutions would not be able to pay all their obligations, so the obligations would need to be reduced in line with their likely revenues.

For other states, where borrowers did not have the option of walking away from their loans, there would be a different issue. Borrowers would be obliged to repay the full amounts that they had borrowed, but they would be unable to sell their homes for the amount borrowed. It might be nearly impossible for any real estate transactions to occur. To make it possible for property to be sold when there was not enough value in the property to pay the mortgage, I would recommend that financial institutions be obliged to replace each under-collateralized mortgage with the combination of a mortgage for 100% of the value of the property and a personal loan to the borrower for the remainder. The financial institutions would be little if any worse off, and the borrowers would be able to sell their property.

The point of these details is that recognition of the equal rights of all persons to natural opportunities would have substantial consequences for the social organization within a nation, but would not require a wholesale overturning of society. There would be difficulties, but they could be managed. Private property in things made by human effort could continue. Markets could continue. A system of private titles to parcels of land and other natural opportunities could continue, with the difference that the selling price of such titles for unimproved natural opportunities would be approximately zero.

Equal Rights to the Earth: Consequences beyond a Nation

Recognition by a nation that all people have equal rights to the earth would have consequences beyond that nation, because there is nothing about being outside a nation's borders that makes a person less worthy of a share of rent. There are two principled positions with respect to non-citizens that might be taken by the nation that recognized that all people have equal rights to the earth.

The Less Severe Position   The less severe of the principled positions would be to affirm that it was important for everyone to refrain from appropriating more than their share of natural opportunities. A person's share of natural opportunities can be calculated as global annual rent divided by global population. A nation's share of rent can therefore be calculated as global annual rent multiplied by the nation's share of global population. The principled nation would hire consultants to estimate the amount, if any, by which its appropriation of global rent exceeded its share. When informed of this amount, the nation would make a corresponding transfer for the benefit of those who received less than their shares of global rent.

Such principled action would provide a powerful example that would help the nation persuade other nations to behave the same way. If all nations could be persuaded to behave in this way, then global rent would be shared equally.

The More Severe Position   The more severe principled position would be that in a world where the equal rights of all persons to the earth are widely unrecognized, those who do recognize the equal rights of all have an obligation to share the available rent equally among all who are being deprived of their shares. From this perspective, the share of rent that can justly be claimed by each citizen of the nation that recognizes that all have equal rights to the earth is much smaller. It is the amount of the nation's rent that each can receive while also raising to that amount the shares of all persons in other countries who have less.

This more severe position would serve as an even more powerful symbol of justice than the less severe position. A nation that took such a position would be in a very strong position to urge other nations to follow its example. Every time another nation made a commitment to accept the consequences of the principle that all people have equal rights to the earth, the rent that could be paid to all who accepted the principle and to all who were deprived of equal shares of rent would rise.

In nations where many citizens were receiving payments to compensate for their lack of shares of rent, but where powerful interests were collecting large shares of rent, if there was any democracy there would be strong pressure to join the nations that were sharing rent. When the preponderance of countries had accepted the principle of equal rights to the earth, it would be possible to put pressure on the holdouts through economic sanctions. In this we could eventually achieve a world where it was accepted that all people have equal rights to the earth.

Environmental and Efficiency Consequences of Equal Rights to the Earth

In a world that recognized the equal rights of all to the earth, environmental sustainability would be a nearly automatic consequence. To engage in actions that reduce the usefulness of natural opportunities through

pollution is just as much an appropriation of a natural opportunity as
enclosures of opportunities that keep others out. Thus a nation that recognizes the equal rights of all to natural opportunities would require anyone
engaging in an activity that generated pollution to pay for the harm
caused by that pollution. When an activity (such as emissions of carbon
dioxide) had consequences beyond the borders of the nation, the nation
would recognize that the rest of the world needed to be compensated for
the costs of that activity. The nation would also recognize that if all people
have equal rights to the earth, that means all people in all generations.
The nation would therefore ensure that it acted in such a way as to
reasonably ensure that future generations would have opportunities no
less valuable than those of the current generation.

The recognition of equal rights to the earth would lead to greater efficiency in at least two ways. First, charging people for the consequences
of their actions motivates people to act with appropriate concern for these
consequences, which improves efficiency. Second, collecting the rent from
natural opportunities would make it possible to reduce the taxes now
used. Economists as far back as Adam Smith have recognized that a tax
on land does not discourage economic activity the way other taxes do,
because the amount of tax to be collected cannot be changed by changing
what one does. Thus recognition of the equal rights of all to the earth
would lead to a generally more efficient economy.

Equal Rights to the Earth and Global Peace

For eons, since before we were human, we have been appropriating
territory and resources through fighting. It is nature's way, for creatures
that lack the intelligence to find something better. As humanity struggles
to become creatures who put fighting aside and achieve peace, the question arises: what basic framework will we use? There are two principal
candidates: armistice and equality.

Armistice is a laying down of arms, with everyone allowed to keep what
they have at that time. It is simple, and it respects the relative power of
the combatants. It is what humanity has traditionally sought to use, but
its success has been limited. As the relative power of combatants changes,
the armistice comes under pressure. Old resentments resurface. Maintaining the armistice requires the continued waste of resources in being
prepared to fight. Fighting breaks out occasionally, until a new armistice
is achieved. The new armistice is no better or worse than the previous
one. Eventually, fighting breaks out again. A sequence of armistices

punctuated by occasional fighting is better than continual fighting, but far from ideal. We ought to aspire to a better tool for achieving peace.

The better tool is a commitment to equal sharing of the earth, to the repudiation of claims based on a historical capacity to subdue other combatants. As long as nations insist on keeping the disproportionately large shares of global rent that history has given them, they will be in an ethically weak position when they try to insist that other nations refrain from trying to better their positions. A world order based on the principle that no one gets more than their share of natural opportunities, and no one is obliged to get by on less, has a much better chance than armistice of ending war permanently. If the preponderance of nations assent, the others can be induced to comply through economic sanctions.

> *A world order based on the principle that no one gets more than their share of natural opportunities, and no one is obliged to get by on less, has a much better chance than armistice of ending war permanently.*

Equal Rights to the Earth:
Consequences for Individual Action

Suppose that you are convinced that all people have equal rights to the earth. What should you do? When a political movement to embrace equal rights to the earth emerges, you should support it. But it may be a long time before such a movement has any chance of success. What should you do in the meantime?

Go back to the parallel with ending slavery. The beginning of the end of slavery in the English-speaking world came in the 1740s, when a few Quakers in the Pennsylvania colony became convinced that slavery was wrong. They traveled around the colonies, persuading people to free their slaves. Within a few decades, nearly all Quakers had freed their slaves. The combination of the widespread voluntary freeing of slaves and the Declaration of Independence[3] led to legislation to end slavery in all of the northern states between 1776 and 1887. The initial spark set the moral revolution in motion, and it could not be stopped.

---

3 'We hold these truths to be self-evident, that all men are created equal, that they are endowed by their Creator with certain unalienable Rights, that among these are Life, Liberty and the pursuit of Happiness'.

A somewhat similar movement of individual conscience is occurring today, with respect to carbon emissions. People are deciding to be 'carbon neutral,' to offset their activities that put carbon dioxide into the atmosphere with other activities that withdraw carbon dioxide from the atmosphere. If everyone could be persuaded to be carbon neutral there would be an end to the rising atmospheric concentration of carbon dioxide that promotes climate change. The existence of the 'carbon neutral' movement adds to the pressure for countries to act to limit climate change.

The individual action of conscience that is needed to bring one's life into conformity with the principle of equal rights to the earth is like being carbon neutral, but wider in its application. Individuals must resolve to be 'resource compensating.'

As with a nation embracing the principle of equal rights to the earth, there is a less severe and a more severe version of the resolution. The less severe version of being 'resource compensating' is to resolve to use no more of the world's natural opportunities than everyone could use if these opportunities were shared equally, or to compensate those with inadequate shares if one wishes to use more than others can have. The more severe version of being 'resource compensating' is to recognize that to use no more than those with the least can have in a world where these opportunities are not shared equally, one must compensate for all of one's appropriations of natural opportunities.

The first few people who seek to be resource compensating will need to make their own estimates. They might begin by using the assistance that is available on line for estimating one's carbon footprint. That is one component of one's resource use. Then one should add the pre-development value of the land that one occupies, including one's share of the land for streets, parks, etc. of the polities to which one belongs. Then there is the rent embodied in all of one's consumption purchases and one's share of the rent appropriated by all of the firms in which one has invested. A person seeking to be resource compensating will estimate this amount and make corresponding contributions to organizations like Right Sharing of the World's Resources that help the most deprived people in the world.

When enough people are making the effort to be resource-compensating, someone will set up a Web site to assist people with estimating the value of the natural opportunities that they appropriate and the value that constitutes one person's share. As the amount of compensation that people offer increases, it will become feasible to try to ensure that everyone in the world with an inadequate share of natural opportunities receives some compensation.

As the number of people who embrace resource compensation increases, some city, state or province will adopt the practice for their whole population. They will organize their economy in such a way that the rent of all natural opportunities that are appropriated by their citizens is collected publicly and appropriate compensation is paid, so that individuals do not need to make their own estimates. When enough states or provinces have made the shift, whole nations will begin to do so. When the preponderance of nations have made the shift, it will be possible to apply economic pressure to the remainder to do so. In this way we can attain the global moral revolution of recognizing that all people have equal rights to the earth.

EPILOGUE

Quest for the Authentic Voice of the People

THE AUTHORS IN CONVERSATION WITH MASON GAFFNEY

T HE CONTRIBUTORS to this volume have cleaned up the language of economics and tested, theoretically and empirically, concepts that are suppressed by the neoclassical model of our world. This, in turn, inspires new perspectives on a future of fulfilment through cultural innovation. Grim outlooks are transformed into good news. This is the process of reconciliation that Mason Gaffney taught his students (Gaffney n.d.). Instead of retreating to the dismal politics of austerity, armed with the correct fiscal policy we may all benefit from the solutions and synergies that flow from the hard-headed/human-hearted view of the world. So now it is the turn of our readers. We all share responsibility for rebuilding the fabric of our communities, to emancipate ourselves in the pursuit of authentic personal ambitions and social interests. But how can this process of psycho-social renewal begin? Recovering the will to work for the common good will not occur spontaneously, when this is made to appear to be in conflict with personal interest.

A fundamental shift in the collective imagination is needed. This may be achieved by engaging in a democratic conversation. Conversation can be cathartic. It needs to include the many people who are petty land owners, who need to be assured that their wellbeing is not threatened by

Box 1

The Children's Inheritance

Joan Bakewell is one of Britain's most respected TV broadcasters. She was elevated to the peerage in 2011. But Baroness Bakewell's most valuable prize came with little effort on her part. After living for 52 years in a house which she had bought for £12,000 in North London, she announced that its price had risen to £5m. Aged 82, she wrote about her intentions in a book: *Stop the Clocks: Thoughts on What I Leave Behind* (Virago).

The baroness was unabashed about her legacy. 'I've already told the children that my interest is in spending as much as I can before I go. I've said I intend to spend their inheritance and they're perfectly happy about that' (Craig 2016). In Ms Bakewell's case, she plans to sell her house and enjoy the proceeds.

People like Baroness Bakewell are genuinely dedicated to pursuing what they perceive as the common good. She says she favours a windfall tax on properties, even if it forced her to sell up to 'an oligarch or a hedge fund manager' (Ward 2016). Living off the sale of the house was her pension, she says, 'and I've told my children I'm not stinting'.

reforms that would restore justice to society. A significant part of each nation's net income is captured by those who own small plots of land beneath their homes. Home owners constitute a majority of most populations in the West. They die relatively rich. They do not fit the profile of the aristocratic land-grabber. They work for their living. But many of them also accumulate substantial unearned fortunes, which are bequeathed to their offspring. That is a powerful inducement to remain anaesthetised to the welfare of other people's future generations (Box 1).

Central to the future welfare of all societies are the challenges that cannot be resolved without framing them in terms of the norms of justice. Those practical issues need to be explored and peacefully resolved. To illustrate the scale of the task, we may emphasise the failure to reform the financial institutions that were at the heart of the Crash of 2008. Policy-makers have confined their 'reforms' to superficial regulatory initiatives in the banking sector, made possible by the ill-informed understanding of the root cause of the financial sector's anti-social behaviour. As a consequence, everyone remains vulnerable to the disasters of the next property boom/bust.

Following the events of 2008, the Occupy movement registered the anger that was felt by people of all ages and classes around the world. They camped in public spaces to register their protests. The lightning conductors for people's frustrations were the bankers, who were blamed for mass unemployment and the repossession of millions of homes. But the dysfunctional financial sector is just one manifestation of a warped politico-economic template. That template was created to serve the narcissistic interests of a corrupted class of patricians and the monarchs who had ceased to honour their role as guardians of the welfare of their subjects. How financiers came to feast from the spoils of what then happened needs to be understood if a reappraisal of contemporary institutions and financial practices is to lead to effective reforms. The historical context is the starting point for a public conversation about the role of modern banks.

When Europe's aristocracies accelerated the commercialisation of common land in the 16th century, they needed a financial mechanism that would support their new lifestyles of leisure. Land had to be transformed into a marketable commodity. Goldsmiths and merchants facilitated this need: they created the embryonic financial sector in what was still the agricultural era. Through their mortgages they were able to appropriate a portion of an economy's net income. Monarchs were complicit. Because they allowed their kingdom's rents to be privatised, they had to turn to moneylenders for the cash they needed to conduct the affairs of state. This transferred a new layer of influence to the early financiers. It gave them the power to name their price for conniving with what was becoming an increasingly pathological relationship between monarchy and aristocracy. Trapped in the middle of this power struggle were the people at large, and the productive economy.

The outcome was the nexus of rent-seekers and political authority, consolidated in the formation of the template of power that became the modern nation-state. Financiers, instead of providing a valuable support service to both the administrators of the state and the producers of wealth, were able to feast on the labours of the working population. They exacted 'interest' on the credit they advanced to entrepreneurs and to cash strapped governments. That interest was, in fact, economic rent. Thus, banks acquired extra-ordinary – and extra-judicial – power over the population at large, and direct influence over political decision-making. But this influence was not 'natural' or inevitable, and therefore beyond democratic reform. It arose by default: the twin failure of governance to

✔ employ revenue policies that ensured financial viability within the
   state sector, while
✔ freeing people to keep the value that they created while paying for
   the services they personally received from the state.

By yielding themselves to the money-lenders, law-makers weakened their
power to act as guardians of the public's welfare. Financiers now act as
they do because they were presented with the opportunity to arbitrage
the failure of public policy. Therefore, confining policy reforms to the
re-regulation of the financial sector is to ignore the source of the problem:
tax policies that determine how a nation's income is distributed.

Western banks did behave badly, both before and after 2008. They paid
hundreds of millions of dollars in fines for their misdemeanours. But
the episodes of malfeasance are not the systemic problem that requires
forensic attention. If the fiscal system is not restructured, banks will
continue to lend to people who wish to buy real estate, and lend to
governments that struggle with budgetary deficits. This will ensure the
continuity of a crippled society. Joseph Stiglitz lamented the grotesque
nature of this situation.

> [H]ow could something that was a means to an end become the centre of
> a New Economy? We should have recognised that the outsized proportions
> of the financial sector – in the years before the crisis, some 40% of
> corporate profits were in that sector – indicated that something was wrong.
>
> (Stiglitz 2010: 188)

A therapeutic conversation would be directed at empowering people to
come to terms with ugly truths.

➢ High Finance ought to have evolved into an honourable service
   that supported the wealth creators. Instead, a monstrous predator
   was unleashed on society, its primary target a share of net income.
➢ Almost everyone is now implicated in this predatory process. About
   70% of the populations of most western nations exercises claims on
   rents that ought to fund the social interests of everyone.

Banks happen to be the most visible agents in this process of avarice.
They mediate the arrangements between governments and rent-seekers.
But they cannot be repositioned as a socially responsible service industry
without first amending the culture of rent-seeking. The post-industrial

society needs a viable commercial financial sector. It would evolve in response to corrective reforms directed at the way governments collect the public's revenue.

Do Nothing is Not an Option

Re-visualising the future can feel dangerous to one's personal interests. Retreat to the safety of 'the devil you know' is the default position. *Do nothing!* One realm of reality, however, is safe territory: the past. We can look backwards and ask what historians call counterfactual questions. This is an exercise in imagination.

> ➤ If the medieval barons had not violated the rights and lives of the peasants, might the Good Life have been accessible to everybody?
> ➤ If rents had been recycled back into their communities for the equal benefit of everyone, how might communities have evolved?

True, excavating the pain of the past is an assault on our senses. But do we not owe it to the victims to retrieve and reassess their histories? In doing so, we transform the injustices they endured into gifts from the millions of people who were deprived of their right to live as fully paid-up humans. Their stories become vehicles for visualising a better future for the children of our children.

Asking awkward questions reminds us that life does not move along a straight path. This is a disturbing thought. It means the future could be radically different from the one that is predicated on the current trajectory. Counterfactual history opens up the present and the future, beginning with the past.

Winston Churchill and David Lloyd George demonstrated how this could be done. They were the guides who, in the early years of the 20th century, championed the restoration of rent as the public's revenue. Their inspirational speeches in town halls and pubs up and down the British Isles enabled people to *engage in conversation* on the rights of the individual and the obligations of government. The mechanism that linked these two issues – rights and obligations – was tax policy. Should the public's finances be democratised or demonised? In 1909, legislation was enacted to begin the process of democratising the nation's net income. The land-lords blocked the law from being implemented. Has the time come to renew the conversation?

Today, Mason Gaffney is one of the best informed guides for such a conversation. His reflections of a lifetime are freely available on his website: http://masongaffney.org/ To affirm that history does not evolve along a linear path, we engaged him in conversation. Our themes were the potential turning points in history, *the junctures that might have redirected the United States towards a poverty-free status if governments had behaved responsibly in the way they funded public services.* Equipped with the knowledge of such episodes, our readers may initiate their own conversations, of imagining how the many opportunities in the past could have been grasped for history to evolve along a different course. Our hope is that such conversations will strengthen the democratic will to confront the challenges of the 21st century.

A Conversation with Mason Gaffney

Authors: At the time when American colonists were opposing the tax policy imposed on them by Parliament in Westminster, Adam Smith published *The Wealth of Nations* (1776). In this, he explained why ground rent was the most suitable source of government revenue. Americans also had access to Thomas Paine's sensational pamphlet, in which he identified how land could be used for the welfare of everyone. He wrote, in *Common Sense* (1776: 36):

> Another reason why the present time is preferable to all others is, that the fewer our numbers are, the more land there is yet unoccupied, which, instead of being lavished by the king on his worthless dependents, may be hereafter applied, not only to the discharge of the present debt, but to the constant support of government. No nation under Heaven hath such an advantage as this.

Paine explained (in *Rights of Man*) the virtues of a public charge on the rent of land. The belief was that the US economy would have assumed a different character if, after the war for independence, American governments had recycled the rents of the New World back into communities for the equal benefit of everyone.

MG: The Peace Treaty with Britain, followed by European powers' preoccupation fighting each other, and the extraordinary Louisiana

Purchase, suddenly endowed the new nation with vast raw lands to occupy and defend at low cost. Jefferson's Ordinance of 1787 arranged to let settlers pour into the new lands on small holdings, and as President he extended credit for them to buy land titles on long and easy credit. His and succeeding administrations turned the new States loose to fend for themselves financially, which the northern ones did mostly by taxing real estate, and borrowing (often foolishly) on that power. American farm and industrial production and commerce flourished; European capital and people immigrated *en masse*.

Washington financed itself in large part by selling parts of the national domain at advanced prices. This could be construed, and was by many, as resembling Paine's proposals, but the similarity was only superficial, because Congress thus in effect gave away, by failing to assert, its long-term power to tax land. Later generations were to pay the price as the nation gradually, step by step, turned to taxes on commerce, imports, wages and salaries, 'consumer' spending by parents to raise children, incomes from real capital, inflationary confiscation of wealth and interest and pensions fixed in dollars, high tuition at State Universities and Colleges once open free to qualified students, sanitary engineering to provide potable water and dispose of sewage ... all the things Paine and the Physiocrats would un-tax. More and more of these tax revenues went to pay interest on the soaring national debt as the nation, instead of taxing the rentiers, borrowed from them.

Authors: The Founding Fathers based their sacred documents, in part, on the natural law doctrine of John Locke. Locke argued, in *Two Treatises on Government* (1689), that people had the natural right to 'life, liberty and estate [land]'. The political structure in the United States was based on a tension between the federal and state governments, with Amendments to the Constitution constraining what the central government could do. One result was that the federal government had to turn to 'the private sector when it wanted to build a transnational railroad' (Gerstle 2015: 93). Vast swathes of public land were handed over to private interests as the inducement to build the railway network. This skewed economic opportunities for future waves of migrants, and it compromised the revenue system. Ideally, the Founding Fathers should have constructed governance (the relationship between federal, state and municipal institutions) on the principle of funding the infrastructure of the new communities out of the rents that they generated.

MG: That is what they did in part, and for many years. Thus the Erie
Canal, the Golden Gate Bridge, Chicago's drainage system, early water
supply and irrigation works like the high Don Pedro Dam on the
Tuolumne River, the state highway system, our K-12 system of free public
education, New York's and many other cities' low-fare mass-transit systems, bridges and tunnels everywhere, State and city parks, Milwaukee's
public swimming pools, were paid in whole or part by taxes on benefited
lands or oil revenues. Only in the later 20th century did the custom
change so that today some States (LA, KS, and MI) are seriously considering defunding their football teams – a desperate last resort indeed
in our culture, or what is left of it!

Authors: Early in the 19th century in Britain the engineer-inventors
based their new technologies on steam power. If government had imposed
a charge on the dumping of pollutants onto communities, that would
have encouraged them to seek clean technologies at the beginning of the
Industrial Revolution. Would that have been an incentive to reduce
the use of nature's capacity to absorb waste from fossil fuels?

MG: Yes, but it's never too late to begin. Early attempts to curb
pollution were crude, clumsy, and arbitrary. They generally mandated
the use of devices like 'scrubbers' or filters applied at the end of a process
that generated toxic wastes. Rather than scattering them broadcast in our
common air or water they would be compacted and moved away from
people.

Economist A.C. Pigou in 1929 came up with a better idea, the 'effluent
charge': effluents were to be metered for volume and toxicity, and the
polluters charged accordingly. Areas affected were defined, and the
'damage functions' calculated. Pigou's idea called for some sophisticated
science, economics, engineering and understanding. The simple idea,
however, was basic economics. To avoid the charge, polluters would have
more options than to depend solely on 'Tail-end Charlies'. They would
modify both processes and products so fewer pollutants would reach the
tail end (smokestack or outfall). Allen Kneese and his disciples developed
this concept and its details in the 1960s; some major foundations and
polls got behind it. Even some conservative economists liked it, and some
still do.

They reckoned ill, however, by discounting the power of polluting
interests, rent-seekers, and allied libertarian ideologues. These put their

broad shoulders behind an idea advanced by Ronald Coase and endorsed by Friedman and his Chicago disciples. Their idea is to grant tradable pollution permits to polluters. These permits are not even to be sold to the highest bidder at auction. They are based on their histories of pollution, thus making them 'grandfather rights', established by having pioneered in polluting the common air and waters in the past! They are not even called 'property', because then they might be taxed as such. The policy is now called 'cap and trade', and has spread like the plague that it is. It could only have happened after generations of 'deep lobbying' by tax-exempt think-tanks had turned 'privatization' into a popular panacea.

But now we are stuck with 'cap and trade', and a dismal choice – the kind that economists and vested interests like to stick us with. Its cap-n-trade or its pollution and suffocation, take your pick. I prefer a third choice: resurrect Pigovian effluent charges and make them work. The now-popular 'carbon tax' is the modern incarnation of Pigou's inspiration.

Effluent charges are no panacea either. There is 'non-point pollution' to deal with, calling for wider departures from the price system.

Authors: The factory mode of production required the provision of new urban settlements. The rise in productivity increased the net income (rents). If those rents had been recycled back into those communities, working families would not have become victims of the 'dark satanic mills'. How would the housing stock have been transformed? Would municipal governments have increased their investments in water and sewage systems? How would rural hamlets, villages and market towns have flourished?

MG: Some urban settlements attracted workers faster than they did capital for housing and infrastructure, resulting in overcrowding and unsanitary, even filthy living and working conditions. These evoked strong reactions during the Progressive Era. Idealists and machine politicians, often working in tandem in some cities, used their power to raise property taxes to supply better infrastructure, so that many cities with higher tax rates attracted more and better infrastructure then those with lower tax rates, with the result that during the Progressive Era high-tax cities grew faster than low tax cities, as documented in my *New Life in Old Cities*. Fast-growing high-tax cities included New York, Cleveland, Detroit, Chicago, Milwaukee, The Twin Cities, Seattle, Portland, San Francisco,

Los Angeles, San Diego, San Jose, dozens of smaller farm towns, and in Canada Vancouver, Calgary, Winnipeg, Edmonton, and others. Stagnant cities with low tax rates included Cincinnati, St. Louis, Buffalo, Philadelphia, and others.

Authors: Workforces in factories were exploited, which is why many were attracted to the utopian ideas of socialists like Karl Marx. If the rents of land had been reserved for public use, as Marx had proposed in his *Communist Manifesto*, would employee institutions like trade unions have taken a different shape? Would industrial relations between employer and employee have been different? Might this have led to a different outcome to the one endured in the 20th century, in which people like Lenin exploited the workplace discontent to lead a bloody revolution?

MG: Clearly, yes. There was no such bloody revolution in the fast-growing cities named above, although there were many aggravations and incidents that might have triggered one.

Authors: At the end of the 19th century, Henry George spelt out the model for tax justice. How might the depression that afflicted the western economy in the 1870s have panned out if statesmen had restructured the tax regime along the lines he proposed?

MG: It might have flattened out and simmered down, like the ensuing one of the 1890s which was tempered and cured by reforms of The Progressive Era. Those reforms held a good deal of Georgist inspiration and content. It was less than landlords and monopolists feared, but a lot more than they wanted. It served to shift tax burdens to corporations and the personal income of property owners (wages and salaries were virtually exempt from the early personal income tax, 1913-40.)

Authors: The rent-seeking model had exhausted the possibilities for spatial expansion into new colonies by the end of the 19th century. A new lease of life was granted by the intervention of the mouthpieces who gave respectability to the Robber Barons. Cumulatively, these and other events opened the way to the chaos of a World at War with itself at the beginning of the 20th century. Might peace have reigned if, instead, nations had rescued themselves with the program advocated by Henry George?

MG: Probably, although there are cross currents to consider. On one hand, the mad quest for land and empire would have been abated had each nation made better use of the lands it already contained. On the other hand, a nation with a strong fiscal system is in a position to finance strong military ventures, both offensive and defensive. This seems to have been the case in World War I, which helps explain why the war lasted so long.

All sides used their strong tax bases as collateral for borrowing, but the USA, whose new corporate income tax exempted labor income, and whose personal income tax exempted almost all wage and salary income until 1939, paid for its share of the war less from borrowing than the other belligerents. That was done consciously: economic journals of the times featured debates between champions of 'pay as you go' vs. champions of borrowing.

In the end, the USA, having begun the war as a debtor nation, ended it as the world's major creditor. That testified to the taxable capacity of property, for the Progressives who drafted the early personal income tax for Congress in 1916 were Georgists, notably Congressmen Henry George, Jr. of Brooklyn, and Warren Worth Bailey of Johnstown, PA. They saw to it that labor income was mostly exempt.

As we now know, the things we did right did not protect us from the things we did wrong in the 1920s. We succumbed to the perils of prosperity, and failed to foresee the rise of fascism. Georgist policies alone can help guarantee peace, but some more wisdom in statecraft is called for.

Authors: The First World War solved nothing. In economics, the void was filled by John Maynard Keynes, the Cambridge economist who grappled with the problem of unemployment during the Great Depression. He had concluded that 'the land question' had been solved (Harrison 1983: 300). If he had used his *General Theory of Employment, Interest and Money* (1937) to draw attention to the role of land in the market economy, how might the economic paradigm of the 1930s have been amended to deliver different outcomes?

MG: Keynes is often said to have overturned the neoclassical paradigm, but he swallowed its trivialization of land, hook line and sinker. He dismissed concerns about monopoly and tax biases as mere 'structural' matters, so trivial next to monetary and aggregate fiscal policies they might be ignored. To him, 'fiscal' policy dealt only with the sum of all taxes of all kinds, with no distinctions. He led economists into seeing all the causative forces in boom and bust as purely monetary, blinding them to the long history of major cycles in real estate, and banking expansion and contraction caused by and interacting with boom and bust in real estate. Whether he led them down blind alleys, or validated their wandering where they wanted to stray anyway, we may never know. Either way he helped to create what became 'The New Economics', dealing with abstractions far above and removed from concrete realities.

To his credit he focused on the need to raise the *marginal* returns to investing in *new* capital – thus excluding land rents. But he blurred the meaning by calling it 'efficiency' of capital, which he never followed up. To his further credit he put *unemployment* in the very title of his major work, and saw it as a major problem that needed to be solved. That has not, however, stopped recent academic elites from redefining unemployment as leisure, a form of taxable (!) income, and ushering us into a condition they seriously call 'jobless prosperity' – an oxymoron to end all oxymorons!

Authors: The decades after World War II were marred by cyclical booms and busts driven by speculation in land. Would those cycles have been smoothed if, instead of Keynesian pump priming, western governments had changed tax incentives to favour full employment? Would the economy have flourished in circumstances in which the real estate sector was free to operate as the provider of services people needed – new homes – rather than the opportunity to reap unearned capital gains?

MG: Yes, of course, but Georgists need to look deeper into the mysteries of financing real estate, especially land, most of which we expect to last for ages longer than we do. So land is more than a place to stand, to dwell, to farm, to trade, to work, to produce, to grow timber, to load and unload ships and trucks, to park vehicles, to store wares and materials, to launch and land aircraft, to hunt and fish, to dine, to meet, to worship, to exercise, to mine, to draw water, to pave and drive, to heal and rest, during our brief sojourns on earth. It is all those, but it is also itself a 'store of value' for individual and institutional owners. To buy the present and near-future use rights one must also buy the perpetual future rights, whose present discounted value is often more than that of the current use.

That in turn calls for a steep payment 'up front', more than most people can advance, especially if they are young and just getting started. So they borrow, but here we run into Schikele's Law: 'The basis for allocating credit is not marginal productivity, but collateral security.' Thus the real estate sector is rarely 'free to operate (solely) as the provider of services people need'. It is more like a tie-in sale, where buying current use-rights is linked to investing in rights to the far future of land. Debt service is then greater than the current use-value of land, and the ability to borrow at low rates for long terms dominates land markets.

Heavy taxes based on land values tend to offset the differential advantage of borrowers with better collateral security, but the relationship is not so simple. The prospect of *future* land-value taxes is the greater equalizer.

Authors: You have repeatedly emphasised how a restructured tax system would become a self-regulating fiscal mechanism that delivered an efficient market economy. If, at the end of the 20th century, banks had been disciplined by the loss of rents (which they extract through mortgages), would the crisis of 2008 have been averted?

MG: Yes. The preceding boom, 2002-07, was a classic spiral of banks' lending on land, land prices' soaring with the easy long-term credit, and banks' lending more on the collateral of the land prices that their own lending had boosted and was continuing to boost. Appraisers and credit agencies joined and supported the circular reasoning by basing collateral valuations on sales of 'comparable' real estate, ignoring the power of the new easier credit to overprice (under-discount) future 'R' (Recycling) values of land, the most durable and re-usable of assets. Economists joined in with a fashionable new name for mass delusion, calling it 'rational expectations' (and variations), good for Nobel Laureates for Robert Lucas (1995) and Thomas Sargent (2011). Such recognition was evidence that delusion was not only 'mass', but 'respectable', and honoured by the elites.

You might think that the several earlier warning crashes (like American farmland in 1987, Japan in 1990, and the 'dot-com' bust in 2,000) would have spooked American financiers and speculators to the dangers ahead. It was not to be, however. The lesson seems to be that mere risk of private losses, however severe, does not sober lenders and buyers nearly as much as the visible outgoing cash flow of property taxes.

Authors: The academic community did not regale itself with glory in the run up to the financial crisis of 2008. There were notable exceptions. Joseph Stiglitz did repeatedly advocate the need to reform fiscal policy. But, in the main, evidence that the economy was going wrong was not honestly monitored by academics. Are universities detached from reality?

MG: Many academics are quacks, but so are many loan officers, securities analysts, and clergymen. The problems with all such professional frauds and lemmings are combined corruption and herd behavior. Personal advancement and security, financial and social, to them are 'reality' of life, which they would only jeopardize were they to 'tell it like it is'. The syndrome is so ingrained in their social settings and value systems that most of them do not even recognize it in themselves. They have lost the moral fibre of being 'inner-directed', of taking chivalric attitudes to heart. They may flock to enjoy *The Man of La Mancha* dreaming the impossible dream, but they themselves would never even tilt at windmills. They scoffed at prophet and Cassandra Nouriel Roubini as 'Dr. Doom', dismissing his forecasts as though they were just a personal psychosis.

Authors: Instead of overdosing on 'quantitative easing', what if western governments had opted for an honest approach to reforming the credit-creating system? Would we now be facing a bleak Japan-style deflation across the western world? Or should we view the intransigence of policy-makers as the opportunity for people to reclaim their democratic right? That is, the right to mandate a coherent exit out of the chaos?

MG: I question the wisdom of junking the whole money and credit system we have today and starting from scratch. We have seen the results of that approach in nations like Poland and Russia emerging from Communism, with the people's deep ignorance of banking and credit. There is a less drastic way to make the present system work better. That is to shorten the allowable terms of bank loans on which our deposit system is based. And the way, in turn, to do that is to ring out the power of banks to accept land as collateral.

And now, Dear Reader ...

We conclude by recognising that responsibility for the future rests with you. Turning points in history provide illuminating themes for discussion, either in the privacy of the home, or as collaborative projects in schools or social clubs, or informally in chance meetings in cafes and pubs. How might life be different for you if the rents that you help to create are shared by everyone who created them, in return for which the taxes on your salaries and savings were abolished?

References

Craig, Olga (2016), 'Joan Bakewell: House I bought for £12,000 is worth £5m ... and I'm spending the children's inheritance', *Mail on Sunday*, January 24.

Gaffney, Mason (2009), *After the Crash: Designing a Depression-Free Economy*, Editor: Cliff Cobb, Chichester: Wiley-Blackwell.

— (n.d.) 'George's Economics of Abundance: Replacing dismal choices with practical resolutions and synergies', http://www.masongaffney.org/essays/Georges_Economics_of_Abundance.pdf

Gerstle, Gary (2015), *Liberty and Coercion: The Paradox of American Government*, Princeton: Princeton University Press.

Harrison, Fred (1983), *The Power in the Land*, London: Shepheard-Walwyn.

— (2015), *As Evil Does*, London: Geophilos.

Paine, Tom (1945), *The Selected work of Tom Paine*, Howard Fast (ed.), New York: Duell, Sloan and Pearce.

Stiglitz, Joseph E. (2010), *Freefall: Free Markets and the Sinking of the Global Economy*, London: Allen Lane.

Ward, Victoria (2016), 'Sell house and enjoy the cash, Lady Bakewell tells pensioners', *Daily Telegraph*, February 2.

About the Authors

Mary M. (Polly) Cleveland is Adjunct Professor of Environmental Economics, Columbia University School of International and Public Affairs. She received a PhD in Agricultural and Resource Economics from the University of California, Berkeley. Her dissertation, *Consequences and Causes of Unequal Distribution of Wealth*, addressed Henry George's basic questions using modern mathematical modelling.

Terry Dwyer BA (Hons) BEc (Hons) (Syd.) MA PhD. (Harvard), Dip. Law (Syd.), CTA, runs his firm of chartered tax advisory service from his legal firm in Sydney, Australia. He is a Visiting Fellow at the Asia Pacific School of Economics and Management, Australian National University, Canberra. His *Taxation: The Lost History* was published in 2014 as the annual supplement of the *American Journal of Economics and Sociology* (Vo.73[4]).

Kris Feder is Associate Professor of Economics and Director of the Environmental and Urban Studies Program at Bard College, Annandale on Hudson, New York. She received her PhD from Temple University, and she serves on the Boards of Directors of the Robert Schalkenbach Foundation and the *American Journal of Economics and Sociology*.

Fred Foldvary teaches at San Jose State University, California. He received his PhD in Economics from George Mason University. He is known for his research on community associations and for accurately predicting the recession of 2008 in 1997. His weekly column appears in The Progress Report <www.progress.org> His books include *Soul of Liberty* (1980), *Public Goods and Private Communities* (1994).

Ted Gwartney, MAI, was Assessment Commissioner (Chief Executive of BC Assessment) in British Columbia, Deputy County Assessor in Sacramento, CA, Assessor in Southfield, Michigan, Hartford, Bridgeport and Greenwich, Connecticut, Commercial Appraiser at Bank of America and City National Bank in Los Angeles. He is President of the Robert Schalkenbach Foundation, and has served as Professor of Real Estate Appraisal, at Baruch College, NY.

Fred Harrison is a graduate of the Universities of Oxford and London. He is Executive Director of the Land Research Trust, London. His first book (*Power in the Land*, 1983) relocated the 18-year land value cycle in macroeconomic analysis. His *Handbook on Humanity* trilogy (Vol 1: *As Evil Does*, 2015) explores the existential risks to civilization arising from what he called the "culture of cheating" (*The Traumatised Society*, 2012).

Dirk Löhr is a Professor of Taxation and Ecological Economics at the Trier University of Applied Sciences, Germany. He has worked as a tax adviser, lecturer at a private real estate academy, and a consultant for the German International Cooperation (GIZ) in Cambodia. He is a member of the public real estate assessment board of Rheinhessen-Nahe, and is a member of the supreme public real estate assessment board of the state of Rhineland-Palatinate. He heads the Center for Soil Protection and Land Use Policy (Trier/Birkenfeld).

Francis K. Peddle, JD, PhD, is Professor of Philosophy, Dominican University College, Ottawa, Canada. He has represented clients in tax and business cases before the Tax Court of Canada, the Federal Court of Appeal and the Ontario Superior Court of Justice and Court of Appeal. Dr. Peddle has appeared before numerous tax commissions and task forces, notably the Bédard Commission (Montreal, 1999). He authored *Cities and Greed: Taxes, Inflation and Land Speculation* (1994) and *Henry George and the End of Tax Commissions* (1994).

Duncan Pickard received his BSc and PhD from the University of Nottingham. He was a Lecturer in Animal Physiology and Nutrition at the University of Leeds before turning to farming. He has farmed in Fife, Scotland, since 1992 in partnership with his wife Barbara and two of their sons and their wives. They own 650 acres and farm another 1,000 acres on contract or on short-term leases. Dr. Pickard is the author of *Lie of the Land* (2004, Land Research Trust).

Roger Sandilands is Emeritus Professor of Economics, University of Strathclyde, Glasgow, UK. His PhD was on inflation and housing finance in Latin America where he worked for four years following graduate studies in Canada. He taught at the National University of Singapore for six years and at universities in Sweden, Tokyo and Beijing. He is the author of *The Life and Political Economy of Lauchlin Currie: New Dealer, Presidential Adviser, and Development Economist* (1990).

Fernando Scornik Gerstein graduated as a lawyer in the University of Buenos Aires. He was advisor to the Argentinean Ministry of Economy and to the Secretary of State for Agriculture where he chaired the Commission to implement the taxation of the rent of agrarian land. For political reasons he sought refuge in Spain in1976, when he established his legal practise in Madrid and London. He has served as President of the Spanish Association for the Study of Land and National Resources Regimes.

Peter Smith received his MSc in Conservation Biology from the Durrell Institute of Conservation & Ecology. He is Founder and Chief Executive of the Wildwood Trust, a nature conservation charity with sites in Kent and Devon. His mission is the reintroduction of beaver, wild horses, lynx and wolves to the wild. He is a contributor to TV wildlife programmes such as BBC's *Countryfile*. He leads an ecological consultancy that specialises in rewilding and habitat restoration.

Nicolaus Tideman is Professor of Economics at Virginia Polytechnic Institute and State University. He received a bachelor's degree from Reed College and a Ph.D. in economics from the University of Chicago. He was an Assistant Professor of Economics at Harvard University from 1969-1973, during which time he was a Senior Staff Economist for the President's Council of Economic Advisors. He has published over 100 professional articles and is author of *Collective Decisions and Voting: The Potential for Public Choice* (2006).

Index

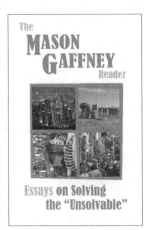

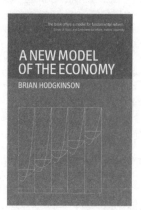